Katherine Anne Porter

A Critical Symposium

Katherine Anne Porter

A Critical Symposium

Edited by Lodwick Hartley and George Core

Published by the University of Georgia Press, Athens

For Harry Kitsun Russell

Preface / viii
Introduction / xi

I

An Interview / BARBARA THOMPSON / 3
Katherine Anne Porter Personally / GLENWAY WESCOTT / 24

II

Irony with a Center / ROBERT PENN WARREN / 51
The Fictions of Memory / EDWARD G. SCHWARTZ / 67
Another Look at
    Katherine Anne Porter / JAMES WILLIAM JOHNSON / 83
Art and Passion in Katherine Anne Porter / JOHN W. ALDRIDGE / 97
The Eye of the Story / EUDORA WELTY / 103

III

On 'The Grave' / CLEANTH BROOKS / 115
Symbol and Theme in 'Flowering Judas' / RAY B. WEST, JR. / 120
Structure and Imagery in
    'Pale Horse, Pale Rider' / SARAH YOUNGBLOOD / 129
Reflections in
    'The Cracked Looking-Glass' / BRO. JOSEPH WIESENFARTH / 139
'Holiday' A Version of Pastoral / GEORGE CORE / 149

IV

The Lady and the Temple / LODWICK HARTLEY / 161
The Way of Dissent / EDWARD G. SCHWARTZ / 169

V

The Responsibility of the Novelist / M. M. LIBERMAN / 185
Ship of Fools: Notes on Style / ROBERT B. HEILMAN / 197
Dark Voyagers / LODWICK HARTLEY / 211

A Selective Bibliography / 227
Index / 237

Preface

SPECIAL acknowledgments are made to the following who have granted permission for the reprinting of copyrighted material from the periodicals and books that are here listed: "An Interview" by Barbara Thompson originally appeared as "The Art of Fiction, XXIX—Katherine Anne Porter: An Interview" in the *Paris Review* (Winter–Spring 1963). Reprinted by permission of the *Paris Review* and the Viking Press, Inc.

"Katherine Anne Porter Personally" by Glenway Wescott appeared in *Images of Truth: Remembrances and Criticism* (New York: Harper and Row, Publishers, Inc., 1962). Reprinted by permission of the author and publisher.

"Irony with a Center: Katherine Anne Porter" by Robert Penn Warren appeared in *Selected Essays* (New York: Random House, Inc., 1958). Reprinted by permission of the publisher.

"The Fictions of Memory" by Edward G. Schwartz appeared in the *Southwest Review* (Summer 1960). Reprinted by permission of the author and the *Southwest Review*.

"Another Look at Katherine Anne Porter" by James William Johnson appeared in the *Virginia Quarterly Review* (Autumn 1960). Reprinted by permission of the author and the *Virginia Quarterly Review*.

"Art and Passion in Katherine Anne Porter" by John W. Aldridge appeared in *Time to Murder and Create: The Contemporary Novel in Crisis* (New York: David McKay Company, Inc., 1966). Reprinted by permission of the author and the publisher.

"The Eye of the Story" by Eudora Welty appeared in the *Yale Review* (Winter 1966). Reprinted by permission of Russell & Volkening, Inc.

"On 'The Grave' " by Cleanth Brooks appeared in the *Yale Review* (Winter 1966). Reprinted by permission of the author and the *Yale Review*.

"Symbol and Theme in 'Flowering Judas' " by Ray B. West, Jr., appeared in *Accent* (Spring 1947). Reprinted by permission of the author.

"Structure and Imagery in Katherine Anne Porter's 'Pale Horse, Pale Rider' " by Sarah Youngblood appeared in *Modern Fiction Studies* (Winter 1959–1960). Reprinted by permission of the Purdue Research Foundation.

"Illusion and Allusion: Reflections in 'The Cracked Looking-Glass' " by Brother Joseph Wiesenfarth, F.S.C., appeared in *Four Quarters* (November 1962). Reprinted by permission of *Four Quarters*.

A part of " 'Holiday': A Version of Pastoral" by George Core appeared in his " 'The *Best* Residuum of Truth' " in the *Georgia Review* (Fall 1966). Reprinted by permission of the *Georgia Review*.

"The Lady and the Temple: The Critical Theories of Katherine Anne Porter" by Lodwick Hartley appeared in *College English* (April 1953). Reprinted by permission of the National Council of Teachers of English.

"The Way of Dissent: Katherine Anne Porter's Critical Position" by Edward G. Schwartz appeared in the *Western Humanities Review* (Spring 1954). Reprinted by permission of the author and the *Western Humanities Review*.

"The Responsibility of the Novelist: The Critical Reception of *Ship of Fools*" by M. M. Liberman appeared in *Criticism* (Fall 1966). Reprinted by permission of the Wayne State University Press.

"*Ship of Fools:* Notes on Style" by Robert B. Heilman appeared in

Four Quarters (November 1962). Reprinted by permission of *Four Quarters*.

"Dark Voyagers: A Study of Katherine Anne Porter's *Ship of Fools*" by Lodwick Hartley appeared in the *University Review* (Winter 1963). Reprinted by permission of the *University Review*.

There remains the pleasant task of thanking the several persons who helped the editors in various ways. First and foremost, we wish to thank Miss Katherine Anne Porter. We are also most grateful to Mr. Seymour Lawrence, Miss Porter's editor and publisher. Finally, we express our appreciation to Mr. Glenway Wescott, Mr. Robert A. Beach, Jr., and Professor Louis D. Rubin, Jr.

Katherine Anne Porter: A Critical Symposium is dedicated to Professor Harry Kitsun Russell who is retiring from the University of North Carolina at Chapel Hill after some forty years of distinguished teaching. The fact that his retirement and the publication of this collection are almost coincidental in point of time is a pleasant fortuity. Needless to say, the dedication is made to the man himself—not to mark any particular stage in a career which the editors believe is far from ending. We wish to honor Mr. Russell both for his accomplishments as a teacher and a scholar and for his invaluable personal qualities—the forthrightness, humility, gentleness, and wisdom of his ways. If for these reasons it is fitting and proper that this book be dedicated to him, there is still a more cogent reason: Harry Russell is a great student and teacher of the art of fiction, the art which Katherine Anne Porter practices so well.

Lodwick Hartley
George Core

January 1969

Introduction

THE "Contributors and Contributions" column of *Asia* for August 1920 carried the following item:

> Katherine Anne Porter is a young American writer who has been on the staff of the Dallas *News* and the *Rocky Mountain News* of Denver. She has written many ballet pantomimes and children's stories and has corresponded for Texas newspapers from the Mexican border.

The piece for which this first biographical notice provided annotation was "The Adventures of Hadji: A Tale of a Turkish Coffee House," an ironic little story ostensibly "retold" by the aspiring journalist.

In 1930, when *Flowering Judas* first appeared, the record of publications by the same writer, though more substantial, was still modest for the achievement of a decade. But the slender volume of stories, carefully selected from a mass of manuscripts ultimately to be discarded, was in itself sufficiently impressive to offset any consideration of previous obscurity. Indeed, it served to establish its author among discriminating readers as a talent fully mature and of first rank, and it won for her a Guggenheim Fellowship for the following year. As late as 1939 Christopher Isherwood apologized for Miss Porter's not being better known in England. (The first English edition of *Flowering Judas* had not appeared until 1936.) In America, admiration for her work had had a steady growth; and, though she did not have a large popular audience, her reputation was firmly established. *Flowering Judas* had been reissued with additions in 1935. By the time it came out in the Modern Library edition in 1940 it was a classic. Moreover, esteem for Miss Porter's work had been by this time further enhanced by the appearance in 1939 of a collection of three short novels published under the title of one of them, *Pale Horse, Pale Rider.*

In the year of the appearance of the Modern Library edition, the first substantial critical article on her work appeared in the *Sewanee Review*. It appropriately pointed out the unusual excellence of the author's prose style, her striking use of the materials of memory, and her uncanny employment of the evocative power of concrete details. If the critic found some small failures and limitations in her art, he nevertheless concluded that she was one of the most talented of living American writers.

In 1942 in the *Kenyon Review* came a major appraisal by a major writer in an essay that has become a classic of criticism: Robert Penn Warren's "Katherine Anne Porter (Irony with a Center)." No other book by Miss Porter appeared until 1944 when *The Leaning Tower,* a short novel combined with narrative sketches and short stories, came from the press. The first reissue of *Pale Horse, Pale Rider* came out in 1949.

This brief survey of the author's publication does not take into account the early or the later publication of her short stories in such magazines as the *Century,* the *Nation, Hound and Horn, New Masses, transition,* and the *Virginia Quarterly Review;* or her poems in *Pagany,* the *Southern Review,* and the *Literary Review.* (The appearance of "María Concepción" in the *Century* for December 1922 is a date of more than ordinary importance since the story was the first genuinely representative example of her talent to appear in a major journal.) Nor does it include the separate publication of such stories as *Hacienda,* published in a limited edition in 1934, before it was reprinted in *Flowering Judas* in 1935; or *Noon Wine,* similarly published in 1937, before it appeared in *Pale Horse, Pale Rider.* More details are included in the bibliography at the end of this volume. For the most complete record of publication before *Ship of Fools* one should see the excellent bibliographical study of Edward Schwartz, which has recently been supplemented by the compilation of Louise Waldrip.

Suffice it to say that until the publication of *Ship of Fools* in 1963, Miss Porter's considerable and in many respects unique reputation had been built on a fictional output containing fewer words than a single long novel of William Faulkner or Ernest Hemingway, to whose generation she belonged, and considerably fewer than the published works of competent contemporaries working in the same genre like Kay Boyle or Caroline Gordon or a younger writer like Eudora Welty whose first volume of stories Miss Porter introduced to the public.

Before the appearance of Miss Porter's full-length novel, the publication of critical essays and miscellaneous pieces under the title of *The Days Before* in 1952 had reminded her readers that her talent as a literary critic, apparent even in her earliest reviewing, was not only an invaluable key to her fiction but also an illuminating body of comment of a brilliant and incisive mind worthy of its own place in the history of American criticism.

The appearance of *Ship of Fools* more than doubled the bulk of Miss Porter's published works. In doing so it inevitably invited a reappraisal of her total accomplishment. In some respects, the reappraisal was agonizing. The earliest reviews—particularly Mark Schorer's in the *New York Times Book Review*—tended to make confident and even glowing reaffirmations of the writer's importance. The later reviews often ranged from gentle skepticism to outright attack.

The impetus toward reappraisal continued with the publication of the *Collected Stories* in 1965. Again, in reviews by well-established critics like Denis Donoghue and J. W. Aldridge, the overall evaluation involved reservations that indicated less than enthusiastic approval. Yet there have remained many readers and critics who have continued to view the volume—augmented as it was by "Holiday," originally published in the *Atlantic Monthly* in 1960—as sufficient evidence for regarding Miss Porter as one of the finest living masters of short fiction.

It would, indeed, be surprising if Miss Porter who has appeared on so many college campuses as reader and lecturer had been neglected by the academic critics and/or if she had not been subjected to analysis in a number of theses and dissertations. Though such theses were written, it was not until the 1960s that pamphlets and monographs treating her work comprehensively and in detail began coming from the presses. Their authors—Harry John Mooney, Jr., Ray B. West, Jr., George Hendrick, William Nance, and Winfred S. Emmons—have all made their contributions. But, ranging as they do from elementary synopsizing to penetrating and illuminating analysis, they are by no means all of equal value. West's pamphlet has particularly successful parts without being equally satisfying as a whole. Although Hendrick's study is useful as the most detailed treatment to date, it leaves something to be desired both in factual material and in interpretation. Mooney's pamphlet is subject to the same sort of inadequacies; and Emmons's is too limited in scope and in originality to be of first importance. Though Nance's thoroughgoing and well-written book is in some ways the best of the lot, it suffers from the limitation of its thesis. In short, no definitive reading of Miss Porter's work by a single author in a single volume is yet available. Such a situation has seemed to make desirable a volume of essays by a number of critics whose work as a whole may give the reader a valuable comprehensive view.

When Miss Porter received the honorary degree of Doctor of Letters from the University of North Carolina at Greensboro in June 1949, her citation mentioned that she was "born in Texas, brought up in Texas and Louisiana, and educated in small Southern schools," that she had lived and traveled extensively in Mexico and in Europe, that she had received many fellowships and awards (including two Guggenheim Fellowships and the Fellowship of Regional American Literature in the Library of Congress), that she had served a stint in Hollywood, and that she had for one reason or another been an ornament to college campuses throughout the country.

Such incidental biographical details, as well as those in lengthier accounts including what may be called her domestic life, seem destined to have limited relevance. From the beginning, Miss Porter has been a legend. Few writers have ever lived so much in and for their art; and of no writer can it be so accurately said that all we actually need to know of her life is what she has transmuted into literature.

In Texas as a child, we are led to believe, she was a good deal of a tomboy. She liked to ride horseback and to follow her brother, much to his annoyance, when he went squirrel hunting. Often she wanted to

shoot his gun—not particularly, however, because she could hit anything or wanted to hit anything. In the exquisite little story called "The
Grave," she has Miranda (who is in many respects herself) say: "What
I like about shooting is pulling the trigger and hearing the noise." Here
is a revealing bit of philosophy and humor that gives the reader an
insight into the writer's character as well as into her art.

Again, we learn that what systematic education Miranda got came
from convents. In "Old Mortality" we see her "immured" in a convent
in New Orleans, paying as little attention as possible to her studies,
thinking chiefly of weekends when she might be taken to the horse
races, and wishing very much that she could be a jockey. Miss Porter
has said of herself at this stage that she was "precocious, nervous,
rebellious, and unteachable." But—we are forced to observe—the style
of writing that she ultimately achieved is not that of the unteachable or
the untaught or even the incorrigibly rebellious. The sisters to whom
her education was entrusted must have labored better than either she or
they knew, for she shows the restraint and order of style that a classical
education and an authoritarian regimen are capable of giving. Moreover,
though the effect of her religious training in the Catholic Church is
rarely obtrusive in her writing, it is everywhere a felt presence.

Her work as a newspaper reporter in Dallas and in Denver and her
falling victim to the influenza epidemic of 1918 are reflected in "Pale
Horse, Pale Rider." Her Mexican residence is implicit in such stories as
"María Concepción" and "Hacienda." Her experiences in Germany in
the 1930s are revealed in "The Leaning Tower." And so on.

Miss Porter has herself summed up her life in a few remarkable
sentences written some decades ago:

> My personal life has been the jumbled and apparently irrelevant mass
> of experiences which can only happen, I think to a woman who goes with
> her mind permanently absent from the place she is. . . . I have no time sense
> and almost no sense of distance. I have no sense of direction and have seen
> a good deal of the world by getting completely lost and simply taking in
> the scenery as I roamed about getting my bearings.

The author deserves to be taken at her word; and her statement
must be regarded as a cogent comment not only on her attitude toward
living but eventually on the way in which she uses materials from her
own experience for her stories. Perhaps, to be sure, it is only a partial

explanation of her artistic method. If her mind is always "permanently absent from the place she *is*," we may comment, it has a most remarkable faculty of being able to return to the places where she has *been*. The handmaiden of art remains, as it always has been, memory; and in this respect Miss Porter has been more than ordinarily endowed. Her own essay, " 'Noon Wine': The Sources" (1956), written almost precisely twenty years after the story, provides the best evidence. As she says, "In this endless remembering which surely must be the main occupation of the writer, events are changed, reshaped, interpreted again and again in different ways, and this is right and natural because it is the intention of the writer to write fiction, after all—real fiction, not a *roman à clef*, or a thinly-disguised personal confession which better belongs to the psychoanalyst's séance." Never suffering from total recall, she has been able with uncanny skill to select details from the past and invest them with beauty, immediacy, and significance. In this talent she has few peers. Hence, as she said in 1939, "All my past is 'usable,' in the sense that my material consists of memory, legend, personal experience, and acquired knowledge." These elements, most readers will agree, are best brought into play and most fully realized in *The Old Order* together with "The Jilting of Granny Weatherall," the short novels in *Pale Horse, Pale Rider*, and "Holiday"—in short, her stories of the Southwest.

This "summer country" of her childhood she has described in a prose paragraph of great beauty: the "landscapes shimmering in light and color," "the sound of mourning doves in the live oaks," the vision of buzzards hovering in the "high blue air"; the rivers she remembered ("the San Antonio, the San Marco, the Trinity, the Neuces, the Rio Grande, the Colorado," and, of course, that small clear branch of the Colorado, Indian Creek, full of colored pebbles); the colors and tastes "that all had their smells" of the places she knew, from the bitter whiff of odor from an animal skeleton after the buzzards had left it to the "sickly sweetness of the chinaberry florets," and on to the "smells and flavors of roses and melons, and peach blossoms and ripe peaches"—in summary, "all the life of that soft backland country" of her childhood. Of equal importance were the people—many of whom would at one time or another contribute something to the fiction. "I was one of four children," Miss Porter writes, "brought up in a household full of adults of ripening age; a grandmother, a father, several Negro servants, among them two aged, former slaves, visiting relatives, uncles, aunts, cousins; grandmother's other grandchildren older than we, with always an ill-identified old soul or two, male or female, who seemed to be guests but helped out with stray chores." If it was the grandmother who emerged most vividly and forcefully both as symbol and character—and to a lesser degree the father and a Negro servant or two—there were God's plenty of others to provide enough characters for a lifetime's writing in fiction or non-fiction.

The way in which the author's life and philosophy have emerged from the "Miranda stories" has been treated more fully elsewhere. But the pursuit of the identity of the artist in a single character has had inherent dangers, and insistence upon equating her life and her art has produced obvious critical excesses. Katherine Anne Porter and Miranda have much in common, as we have seen. But beyond this assumption one must proceed with extreme caution. The code that Miss Porter has accepted for her personal life may in many ways be like that which she has applied to her art, and the two may seem to reveal similar aspects: decorum, grace, toughmindedness, and control, to mention only a few. But a confusion between art and life is rarely made in her mind—and neither should it be made in ours. Whereas for Miss Porter life is always of more importance than any fictive version of it, life can be best understood, not through a transcription of experience in its undifferentiated chaos, but in the ordered artistic record.

One day the standard kind of biography of Katherine Anne Porter will doubtless appear, and many of factual matters now obscure will doubtless be established in a book which there is no reason to believe will not be entirely competent. But, understandably enough to all real students of the writer, a full-dress biographical treatment seems at the moment to invoke no urgency. This is particularly true since we have the delightful and enticing prospect of being able to read a selection of Miss Porter's letters in the not too distant future, as well as a new collection of her criticism and miscellaneous prose. So at the present time Glenway Wescott's warm and searching reminiscence and Barbara Thompson's penetrating interview are perfectly adequate for the purpose and scope of this collection, devoted essentially to the illumination of Miss Porter's art.

In view of the purity of Miss Porter's style and the finish of her work, it may seem a little strange that classification of her fiction has posed some difficulty. As the recent debate over *Ship of Fools* may demonstrate, attempts at categorizing have not always been profitable. In the latter instance, the author herself has with ample justification shown some impatience over the discussion about whether or not she has, indeed, written a "novel." Other *genres* have also been involved in equally fruitless discussion in the past.

Flowering Judas was quite plainly intended as a collection of short stories; whereas the pieces in *Pale Horse, Pale Rider* were labeled short novels. The title story of *The Leaning Tower* was also obviously intended for the latter category. If then the vexing question of the difference between the short story and the short novel arises, the safest course may be to ride on the horns of the dilemma. Limited range and concentration of material, the usual characteristics of the "short story," are everywhere apparent in *Flowering Judas*. When the narrative turns on a specific psychological problem as it does in "Rope" or on a highly-particularized situation as it does in "Magic," no problem of *genre* may seem apparent. But with all their compactness, several of the stories—"The Cracked Looking-Glass," for example—become remarkably expansive in implication and one sometimes has the feeling that they are actually small novels with all the extraneous materials rigidly excised. "Hacienda" similarly defies easy generalization.

"Old Mortality" with its three distinct parts ranging over a period of more than two decades in the life of the heroine in relation to her family suggests the chronicle novel. "Pale Horse, Pale Rider," a tragic love story told with great skill against a background of World War I, accomplishes in its way something like what Hemingway's *A Farewell to Arms* achieves in considerably more space, even though Miss Porter's economy of means may seem to suffer from the long account of Miranda's febrile cerebration at the end. "Noon Wine" is such a structural triumph that its classification seems to be of little importance. But its astonishing comprehensiveness combined with equally astonishing concentration entitles it a place among short novels of the first rank. The structure of "The Leaning Tower" is far less taut and its total effect as a short novel is not quite so impressive. On the other hand, it could hardly be called a short story.

So far as the comparison of Miss Porter with other writers, past and present, is concerned, one may observe that from the outset she has been mentioned in the same breath with Flaubert and Maupassant, with Chekhov and Turgenev, and with Katherine Mansfield—in short, with the best of antecedent craftsmen. Such associations are both flattering and just, especially if one remembers that there is absolutely no suggestion that Miss Porter's art is in any way derivative. But perhaps on this matter J. F. Powers, himself a first-rate short-story writer, has said the final word:

> It is unprofitable to compare Katherine Anne Porter with other writers. The only one she is really like is herself. From the very first, she seems to have known what she was doing—that only her best would be good enough for her. She hasn't written any "yarns," and she hasn't let the daemons take over. She has approached life reverently in her stories, and it lives on in them. She has been given a very great gift, and she has kept it—by risking it. Nobody else could have written the story "Holiday," published a couple of years ago. One could say this about other stories of hers, and about stories by others, I know, but I think Katherine Anne Porter has usually worked on a higher wire than others: she has seen and felt more above *and* below, and, without huffing and puffing, has given us more—the nearest thing yet to reality in American fiction.

The effort to establish a philosophical unity for all Miss Porter's work has stimulated a considerable amount of comment. Undoubtedly the boldest attempt in this direction has been made by William Nance, who divides Miss Porter's short fiction into two groups: first, those stories centered around what he regards as the isolated autobiographical heroine most often named Miranda; and, second, those stories employing characters inferior to Miranda and separated from her by ironic criticism. The critic sees the total pattern of rejection in the stories as consisting of themes involving repeated escapes from several sorts of oppressive unions: family, marriage, and various other associations with people. Though the protagonist may seek to compensate by a search for truth and beauty (the artistic quest), she encounters disillusionment everywhere and she finally flees from human oppressiveness. The same kind of pattern, Nance finds, reappears and is repeated (even to the point of monotony) in the novel, *Ship of Fools*.

In Miss Porter's (or her typical heroine's) rejection of organized religion and human relationships in favor of a search for life and truth in art, Nance sees an effective rejection of all reality and a "downward path" to ignorance, despair, and death—of which the writer herself may not always be aware. Sometimes, Nance argues, the rejection theme coincides with the surface plot and meaning; at other times it operates beneath the surface in opposition to evident dramatic and thematic elements. Since the result may be negativism and narrowness, Miss Porter is most successful in those stories in which she allows faithfulness to reality to transcend the theme.

To this kind of argument, Caroline Gordon has made the most spirited answer. Rejecting completely Nance's contention concerning Miss Porter's negativistic and tragic vision of life, Miss Gordon argues that the short stories involving Miranda actually comprise a "Comédie Humaine" in which the protagonist's predicament is simply mortality and the only apparent resolution is death—or a "divine comedy" in which Miranda is cast not in the role of adventurer but of a pilgrim. Similar polarities may be found often in interpretations of *Ship of Fools*, and indeed they are abundantly present.

On another level, the attitude of the writer toward her Southern or regional materials has also stimulated some diversity of opinion. No one can doubt that at times she can most impressively reveal her deep emotional involvement with Southern culture and that she has most effectively used her own to her family experience in her fiction. Allen Tate once observed about the ending of "Old Mortality" that a weakness in Miss Porter's art may lie in some instances in a confusion of personal history and actual observation. Thus, he felt, she ultimately allows Miranda's romanticism to distort the magnificent people in the story because she fails to see that their trouble was not really their sentimental evasion of life so much as the fact that they belonged to a formal society that had lost the material basis to support it. The ending may, therefore, be not only dramatically false but perhaps historically false also. A more recent critic, Denis Donoghue, senses a related difficulty. "Miss Porter, like Miranda," he remarks, "eloped from her tradition and...her elopement, like Miranda's was a failure." In addition, Aldridge's essay, included in this volume, suggests something that can be diagnosed only as "perverse fastidiousness or shyness" that has compelled the writer in the main body of her work "to repress her feelings of intense personal connection" with her Southern experience.

Most of Miss Porter's readers, however, will undoubtedly feel that the skillful way in which the artist has assimilated and universalized her background materials, limited as many of her stories are to an identifiable Southwest, at least renders any sort of classification of her as a regionalist of no particular relevance. If there is in her writing the felt presence of her religious training, there is certainly more than the felt presence of her Southern background and heritage, for she has often made it explicit with great vividness and accuracy. Yet the fictional reflection of young Katherine's years at the home of her Grandmother Porter in the village of Kyle, Texas, between San Marcos and Austin, belongs finally about as much to regional literature as do the experiences of young Marcel Proust in his great aunt's house in the provincial town of Combray or on a holiday with his grandmother in Balbec. In the final analysis, Miss Porter may be accounted as Southern American somewhat in the same way that Proust is Parisian French or Chekhov is Russian of the region around Taganrog or Moscow.

The selection of the materials for any volume of this sort is obliged to involve problems. In this instance, however, the task has been made easier than usual by the fact that certain choices have been inevitable. Happily, such important critics and creative writers as Robert Penn Warren, Eudora Welty, Cleanth Brooks, John W. Aldridge, Ray B. West, Jr., and Robert B. Heilman have written critical essays on Miss Porter's work that are classics and that could hardly have been excluded from any collection. Less well-known critics like James William Johnson, Sarah Youngblood, Brother Joseph Weisenfarth, and M. M. Liberman have provided commentary well deserving attention beyond the limits of the publications in which they originally appeared. Edward Schwartz merits inclusion not only because of the intrinsic value of the essays chosen but because he has long been an authority in the field. Other essays were selected because of their availability to the editors and their appropriateness to the intended scope of the volume. Plainly, many excellent essays had to be passed up for lack of space and for other reasons. Their points of view, however, have in most instances been reflected either in the introduction or in the essays included. Thus the essays of Aldridge and Liberman, for example, serve more than one purpose.

Though the essays were not selected primarily to present a debate on the achievement of Miss Porter, they obviously represent some diversity in point of view. Any attempt to direct a verdict here is entirely unnecessary. What should be clear, nevertheless, is that in any list of the best Southern and even American writers of the twentieth century, Miss Porter deserves a place in the highest rank. In some respects, as we have already suggested, she has few peers. But one does not have— in the true meaning of Shakespeare's phrase—to "protest too much"; for the reputation of a really first-rate writer may thrive on dissent and even in the indication of her limitations the genuine quality of her success may emerge more clearly than ever.

In a perceptive demurrer to regarding Miss Porter as merely a Southern writer, Eudora Welty has rightly observed that she writes always and essentially about her profound sense of the "human encounter," an encounter that is felt not in any particular geographical setting but in the "interior of our lives." Thus, concludes Miss Welty, Katherine Anne Porter achieves "stories of the spirit, and the time that fills these moments is eternity." This is, indeed, in itself an eloquent and comprehensive tribute to Miss Porter's genius.

I

Barbara Thompson

An
Interview

THE VICTORIAN HOUSE *in which Katherine Anne Porter lives is*
narrow and white, reached by an iron-railed stairway curving up from
the shady brick-walked Georgetown street. The parlor to which a maid
admits the caller is an elegant mélange of several aspects of the past,
both American and European. High-ceilinged, dim and cool after the
midsummer glare, the room is dominated by a bottle-green settee from
the period of Napoleon III. Outside the alcove of windows there is a
rustle of wind through ginkgo trees, then a hush.

   Finally, a voice in the upper hallway: its tone that of someone talk-
ing to a bird, or coquetting with an old beau—light and feathery, with
a slight flutter. A few moments later, moving as lightly as her voice,
Miss Porter hurries through the wide doorway, unexpectedly modern in
a soft green suit of woven Italian silk. Small and elegant, she explains
her tardiness, relates an anecdote of the morning's mail, offers a minted
ice tea, and speculates aloud on where we might best conduct our con-
versation.

   She decides on the dining room, a quiet, austere place overlooking the
small enclosed garden. Here the aspect is a different one. "I want to live

in a world capital or the howling wilderness," she said once, and did. The drawing room was filled with pieces that had once been part of the house on rue Notre-Dame des Champs; this one is bright with Mexican folk art—whistles and toy animals collected during a recent tour for the Department of State—against simpler, heavier pieces of furniture. The round table at which we sit is of Vermont marble, mottled and colored like milk glass, on a wrought-iron base of her own design. There is a sixteenth-century cupboard from Avila, and a refectory table of the early Renaissance from a convent in Fiesole. Here we settle the tape recorder, under an image of the great god Horus.

We try to make a beginning. She is an experienced lecturer, familiar with microphone and tape recorder, but now she is to talk about herself as well as her work, the link between, and the inexorable winding of the tape from one spool to the other acts almost as a hypnotic. Finally we turn it off and talk for a while of other things, more frivolous and more autobiographical, hoping to surprise an easier revelation. . . .

INTERVIEWER: You were saying that you had never intended to make a career of writing.

PORTER: I've never made a career of anything, you know, not even of writing. I started out with nothing in the world but a kind of passion, a driving desire. I don't know where it came from, and I don't know why—or why I have been so stubborn about it that nothing could deflect me. But this thing between me and my writing is the strongest bond I have ever had—stronger than any bond or any engagement with any human being or with any other work I've ever done. I really started writing when I was six or seven years old. But I had such a multiplicity of half-talents, too: I wanted to dance, I wanted to play the piano, I sang, I drew. It wasn't really dabbling—I was investigating everything, experimenting in everything. And then, for one thing, there weren't very many amusements in those days. If you wanted music, you had to play the piano and sing yourself. Oh, we saw all the great things that came during the season, but after all, there would only be a dozen or so of those occasions a year. The rest of the time we depended upon our own resources: our own music and books. All the old houses that I knew when I was a child were full of books, bought generation after generation by members of the family. Everyone was literate as a matter of course.

Nobody told you to read this or not to read that. It was there to read, and we read.

INTERVIEWER: Which books influenced you most?

PORTER: That's hard to say, because I grew up in a sort of mélange. I was reading Shakespeare's sonnets when I was thirteen years old, and I'm perfectly certain that they made the most profound impression upon me of anything I ever read. For a time I knew the whole sequence by heart; now I can only remember two or three of them. That was the turning point of my life, when I read the Shakespeare sonnets, and then all at one blow, all of Dante—in that great big book illustrated by Gustave Doré. The plays I saw on the stage, but I don't remember reading them with any interest at all. Oh, and I read all kinds of poetry —Homer, Ronsard, all the old French poets in translation. We also had a very good library of—well, you might say secular philosophers. I was incredibly influenced by Montaigne when I was very young. And one day when I was about fourteen, my father led me up to a great big line of books and said, "Why don't you read this? It'll knock some of the nonsense out of you!" It happened to be the entire set of Voltaire's philosophical dictionary with notes by Smollett. And I plowed through it; it took me about five years.

And of course we read all the eighteenth-century novelists, though Jane Austen, like Turgenev, didn't really engage me until I was quite mature. I read them both when I was very young, but I was grown up before I really took them in. And I discovered for myself *Wuthering Heights*; I think I read that book every year of my life for fifteen years. I simply adored it. Henry James and Thomas Hardy were really my introduction to modern literature; Grandmother didn't much approve of it. She thought Dickens might do, but she was a little against Mr. Thackeray; she thought he was too trivial. So that was as far as I got into the modern world until I left home!

INTERVIEWER: Don't you think this background—the comparative isolation of Southern rural life, and the atmosphere of literary interest —helped to shape you as a writer?

PORTER: I think it's something in the blood. We've always had great letter writers, readers, great storytellers in our family. I've listened all my life to articulate people. They were all great storytellers, and every story had shape and meaning and point.

INTERVIEWER: Were any of them known as writers?

PORTER: Well, there was my sixth or seventh cousin once removed, poor William Sidney. O. Henry, you know. He was my father's second cousin—I don't know what that makes him to me. And he was more known in the family for being a bank robber. He worked in a bank, you know, and he just didn't seem to find a talent for making money; no Porter ever did. But he had a wife who was dying of TB and he couldn't keep up with the doctor's bills. So he took a pitiful little sum—oh, about three hundred and fifty dollars—and ran away when he was accused. But he came back, because his wife was dying, and went to prison. And there was Horace Porter, who spent his whole eight years as ambassador to France looking for the bones of John Paul Jones. And when he found them, and brought them back, he wrote a book about them.

INTERVIEWER: It seems to me that your work is pervaded by a sense of history. Is that part of the family legacy?

PORTER: We were brought up with a sense of our own history, you know. My mother's family came to this country in 1648 and went to the John Randolph territory of Virginia. And one of my great great grandfathers was Jonathan Boone, the brother of Daniel. On my father's side I'm descended from Colonel Andrew Porter, whose father came to Montgomery County, Pennsylvania, in 1720. He was one of the circle of George Washington during the Revolution, a friend of Lafayette, and one of the founders of the Society of the Cincinnati—oh, he really took it seriously!—and when he died in 1809—well, just a few years before that he was offered the post of Secretary of War, but he declined. We were never very ambitious people. We never had a President, though we had two governors and some in the Army and the Navy. I suppose we did have a desire to excel but not to push our way to higher places. We thought we'd *already* arrived!

INTERVIEWER: The "we" of family is very strong, isn't it? I remember that you once wrote of the ties of blood as the "absolute point of all departure and return." And the central character in many of your stories is defined, is defining herself often, in relation to a family organization. Even the measure of time is human—expressed in terms of the very old and the very young, and how much of human experience they have absorbed.

PORTER: Yes, but it wasn't a conscious made-up affair, you know. In those days, you belonged together, you lived together, because you were a family. The head of our house was a grandmother, an old matriarch, you know, and a really lovely and beautiful woman, a good soul, and so she didn't do us any harm. But the point is that we did live like that, with Grandmother's friends, all reverend old gentlemen with frock coats, and old ladies with jet breastplates. Then there were the younger people, the beautiful girls and the handsome young boys, who were all ahead of me; when I was a little girl, eight or nine years old, they were eighteen to twenty-two, and they represented all glamour, all beauty, all joy and freedom to me. Then there was my own age, and then there were the babies. And the servants, the Negroes. We simply lived that way; to have four generations in one house, under one roof, there was nothing unusual about that. That was just my experience, and this is just the way I've reacted to it. Many other people didn't react, who were brought up in very much the same way.

I remember when I was very young, my older sister wanted to buy some old furniture. It was in Louisiana, and she had just been married. And I went with her to a wonderful old house in the country where we'd been told there was a very old gentleman who probably had some things to sell. His wife had died, and he was living there alone. So we went to this lovely old house, and, sure enough, there was this lonely beautiful old man, eighty-seven or -eight, surrounded by devoted Negro servants. But his wife was dead and his children were married and gone. He said, yes, he had a few things he wanted to sell. So he showed us through the house. And finally he opened a door, and showed us a bedroom with a beautiful four-poster bed, with a wonderful satin coverlet: the most wonderful, classical-looking bed you ever saw. And my sister said, "Oh, that's what I want." And he said, "Oh, madame, that is my marriage bed. That is the bed that my wife brought with her as a bride. We slept together in that bed for nearly sixty years. All our children were born there. Oh," he said, "I shall die in that bed, and then they can dispose of it as they like."

I remembered that I felt a little suffocated and frightened. I felt a little trapped. But why? Only because I understood that. I was brought up in that. And I was at the age of rebellion then, and it really scared me. But I look back on it now and think how perfectly wonderful, what a tremendously beautiful life it was. Everything in it had meaning.

INTERVIEWER: But it seems to me that your work suggests someone who was searching for new—perhaps broader—meanings . . . that while you've retained the South of your childhood as a point of reference, you've ranged far from that environment itself. You seem to have felt little of the peculiarly Southern preoccupation with racial guilt and the death of the old agrarian life.

PORTER: I'm a Southerner by tradition and inheritance, and I have a very profound feeling for the South. And, of course, I belong to the guilt-ridden white-pillar crowd myself, but it just didn't rub off on me. Maybe I'm just not Jewish enough, or Puritan enough, to feel that the sins of the father are visited on the third and fourth generations. Or maybe it's because of my European influences—in Texas and Louisiana. The Europeans didn't have slaves themselves as late as my family did, but they *still* thought slavery was quite natural. . . . But, you know, I was always restless, always a roving spirit. When I was a little child I was always running away. I never got very far, but they were always having to come and fetch me. Once when I was about six, my father came to get me somewhere I'd gone, and he told me later he'd asked me, "Why are you so restless? Why can't you stay here with us?" and I said to him, "I want to go and see the world. I want to know the world like the palm of my hand."

INTERVIEWER: And at sixteen you made it final.

PORTER: At sixteen I ran away from New Orleans and got married. And at twenty-one I bolted again, went to Chicago, got a newspaper job, and went into the movies.

INTERVIEWER: The movies?

PORTER: The newspaper sent me over to the old S. and A. movie studio to do a story. But I got into the wrong line, and then was too timid to get out. "Right over this way, Little Boy Blue," the man said, and I found myself in a courtroom scene with Francis X. Bushman. I was horrified by what had happened to me, but they paid me five dollars for that first day's work, so I stayed on. It was about a week before I remembered what I had been sent to do; and when I went back to the newspaper they gave me eighteen dollars for my week's non-work and fired me!

I stayed on for six months—I finally got to nearly ten dollars a day —until one day they came in and said, "We're moving to the coast." "Well, I'm not," I said. "Don't you want to be a movie actress?" "Oh, no!" I said. "Well, be a fool!" they said, and they left. That was 1914 and world war had broken out, so in September I went home.

INTERVIEWER: And then?

PORTER: Oh, I sang old Scottish ballads in costume—I made it myself—all around Texas and Louisiana. And then I was supposed to have TB, and spent about six weeks in a sanitarium. It was just bronchitis, but I was in Denver, so I got a newspaper job.

INTERVIEWER: I remember that you once warned me to avoid that at all costs—to get a job "hashing" in a restaurant in preference.

PORTER: Anything, anything at all. I did it for a year and that is what confirmed me that it wasn't doing me any good. After that I always took little dull jobs that didn't take my mind and wouldn't take all of my time, and that, on the other hand, paid me just enough to subsist. I think I've only spent about ten percent of my energies on writing. The other ninety per cent went to keeping my head above water.

And I think that's all wrong. Even Saint Teresa said, "I can pray better when I'm comfortable," and she refused to wear her haircloth shirt or starve herself. I don't think living in cellars and starving is any better for an artist than it is for anybody else; the only thing is that sometimes the artist has to take it, because it is the only possible way of salvation, if you'll forgive that old-fashioned word. So I took it rather instinctively. I was inexperienced in the world, and likewise I hadn't been trained to do anything, you know, so I took all kinds of laborious jobs. But, you know, I think I could probably have written better if I'd been a little more comfortable.

INTERVIEWER: Then you were writing all this time?

PORTER: All this time I was writing, writing no matter what else I was doing; no matter what I *thought* I was doing, in fact. I was living almost as instinctively as a little animal, but I realize now that all that time a part of me was getting ready to be an artist. That my mind was working even when I didn't know it, and didn't care if it was working or not. It is my firm belief that all our lives we are preparing to be somebody or something, even if we don't do it consciously. And the time comes one morning when you wake up and find that you have become irrevocably what you were preparing all this time to be. Lord, that could be a sticky moment, if you had been doing the wrong things, something against your grain. And, mind you, I know that can happen.

I have no patience with this dreadful idea that whatever you have in you has to come out, that you can't suppress true talent. People *can* be destroyed; they can be bent, distorted, and completely crippled. To say that you can't destroy yourself is just as foolish as to say of a young man killed in war at twenty-one or twenty-two that that was his fate, that he wasn't going to have anything anyhow.

I have a very firm belief that the life of no man can be explained in terms of his experiences, of what has happened to him, because in spite of all the poetry, all the philosophy to the contrary, we are not really masters of our fate. We don't really direct our lives unaided and unobstructed. Our being is subject to all the chances of life. There are so many things we are capable of, that we could be or do. The potentialities are so great that we never, any of us, are more than one-fourth fulfilled. Except that there may be one powerful motivating force that simply carries you along, and I think that was true of me. . . . When I was a very little girl I wrote a letter to my sister saying I wanted glory. I don't know quite what I meant by that now, but it was something different from fame or success or wealth. I know that I wanted to be a good writer, a good artist.

INTERVIEWER: But weren't there certain specific events that crystallized that desire for you—something comparable to the experience of Miranda in *Pale Horse, Pale Rider*?

PORTER: Yes, that was the plague of influenza, at the end of the First World War, in which I almost died. It just simply divided my life, cut across it like that. So that everything before that was just getting ready, and after that I was in some strange way altered, ready. It took me a long time to go out and live in the world again. I was really "alienated," in the pure sense. It was, I think, the fact that I really had participated in death, that I knew what death was, and had almost experienced it. I had what the Christians call the "beatific vision," and the Greeks called the "happy day," the happy vision just before death. Now if you have had that, and survived it, come back from it, you are no longer like other people, and there's no use deceiving yourself that you are. But you see, I did: I made the mistake of thinking I was quite like anybody else, of trying to live like other people. It took me a long time to realize that that simply wasn't true, that I had my own needs and that I had to live like me.

INTERVIEWER: And that freed you?

PORTER: I just got up and bolted. I went running off on that wild escapade to Mexico, where I attended, you might say, and assisted at, in my own modest way, a revolution.

INTERVIEWER: That was the Obregón Revolution of 1921?

PORTER: Yes—though actually I went to Mexico to study the Aztec and Mayan art designs. I had been in New York, and was getting ready to go to Europe. Now, New York was full of Mexican artists at that time, all talking about the renaissance, as they called it, in Mexico. And they said, "Don't go to Europe, go to Mexico. That's where the exciting things are going to happen." And they were right! I ran smack into the Obregón Revolution, and had, in the midst of it, the most marvelous, natural, spontaneous experience of my life. It was a terribly exciting time. It was alive, but death was in it. But nobody seemed to think of that: life was in it, too.

INTERVIEWER: What do you think are the best conditions for a writer, then? Something like your Mexican experience, or—

PORTER: Oh, I can't say what they are. It would be such an individual matter. Everyone needs something different. . . . But what I find most dreadful among the young artists is this tendency toward middle-class-ness—this idea that they have to get married and have lots of children and live just like everybody else, you know? Now, I am all for human life, and I am all for marriage and children and all that sort of thing, but quite often you can't have that and do what you were supposed to do, too. Art is a vocation, as much as anything in this world. For the real artist, it is the most natural thing in the world, not as necessary as air and water, perhaps, but as food and water. But we really do lead almost a monastic life, you know; to follow it you very often have to give up something.

INTERVIEWER: But for the unproven artist that is a very great act of faith.

PORTER: It *is* an act of faith. But one of the marks of a gift is to have the courage of it. If they haven't got the courage, it's just too bad. They'll fail, just as people with lack of courage in other vocations and walks of life fail. Courage is the first essential.

INTERVIEWER: In choosing a pattern of life compatible with the vocation?

PORTER: The thing is not to follow a pattern. Follow your own pattern of feeling and thought. The thing is, to accept your own life and not try to live someone else's life. Look, the thumbprint is not like any other, and the thumbprint is what you must go by.

INTERVIEWER: In the current vernacular then, you think it's necessary for an artist to be a "loner"—not to belong to any literary movement?

PORTER: I've never belonged to any group or huddle of any kind. You cannot be an artist and work collectively. Even the fact that I went to Mexico when everybody else was going to Europe—I went to Mexico because I felt I had business there. And there I found friends and ideas that were sympathetic to me. That was my entire milieu. I don't think anyone even knew I was a writer. I didn't show my work to anybody or talk about it, because—well, no one was particularly interested in that. It was a time of revolution, and I was running with almost pure revolutionaries!

INTERVIEWER: And you think that was a more wholesome environment for a writer than, say, the milieu of the expatriated artist in Europe at the same time?

PORTER: Well, I know it was good for me. I would have been completely smothered—completely disgusted and revolted—by the goings-on in Europe. Even now when I think of the twenties and the legend that has grown up about them, I think it was a horrible time: shallow and trivial and silly. The remarkable thing is that anybody survived in such an atmosphere—in a place where they could call F. Scott Fitzgerald a great writer!

INTERVIEWER: You don't agree?

PORTER: Of course I don't agree. I couldn't read him then and I can't read him now. There was just one passage in a book called *Tender Is the Night*—I read that and thought, "Now I will read this again," because I couldn't be sure. Not only didn't I like his writing, but I didn't like the people he wrote about. I thought they weren't worth thinking about, and I still think so. It seems to me that your human beings have to have some kind of meaning. I just can't be interested in those perfectly stupid meaningless lives. And I don't like the same thing going on now—the way the artist simply will not face up to the final reckoning of things.

INTERVIEWER: In a philosophical sense?

PORTER: I'm thinking of it now in just the artistic sense—in the sense of an artist facing up to his own end meanings. I suppose I shouldn't be mentioning names, but I read a story some time ago, I think it was in the *Paris Review,* called "The McCabes." [1] Now I think William Styron is an extremely gifted man: he's very ripe and lush and with a kind of Niagara Falls of energy, and a kind of power. But he depends so on violence and a kind of exaggerated heat—at least it looks like heat, but just turns out to be summer lightning. Because there is nothing in the world more meaningless than that whole escapade of this man going off and winding up in the gutter. You sit back and think, "Well, let's see, where are we now?" All right, it's possible that that's just what Styron meant—the whole wicked pointlessness of things. But I tell you, nothing is pointless, and nothing is meaningless if the artist will face it. And it's his business to face it. He hasn't got the right to sidestep it like that. Human life itself may be almost pure chaos, but the work of the artist—the only thing he's good for—is to take these handfuls of confusion and disparate things, things that seem to be irreconcilable, and put them together in a frame to give them some kind of shape and meaning. Even if its only his view of a meaning. That's what he's for—to give his view of life. Surely, we understand very little of what is happening to us at any given moment. But by remembering, comparing, waiting to know the consequences, we can sometimes see what an event really meant, what it was trying to teach us.

INTERVIEWER: You once said that every story begins with an ending, that until the end is known there is no story.

PORTER: That is where the artist begins to work: with the consequences of acts, not the acts themselves. Or the events. The event is important only as it affects your life and the lives of those around you. The reverberations, you might say, the overtones: that is where the artist works. In that sense it has sometimes taken me ten years to understand even a little of some important event that had happened to me. Oh, I could have given a perfectly factual account of what had happened, but I didn't know what it meant until I knew the consequences. If I didn't know the ending of a story, I wouldn't begin. I always write my last lines, my last paragraph, my last page first, and then I go back and

---

[1] "The McCabes" was mistakenly not identified as a section from Styron's novel *Set This House on Fire.*

work towards it. I know where I'm going. I know what my goal is. And how I get there is God's grace.

INTERVIEWER: That's a very classical view of the work of art—that it must end in resolution.

PORTER: Any true work of art has got to give you the feeling of reconciliation—what the Greeks would call catharsis, the purification of your mind and imagination—through an ending that is endurable because it is right and true. Oh, not in any pawky individual idea of morality or some parochial idea of right and wrong. Sometimes the end is very tragic, because it needs to be. One of the most perfect and marvelous endings in literature—it raises my hair now—is the little boy at the end of *Wuthering Heights*, crying that he's afraid to go across the moor because there's a man and woman walking there.

And there are three novels that I reread with pleasure and delight— three almost perfect novels, if we're talking about form, you know. One is *A High Wind in Jamaica* by Richard Hughes, one is *A Passage to India* by E. M. Forster, and the other is *To the Lighthouse* by Virginia Woolf. Every one of them begins with an apparently insoluble problem, and every one of them works out of confusion into order. The material is all used so that you are going toward a goal. And that goal is the clearing up of disorder and confusion and wrong, to a logical and human end. I don't mean a happy ending, because after all at the end of *A High Wind in Jamaica* the pirates are all hanged and the children are all marked for life by their experience, but it comes out to an orderly end. The threads are all drawn up. I have had people object to Mr. Thompson's suicide at the end of *Noon Wine*, and I'd say, "All right, where was he going? Given what he was, his own situation, what else could he do?" Every once in a while when I see a character of mine just going towards perdition, I think, "Stop, stop, you can always stop and choose, you know." But no, being what he was, he already *has* chosen, and he can't go back on it now. I suppose the first idea that man had was the idea of fate, of the servile will, of a deity who destroyed as he would, without regard for the creature. But I think the idea of free will was the second idea.

INTERVIEWER: Has a story never surprised you in the writing? A character suddenly taken a different turn?

PORTER: Well, in the vision of death at the end of "Flowering Judas" I knew the real ending—that she was not going to be able to face her life, what she'd done. And I knew that the vengeful spirit was going to come in a dream to tow her away into death, but I didn't know until I'd written it that she was going to wake up saying, "No!" and be afraid to go to sleep again.

INTERVIEWER: That was, in a fairly literal sense, a "true" story, wasn't it?

PORTER: The truth is, I have never written a story in my life that didn't have a very firm foundation in actual human experience—somebody else's experience quite often, but an experience that became my own by hearing the story, by witnessing the thing, by hearing just a word perhaps. It doesn't matter, it just takes a little—a tiny seed. Then it takes root, and it grows. It's an organic thing. That story had been on my mind for years, growing out of this one little thing that happened in Mexico. It was forming and forming in my mind, until one night I was quite desperate. People are always so sociable, and I'm sociable too, and if I live around friends. . . . Well, they were insisting that I come and play bridge. But I was very firm, because I knew the time had come to write that story, and I had to write it.

INTERVIEWER: What was that "little thing" from which the story grew?

PORTER: Something I saw as I passed a window one evening. A girl I knew had asked me to come and sit with her, because a man was coming to see her, and she was a little afraid of him. And as I went through the courtyard, past the flowering judas tree, I glanced in the window and there she was sitting with an open book in her lap, and there was this great big fat man sitting beside her. Now Mary and I were friends, both American girls living in this revolutionary situation. She was teaching at an Indian school, and I was teaching dancing at a girls' technical school in Mexico City. And we were having a very strange time of it. I was more skeptical, and so I had already begun to look with a skeptical eye on a great many of the revolutionary leaders. Oh, the idea was all right, but a lot of men were misapplying it.

And when I looked through that window that evening, I saw something in Mary's face, something in her pose, something in the whole situation, that set up a commotion in my mind. Because until that moment I hadn't really understood that she was not able to take care of herself, because she was not able to face her own nature and was afraid of everything. I don't know why I saw it. I don't believe in intuition. When you get sudden flashes of perception, it is just the brain working faster than usual. But you've been getting ready to know it for a long time, and when it comes, you feel you've known it always.

INTERVIEWER: You speak of a story "forming" in your mind. Does it begin as a visual impression, growing to a narrative? Or how?

PORTER: All my senses were very keen; things came to me through my eyes, through all my pores. Everything hit me at once, you know. That makes it very difficult to describe just exactly what is happening. And then, I think the mind works in such a variety of ways. Sometimes an idea starts completely inarticulately. You're not thinking in images or words or—well, it's exactly like a dark cloud moving in your head. You keep wondering what will come out of this, and then it will dissolve itself into a set of—well, not images exactly, but really thoughts. You begin to think directly in words. Abstractly. Then the words transform themselves into images. By the time I write the story my people are up and alive and walking around and taking things into their own hands. They exist as independently inside my head as you do before me now. I have been criticized for not enough detail in describing my characters, and not enough furniture in the house. And the odd thing is that I see it all so clearly.

INTERVIEWER: What about the technical problems a story presents—its formal structure? How deliberate are you in matters of technique? For example, the use of the historical present in "Flowering Judas"?

PORTER: The first time someone said to me, "Why did you write 'Flowering Judas' in the historical present?" I thought for a moment and said, "Did I?" I'd never noticed it. Because I didn't *plan* to write it any way. A story forms in my mind and forms and forms, and when it's ready to go, I strike it down—it takes just the time I sit at the typewriter. I never think about form at all. In fact, I would say that I've never been interested in anything about writing after having learned, I hope, to write. That is, I mastered my craft as well as I could. There is a technique, there is a craft, and you have to learn it. Well, I did as well as I could with that, but now all in the world I am interested in is telling a story. I have something to tell you that I, for some reason, think is worth telling, and so I want to tell it as clearly and purely and simply as I can. But I had spent fifteen years at least learning to write. I practiced writing in every possible way that I could. I wrote a pastiche of other people, imitating Dr. Johnson and Laurence Sterne, and Petrarch and Shakespeare's sonnets, and then I tried writing my own way. I spent fifteen years learning to trust myself: that's what it comes to. Just as a pianist runs his scales for ten years before he gives his concert: because when he gives that concert, he can't be thinking of his fingering or of his hands; he has to be thinking of his interpretation, of the music he's playing. He's thinking of what he's trying to communicate. And if he hasn't got his technique perfected by then, he needn't give the concert at all.

INTERVIEWER: From whom would you say you learned most during this period of apprenticeship?

PORTER: The person who influenced me most, the real revelation in my life as a writer—though I don't write in the least like him—was Laurence Sterne, in *Tristram Shandy*. Why? Because, you know, I loved the grand style, and he made it look easy. The others, the great ones, really frightened me; they were so grand and magnificent they overawed me completely. But Laurence Sterne—well, it was just exactly as if he said, "Oh, come on, do it this way. It's so easy." So I tried to do it that way, and that taught me something, that taught me more than anybody else had. Because Laurence Sterne is a most complex and subtle man.

INTERVIEWER: What about your contemporaries? Did any of them contribute significantly to your development as a writer?

PORTER: I don't think I learned very much from my contemporaries. To begin with, we were all such individuals, and we were all so argumentative and so bent on our own courses that although I got a kind of support and personal friendship from my contemporaries, I didn't get very much help. I didn't show my work to anybody. I didn't hand it around among my friends for criticism, because, well, it just didn't occur to me to do it. Just as I didn't even try to publish anything until quite late because I didn't think I was ready. I published my first story in 1923. That was "María Concepción," the first story I ever finished. I rewrote "María Concepción" fifteen or sixteen times. That was a real battle, and I was thirty-three years old. I think it is the most curious lack of judgment to publish before you are ready. If there are echoes of other people in your work, you're not ready. If anybody has to help you rewrite your story, you're not ready. A story should be a finished work before it is shown. And after that, I will not allow anyone to change anything, and I will not change anything on anyone's advice. "Here is my story. It's a finished story. Take it or leave it!"

INTERVIEWER: You are frequently spoken of as a stylist. Do you think a style can be cultivated, or at least refined?

PORTER: I've been called a stylist until I really could tear my hair out. And I simply don't believe in style. The style is you. Oh, you can cultivate a style, I suppose, if you like. But I should say it remains a cultivated style. It remains artificial and imposed, and I don't think it deceives anyone. A cultivated style would be like a mask. Everybody knows it's a mask, and sooner or later you must show yourself—or at least, you show yourself as someone who could not afford to show himself, and so created something to hide behind. Style is the man. Aristotle said it first, as far as I know, and everybody has said it since, because it is one of those unarguable truths. You do not create a style. You work, and develop yourself; your style is an emanation from your own being. Symbolism is the same way. I never consciously took or adopted a symbol in my life. I certainly did not say, "This blooming tree upon which Judas is supposed to have hanged himself is going to be the center of my story." I named "Flowering Judas" after it was written, because when reading back over it I suddenly saw the whole symbolic plan and pattern of which I was totally unconscious while I was writing. There's a pox of symbolist theory going the rounds these days in American colleges in the writing courses. Miss Mary McCarthy, who is one of the wittiest and most acute and in some ways the worst-tempered woman in American letters, tells about a little girl who came to her with a story. Now Miss McCarthy is an extremely good critic, and she found this to be a good story, and she told the girl that it was—that she considered it a finished work, and that she could with a clear conscience go on to something else. And the little girl said, "But Miss McCarthy, my writing teacher said, 'Yes, it's a good piece of work, but now we must go back and put in the symbols!'" I think that's an amusing story, and it makes my blood run cold.

INTERVIEWER: But certainly one's command of the language can be developed and refined?

PORTER: I love the purity of language. I keep cautioning my students and anyone who will listen to me not to use the jargon of trades, not to use scientific language, because they're going to be out of date the day after tomorrow. The scientists change their vocabulary, their jargon, every day. So do the doctors, and the politicians, and the theologians—every body, every profession, every trade changes its vocabulary all of the time. But there is a basic pure human speech that exists in every language. And that is the language of the poet and the writer. So many words that had good meanings once upon a time have come to have meanings almost evil—certainly shabby, certainly inaccurate.. And "psychology" is one of them. It has been so abused. This awful way a whole segment, not a generation but too many of the young writers, have got so soaked in the Freudian and post-Freudian vocabulary that they can't speak—not only can't speak English, but they can't speak *any* human language anymore. You can't write about people out of textbooks, and you can't use a jargon. You have to speak clearly and simply and purely in a language that a six-year-old child can understand; and yet have the meanings and the overtones of language, and the implications, that appeal to the highest intelligence—that is, the highest intelligence that one is able to reach. I'm not sure that I'm able to appeal to the highest intelligence, but I'm willing to try.

INTERVIEWER: You speak of the necessity of writing out of your own understanding rather than out of textbooks, and I'm sure any writer would agree. But what about the creation of masculine characters then? Most women writers, even the best of them like George Eliot, have run aground there. What about you? Was Mr. Thompson, say, a more difficult imaginative problem than Miranda?

PORTER: I never did make a profession of understanding people, man or woman or child, and the only thing I know about people is exactly what I have learned from the people right next to me. I have always lived in my immediate circumstances, from day to day. And when men ask me how I know so much about men, I've got a simple answer: everything I know about men, I've learned from men. If there is such a thing as a man's mind and a woman's mind—and I'm sure there is—it isn't what most critics mean when they talk about the two. If I show wisdom, they say I have a masculine mind. If I am silly and irrelevant—and Edmund Wilson says I often am—why then they say I have a typically feminine mind! (That's one thing about reaching my age: you can always quote the authorities about what you are.) But I haven't ever found it unnatural to be a woman.

INTERVIEWER: But haven't you found that being a woman presented to you, as an artist, certain special problems? It seems to me that a great deal of the upbringing of women encourages the dispersion of the self in many small bits, and that the practice of any kind of art demands a corralling and concentrating of that self and its always insufficient energies.

PORTER: I think that's very true and very right. You're brought up with the notion of feminine chastity and inaccessibility, yet with the curious idea of feminine availability in all spiritual ways, and in giving service to anyone who demands it. And I suppose that's why it has taken me twenty years to write this novel; it's been interrupted by just anyone who could jimmy his way into my life.

INTERVIEWER: Hemingway said once that a writer writes best when he's in love.

PORTER: I don't know whether you write better, but you feel so good you *think* you're writing better! And certainly love does create a rising of the spirit that makes everything you do seem easier and happier. But there must come a time when you no longer depend upon it, when the mind—not the will, really, either—takes over.

INTERVIEWER: In judging that the story is ready? You said a moment ago that the actual writing of a story is always done in a single spurt of energy—

PORTER: I always write a story in one sitting. I started "Flowering Judas" at seven p.m. and at one-thirty I was standing on a snowy windy corner putting it in the mailbox. And when I wrote my short novels, two of them, I just simply took the manuscript, packed a suitcase and departed to an inn in Georgetown, Pennsylvania, without leaving any forwarding address! Fourteen days later I had finished *Old Mortality* and *Noon Wine*.

INTERVIEWER: But the new novel *Ship of Fools* has been in the writing since 1942. The regime for writing this must have been a good deal different.

PORTER: Oh, it was. I went up and sat nearly three years in the country, and while I was writing it I worked every day, anywhere from three to five hours. Oh, it's true I used to do an awful lot of just sitting there thinking what comes next, because this is a great big unwieldy book with an enormous cast of characters—it's four hundred of my manuscript pages, and I get four hundred and fifty words on a page. But all that time in Connecticut, I kept myself free for work; no telephone, no visitors—

oh, I really lived like a hermit, everything but being fed through a grate! But it is, as Yeats said, a "solitary sedentary trade." And I did a lot of gardening, and cooked my own food, and listened to music, and of course I would read. I was really very happy. I can live a solitary life for months at a time, and it does me good, because I'm working. I just get up bright and early—sometimes at five o'clock—have my black coffee, and go to work.

INTERVIEWER: You work best in the morning, then?

PORTER: I work whenever I'm let. In the days when I was taken up with everything else, I used to do a day's work, or housework, or whatever I was doing, and then work at night. I worked when I could. But I prefer to get up very early in the morning and work. I don't want to speak to anybody or see anybody. Perfect silence. I work until the vein is out. There's something about the way you feel, you know when the well is dry, that you'll have to wait till tomorrow and it'll be full up again.

INTERVIEWER: The important thing, then, is to avoid any breaks or distractions while you're writing?

PORTER: To keep at a boiling point. So that I can get up in the morning with my mind still working where it was yesterday. Then I can stop in the middle of a paragraph and finish it the next day. I began writing *Ship of Fools* twenty years ago, and I've been away from it for several years at a time and stopped in the middle of a paragraph—but, you know, I can't tell where the crack is mended, and I hope nobody else can.

INTERVIEWER: You find no change in style, or in attitudes, over the years?

PORTER: It's astonishing how little I've changed: nothing in my point of view or my way of feeling. I'm going back now to finish some of the great many short stories that I have begun and not been able to finish for one reason or another. I've found one that I think I can finish. I have three versions of it: I started it in 1923, and it's based on an episode in my life that took place when I was twenty. Now here I am, seventy, and it's astonishing how much it's like me now. Oh, there are certain things, certain turns of sentence, certain phrases that I think I can sharpen and make more clear, more simple and direct, but my point of view, my being, is strangely unchanged. We change, of course, every day; we are not the same people who sat down at this table, yet there is a basic and innate being that is unchanged.

INTERVIEWER: *Ship of Fools* too is based upon an event that took place ten years or more before the first writing, isn't it? A sea voyage just before the beginning of the European war.

PORTER: It is the story of my first voyage to Europe in 1931. We embarked on an old German ship at Veracruz and we landed in Bremerhaven twenty-eight days later. It was a crowded ship, a great mixture of nationalities, religions, political beliefs—all that sort of thing. I don't think I spoke a half-dozen words to anybody. I just sat there and watched —not deliberately, though. I kept a diary in the form of a letter to a friend, and after I got home the friend sent it back. And, you know, it is astonishing what happened on that boat, and what happened in my mind afterwards. Because it is fiction now.

INTERVIEWER: The title—isn't it from a medieval emblem?—suggests that it might also be an allegory.

PORTER: It's just exactly what it seems to be. It's an allegory if you like, though I don't think much of the allegorical as a standard. It's a parable, if you like, of the ship of this world on its voyage to eternity.

INTERVIEWER: I remember your writing once—I think in the preface to *Flowering Judas*—of an effort to understand what you called the "majestic and terrible failure" of Western man. You were speaking then of the World War and what it signified of human folly. It seems to me that *Ship of Fools* properly belongs to that investigation of betrayal and self-delusion—

PORTER: Betrayal and treachery, but also self-betrayal and self-deception—the way that all human beings deceive themselves about the way they operate. . . . There seems to be a kind of order in the universe, in the movement of the stars and the turning of the earth and the changing of the seasons, and even in the cycle of human life. But human life itself is almost pure chaos. Everyone takes his stance, asserts his own rights and feelings, mistaking the motives of others, and his own. . . . Now, nobody knows the end of the life he's living, and neither do I. Don't forget I am a passenger on that ship; it's not the other people altogether who are the fools! We don't really know what is going to happen to us, and we don't know why. Quite often the best we can do is to keep our heads, and try to keep at least one line unbroken and unobstructed. Misunderstanding and separation are the natural conditions of man. We come together only at these pre-arranged meeting grounds; we were all passengers on that ship, yet at his destination, each one was alone.

INTERVIEWER: Did you find that the writing of *Ship of Fools* differed from the writing of shorter fiction?

PORTER: It's just a longer voyage, that's all. It was the question of keeping everything moving at once. There are about forty-five main characters, all taking part in each others' lives, and then there was a steerage of sugar workers, deportees. It was all a matter of deciding which should come first, in order to keep the harmonious moving forward. A novel is really like a symphony, you know, where instrument after instrument has to come in at its own time, and no other. I tried to write it as a short novel, you know, but it just wouldn't confine itself. I wrote notes and sketches. And finally I gave in. "Oh, no, this is simply going to have to be a novel," I thought. That was a real horror. But it needed a book to contain its full movement: of the sea, and the ship on the sea, and the people going around the deck, and into the ship, and up from it. That whole movement, felt as one forward motion: I can feel it while I'm reading it. I didn't "intend" it, but it took hold of me.

INTERVIEWER: As writing itself, perhaps, "took hold" of you—we began by your saying that you had never intended to be a professional anything, even a professional writer.

PORTER: I look upon literature as an art, and I practice it as an art. Of course, it is also a vocation, and a trade, and a profession, and all kinds of things; but first it's an art, and you should practice it as that, I think. I know a great many people disagree, and they are welcome to it. I think probably the important thing is to get your work done, in the way you can—and we all have our different and separate ways. But I look upon literature as an art, and I believe that if you misuse it or abuse it, it will leave you. It is not a thing that you can nail down and use as you want. You have to let it use you, too.

Glenway Wescott

Katherine Anne Porter
Personally

*The only real voyage is not an approach to landscapes but a
viewing of the universe with the eyes of a hundred other people.*
—MARCEL PROUST

HAVING had the pleasure of lifelong friendship with Miss Porter, I find
it irksome to call her "Miss Porter." It has been mainly a comradeship
of the literary life, and on that account perhaps, in conversation and in
correspondence, I often address her as "Porter." A host of her fellow
writers and others speak of her and to her as "Katherine Anne," with
or without a basis of intimacy. Somewhat like Jane Austen, or like
Colette, she has an unassuming sort of celebrity that invites or at least
inspires friendliness. Let me now also take the fond informal tone,
to celebrate the publication of her novel *Ship of Fools*, twenty years in
the making.

First, some facts: She was born on May 15, 1890, in Texas, in "soft
backland farming country, full of fruits and flowers and birds," on the
banks of a branch of the Colorado River denominated Indian Creek,
small and clear, unimportant but unforgettable. She went to a convent
school, perhaps more than one, and was an uneven student: A in history
and composition and other subjects having to do with literature, but,
she admits, "D in everything else, including deportment, which sometimes went down to E and stopped there."

She spent an important part of her girlhood in New Orleans, and afterward lived in New York City and in Mexico City and in Paris and in Baton Rouge, Louisiana, and in more recent years, in upper New York State and in southern California and in Connecticut and in Washington, D.C. Prior to *Ship of Fools*, she published five short novels or nouvelles, and approximately twenty short stories (my count), and several dozen essays and criticisms and historical studies; quality always instead of quantity. She is an incomparable letter writer, sparkling, poignant, and abundant, and a famous conversationalist.

Now let me try to describe her, as to her physical presence and personality. Like many women accustomed to being loved, she dreads and disapproves of photographers, although in fact usually she has lent herself well to their techniques, and they have been on her side. I remember one of her diatribes, some years ago, against a photographer and an interviewer sent by one of the news weeklies, who, she said, had caught her unawares and committed a misrepresentation of her. In the photograph in question when it appeared she looked (to me) like Marie Antoinette young, her hair perfectly coifed and powdered-looking, playing her typewriter as though it were a spinet. And it amazed me to note how skillfully she had been able to simplify the record of her life for the interviewer also.

She has in fact a lovely face, of the utmost distinction in the Southern way; moonflower-pale, never sunburned, perhaps not burnable. She is a small woman, with a fine figure still; sometimes very slender, sometimes not. Her eyes are large, dark, and lustrous, and they are apt to give one fond glances, or teasing merry looks, or occasionally great flashes of conviction or indignation. Her voice is sweet, a little velvety or husky. In recent years she has familiarized a great number of appreciative fellow Americans with it, by means of reading and speaking engagements, and phonograph recordings.

I remember hearing her read her finest nouvelle, "Noon Wine," one summer afternoon in 1940, at a time of cruel setbacks in her personal life, in a little auditorium on the campus of Olivet College planted with oak trees. It was hot and the windows stood open. The oak trees were full of bluejays, and they were trying to shout her down. Were they muses in bird form, I remember humorously asking myself, inspiring her to cease publicly performing old work, to start writing something new? (In fact it was later that year that she began *Ship of Fools*, then temporarily entitled *No Safe Harbor*.)

She must have had a bout of bronchitis that spring or summer; she almost whispered the great tale, breathing a little hollowly, with an uneasy frayed sound now and then. Certainly there were not as many decibels in her voice as in the outcry of the jays. Nevertheless, her every tone carried; her every syllable was full of meaning and easy to understand, just as it is in print.

Certainly not muses, she protested years later, when I had written her a reminiscent letter about our brief sojourn together on that campus: "Jays are the furies, never trust them, never be deceived by them."

They congregated on the hilltop in Connecticut where she then lived, "thieving and raiding and gluttonizing everything in sight," depriving even the squirrels of their peanuts, and of course driving away from the seed table "all the little sweet birds" that she especially wanted to feed and save.

Characteristically, she had in mind a certain hierarchy of the bird world, poetical but perhaps not just. One day she looked up and discovered hawks hovering over the wooded-lot and the meadow, closer and closer, and it came over her with dismay that by drawing the small birds together she was simply facilitating matters for the predators. That was the underlying theme of "Flowering Judas," the story that made her reputation in 1930, a theme of intense concern to her all her life: involuntary or at least unintentional betrayal.

But, she wrote, the songbirds of Connecticut "were skilled and quick, and we know that they can make common cause and chase a hawk away; we have seen that together, have we not? And in some way, I cannot hate a hawk; it is a noble kind of bird who has to hunt for living food in order to live; his risks and privations are great. But the jay! there is no excuse for his existence, there should be a bounty on every ugly hammerhead of that species!"

Throughout human history hawks have been thought godlike, or at least comparable to the greatest men of action, our heroes, our lords and masters. In this letter Katherine Anne seemed to make some identification of the small birds with men and women of letters and of the arts, a somewhat more modern fancy. In a later letter she referred once more to *Cyanocitta cristata*, the middle-sized hammerheaded ones, as emblematic of certain intrusive parasitic persons who devote themselves to writers, perhaps to her more than the average. "They are as rapacious and hard to fight off as the bluejays," but, she boasted, "I have developed a great severity of rejection that I did not know I was capable of. We were all brought up on the Christian and noble idea that we have no right to deny our lives and substance to anyone who seems to need either or both. Never was a fonder delusion." And then with characteristic love of justice, even in the midst of irritation, she reminded herself that, to some extent, life and substance had been contributed to her by certain persons in her day; how had those persons known that she was a songbird? Are there, for human beings also, what ornithologists call "field marks"?

One of her "field marks," I think, is a profound, inward, hidden way of working; not just thoughtfully, methodically, as perhaps prose writers ought to be able to work, as indeed in her case the finished product suggests that she may have done. "I spend my life thinking about technique, method, style," she once told me. "The only time I do not think of them at all is when I am writing."

※   ※

. . . Literary critics and historians have often remarked the mighty contributions of the female sex to literature, far and wide and always. For the most part those who have done the contributing have been spinsters, nuns, courtesans, invalids, a little exempt from the more distracting, exhausting aspects of womanhood as such. Katherine Anne, throughout her youth and middle age, led a maximum life, concomitantly with her perfect, even perfectionist story writing. As I have remarked, she seems to like to simplify a part of the record of her existence for any sort of questioner. In fact, except for essentially private matters of love and marriage and ill-health and economics, it really has been simple. And therefore I (and other friends), instead of concentrating on ascertaining all the realities, the dates and the names and the locations and so on, have always interested ourselves in what might be called story material about her, somehow more characteristic than her mere biography.

For example, when she was a girl somewhere in the South, she had to spend months and months in a sanitarium with a grave pulmonary illness, diagnosed as one of the baffling, uncommon forms of tuberculosis. She was too ill to have visitors. Letters also evidently were over-stimulating and exhausting. Even books seemed not good for her; her reading had to be rationed, just a few pages at a time. Then it was discovered that the intense restlessness of her bright eyes gazing at the ceiling, examining and re-examining the furniture, staring at the solitude, gave her a temperature. Her doctor therefore prescribed that a restful green baize cloth be placed over her face for an hour or two every morning and every afternoon, as one covers the cage of a canary when one doesn't want it to sing. I feel convinced that if anything of the sort were done to me I should give up the ghost, on account of the auto-suggestion and the discouragement. Not Katherine Anne! That was only the beginning of a lifetime of delicate health and indomitable strength.

All this balance of physiology in her case, strong constitution, poor health, has mystified those who care for her. Perhaps the physicians whom she happened on here and there—"the pulse-takers, the stetho-scope-wielders, the order-givers," as she has called them—have been mystifiers in some measure. One of them, in upstate New York, told her that her trouble was all a matter of allergies, and when she inquired, "What allergies?" his answer was, "You're allergic to the air you breathe."

Another, in California, she wrote me, "set out to change my chemistry, which made him say tst, tst, after a very thorough going-over, and he aims to supply all my lacks and to suppress all my internal enemies. There is about the whole project something so blithely Californian that I cannot but fall in with it."

Still another, a young one in Connecticut, pleased her by practicing "real materia medica," and not saying anything at all about her state of mind or her nervous condition. She has always objected to having strangers, even specialists, fussing around in her psychology, comparing them to the most disrespectful, disrupting type of cleaning woman. "They mess the place up; they don't know where things belong, or what goes with what."

One year at Christmastime, when she had been felled for ten days by some form of influenza and had been taking one of the sulfa drugs, she got up out of bed, though in mortal weakness; took a look at herself: prettily dressed, with "her hair in a curl or two, with an expression on her face which she could not quite make out, "distinctly remote, disengaged, full of mental reservations"; and then in a longish letter undertook to make clear to me her whole view of life. But it was unclarifiable, inexplicable, she had to admit, even to herself as she was living it, "because its truth or falseness cannot be known until the end."

Therefore, instead, she concluded that letter with an account of the medicines she had been taking: "a fantastic row of apothecary's powders, pills, and potions, all of them in the most poisonously brilliant colors, amethyst and sapphire and emerald and purple, each with its own mission of soothing or elevating the spirits, calming the heart or stimulating it, loosening the phlegm and tightening the nerves, stopping the cough and lowering the fever.

"As for the sulfa, I have had to take a tablet every four hours for two nights and two days, and never once did my mind fail to wake me at the right hour, on the hour, like a little radio station. Once I slept stubbornly, and was waked finally by a sharp rapping at my door. It was four in the morning; the whole house was asleep and quiet. I sat up in bed, knowing Who had done it."

It is hard to read this slight incident rightly, with its capitalized Who, suggestive of the commissioning of Mozart's never-finished Requiem by Whoever that was, a being never seen again, and of other such myths. But, stop and think, if that rapper at Katherine Anne's door at four in the morning had been Death, He would have stayed his hand and let her sleep and skip the sulfa. That was in 1943; it is pleasant to think that the greater part of *Ship of Fools* was written on time borrowed from Him.

No doubt about it, there are warring forces in Katherine Anne. Is it that her physique wearies of having to house a spirit so strenuous and emotional, and now and then tries to expel it or to snuff it out? Or is it instinctive in her soul to keep punishing her body for not being superhuman, for not being ideal, for not being immortal? Neither has ever exactly prevailed over the other; both have been invincible. Nothing has come of the great dichotomy; or, to be exact, literature has come of it.

"Every force of instinct and every psychic evil in us," she once wrote, "fight the mind as their mortal enemy; but in this as in everything else I have known from the beginning which side I am on, and I am perfectly willing to abide by my first choice until death; indeed I can't do otherwise. For death it must be in the end, so far as the flesh is concerned; but what lives on afterward can be honorable." To wit, twenty-six works of fiction of different lengths, honorable and (I am sure) durable; and more to come.

She lived in Mexico for a good while when she was young, and a number of the men who revolutionized that intense and artistic though primitive nation were her friends. In 1922 she brought the first exhibition of Mexican-Indian folk art north of the border, but only as far north as Los Angeles. One of the revolutionaries wrote a song about her, "La Norteña," which, I have heard tell, has become a folk song; little companies of young singers, mariachis, like boy scouts in a dream, sing it in the streets. I understand that another lady also lays claim to it. Be that as it may, "Flowering Judas" softly resounds with music of that kind, strummingly accompanied and perhaps mortally seductive.

Some years later in Paris she wrote another Mexican tale, a nouvelle in memoir form, "Hacienda." It is a rarity in her lifework in that it is all à clef; mainly a portrait of the great Russian film maker, Eisenstein, with others of note, helpers and hinderers of his work in Mexico, clustered around. It has a singularity of style also, somehow an outdoor style, leafy and tendrilous, seeming to weave itself into a fabric without her usual touch; soft breezy sentences, with a warmth and animation unlike her earlier writing.

Certainly it points toward *Ship of Fools*. For some mysterious reason, perhaps nothing but the timing in her life, her recollection of Mexico evidently has lapsed less for her, subsided less, than that of other places she has lived. "Flowering Judas" had an odd, almost painful dreaminess, with only present-time verbs; and in the first twenty pages of *Ship of Fools*, when the passengers are assembling and waiting to sail, as in "a little purgatory between land and sea," the half-Indian world seems to reach out after them, overstimulatingly, and it haunts the entire volume, across the ocean, though its subject matter is mainly German and American.

In another way the latest of her nouvelles, "The Leaning Tower," must also have served as a study for the future greater undertaking: a tale of Berlin on the eve of the Nazi revolution, when in fact Katherine Anne spent a winter there, and saw the dangerousness of the Germans, and understood how risky it was to fear them or, on the other hand, to be too simply prejudiced against them. Doubtless also, while writing it, during World War II, she was aware of the aesthetic pitfall of propagandizing in any sense, with the excitement of the time. She holds her breath in it.

Now to turn to another area of the legendry of Katherine Anne's life, which she has not perpetuated in any of her fiction.—Someone, years ago, used to say that at an early age she had been in the movies as a Mack Sennett bathing girl, along with Gloria Swanson and Mabel Normand et al. Certainly she was as good-looking as they, whether or not she could have performed as funnily. For some reason I never quite like to question or cross-question her about things; but I once ventured to do so about this. It was a matter of journalism, she explained, not show business. Commissioned to write an article for some newspaper or magazine she pretended briefly to be a comedienne for the sake of the realistic detail and local color.

Not so long ago she had a try at earning her living by script writing. Her first Hollywood assignment was not so much to write as to be attached in an Egeria-like or muse-like capacity to a famous producer, now dead. For a while this amused her; at least she sent back to the Eastern seaboard amusing reports of it. "One or the other of us," she reported—he had another salaried writer also at his beck and call, perhaps more than one—"tosses a tiny shred of an idea at him. He seizes it out of the air and without stopping for breath constructs a whole scene. He then asks us what we think of it, and as we open our mouths to answer, he says, 'It's a wonderful scene. Now what else have you got in mind?' And the thing is repeated; sometimes we just sit there for two hours." What he had in mind, or perhaps I should say, in the works, was a film about Queen Elizabeth I.

Presently she began to feel like "a fox with his leg in a trap," gnawing away at it; and by the end of the thirteen-week stint contracted for in the first place she had persuaded her famous man that she was not the inspirer he needed. A part of their maladjustment, she sensed, was the fact that he was a Christian Scientist, whereas she had been brought up a Roman Catholic. During the thirteen weeks he had seemed deeply disapproving of the large salary that he or his studio had been paying her; but suddenly, she wrote, when she was on her way, he "began to worry about my future. What on earth was I going to do now?

where was I going? did I have any money? I was happy to be able to tell him that I was relatively rich and wasn't going anywhere."

In fact she was relatively poor; apparently they had been paying her in Confederate money or fool's gold or something. Not seeing any other solution for her practical problems just then, she transferred her talents to another studio, where she was put to work on a film about Madame Sans-Gêne.

All her life Katherine Anne has been bewitched by the hope of ceasing to be homeless, of settling somewhere and getting her books and manuscripts and notebooks out of storage and within reach somehow, on shelves and in filing cabinets and in ring-binders. With the evanescent Western money she bought a small segment of mountain for a building site, but could not keep it. One day as she sat peacefully writing in a rented ranch cabin in the Mojave Desert a Western wind arose and tore out a window frame over her desk and slightly fractured her skull; once more, the Furies! But, never forget, the Furies sometimes are on the side of the angels. She did not properly belong out West, at least not then.

In subsequent years, a good deal of the time, at intervals, she has had to depend on the universities and colleges for her livelihood. As a rule, at the beginning of her various stints or bouts on campuses, she has been persuaded by the literature-loving educators who have arranged things, or she has persuaded herself, that not much actual pedagogy would be required of her. Usually, however, they seem to have got the harness on her in some way. I remember a letter from a very great university indeed, in the Middle West, specifying her teaching schedule: only five hours a week actually behind the microphone in the classroom (so specified in her contract) and only about eighty term papers to be read and graded. But she also had to examine the manuscripts of the more creative young persons on campus and to advise them in hour-long sessions; about fourteen of these a week. Also once a week she had to give a spontaneous hour-long lecture to some special class or group or club. It may be that no trained and experienced professional would find this schedule at all onerous or unfair. To Katherine Anne, as a mature woman of genius in delicate health, perhaps somewhat proud and euphoric, with so much creative work of her own not only in mind but partly on paper, and covered by publishers' contracts, it seemed hard; and all too often her university engagements were terminated by illness.

※ ※

As the quantity of my quotations will have suggested to you, I have been rereading my precious file of long letters from her, and another set addressed to Monroe Wheeler, about two hundred in all. She and I made friends in Paris in 1932 and began our correspondence upon my return to this country in the autumn of 1933, and it has been continuous ever since. Yes, yes, probably she should have repressed or restrained this long-distance friendliness somewhat, in order to produce more for publication. But as I peruse her letters, now that much of the circumstantial detail in them has ceased to be of interest, and therefore the main elements and outlines of her mind and her life appear more impressively, as it were a range of hills which the autumn has stripped of leaves, I am struck by something about them that may have conditioned her, even benefited her, in her art of fiction.

It is that they are extraordinarily, uniquely subjective: self-judging and explanatory and disciplinary, and self-defending, with matchless detail and finesse in all these mirrorings of the heart and the mind, shifting and shining, and, in a way, hypnotizing. Whereas in fiction she has been free from herself. In fiction she has maintained a maximum impersonality, a disengagement from any sort of autobiographical point of view, a distinctness between her own ego, her sensitiveness and compulsions and illusions, and those of all the alter egos that she writes about, and an abstention from fantasy and lyricism and rhetoric, of which most novelists, indeed even many journalists and historians, are incapable.

It is almost startling to compare her with other famous twentieth-century women in this respect: Virginia Woolf! Colette! Even reticent and rather cold writers such as Maugham have made use of their shyness, exercised their self-consciousness, almost as a convention or a technique. As for the writing of our more extreme, compendious, sociological novelists, it is a sort of concavity, which almost teases one to deduce what they themselves are, convexly; rather like the shapes of ancient Pompeians in the awful layers of ashes from Vesuvius.

Katherine Anne is not like that at all. The objectivity of her narrative art, if I may apply to her Coleridge's famous formula (only Shakespeare really filled the bill, *he* thought), is a matter of sending herself out of herself; of thinking herself into "the thoughts and feelings of beings in circumstances wholly and strangely different" from her own: *hic labor, hoc opus.*

I believe that her vast self-expressive and confidential first-person communication to her friends, freshly inspired or provoked each time, swiftly produced on the typewriter, and not rewritten, scarcely reread, has served to purify her mind of a good deal of that pride and willfulness and narcissism and excitability by which the life-work of most modern fiction writers has often been beclouded, enfeebled, blemished. Of course her letter writing must have shortened her working days and used up incalculable energy, thus reducing the amount of her production of the more public forms of literature.

In the earliest of her nouvelles, "Old Mortality," a Northerner may mind the extremely regional feeling, the patriotism of the South, which is a group subjectivity. But even this is so much less soft and heady and spicy than the accounts that other fiction writers have given us of that important part of the world, its premises, its problems, that it seems almost bitter, like a medicine, like a lesson. At the end of it the protagonist, Miranda, realizes how much of her girlhood she has spent "peering in wonder" at other people's notions of the past, "like a child at a magic-lantern show," and resolves to close her mind stubbornly to all such secondhand remembrance, spiritual predigestion.

In "Pale Horse, Pale Rider," and in later stories featuring that same somewhat autobiographical Miranda—the best of which is perhaps "The Grave," an episode of almost mystical childhood, having to do with the closeness and connectedness of life and death, womb and tomb (as in medieval religious imagery)—all is self-possessed and responsible, thoughtful and indeed philosophical. What I call her impersonality applies even to the painting of her own portrait, when it is fictitious. And apparently the saving thoughtfulness, the mastery of her mind over every sort of old ideal and dark prejudice and grievance and self-flattery, takes place at the time that she stores things away in her memory, for future use; not just according to her formal intellect and her sense of story pattern when she begins to work. Again, we may see in this something of her classic practical womanly temperament, housewifeliness! Subject matter that she deems worth keeping she simply folds up a little, scales down a little, and deflates and dehydrates, with applications of sense of humor, sense of proportion, sense of justice, as it were against moth and worm and mildew and dust.

It pleases me to recall a conversation that I had with Katherine Anne while she was writing "Pale Horse, Pale Rider" and was having trouble with a passage in it toward the end in which Miranda, desperately ill, almost dead, was to see heaven. She told me that she herself, at the end of World War I, had experienced this part of what she had created this heroine to experience and to make manifest; and because, no doubt, it really was heaven, she found herself unable to re-see it with her lively, healthy eyes.

This conversation took place in a valley in New Jersey where I used to live, which has been turned into a water reservoir, gone forever! It was springtime; the sward or sod was moss green, strewn with little blue shadows under the trees half in leaf; the vistas upstream and downstream were dim, Bavarian-looking; and there were some soprano voices within earshot, I have forgotten whose voices. With characteristic, somewhat superficial helpfulness I proposed to my dear friend and rival, "Why not at that point just write a page about your inability to recede, your impotence to write? Eternal curtain, blinding, effulgence! Let each one of your readers fill in the kind of heaven that his particular life has prepared him to go to, when his turn comes.

"What else is heaven, anyway?" I went on, where angels fear to tread. "What can it be, empirically, but the indescribable; the defeat of literature; the end of empiricism?"

To my amusement and perhaps regret, mingled with a little vanity, Katherine Anne did not take to this suggestion. She let "Pale Horse" go for another year, and turned to other work. She said au revoir to her New York and New Jersey friends and went to live for a while in Louisiana, perhaps waiting all that time to re-see Miranda's heaven.

In due course, "Pale Horse, Pale Rider" appeared in book form, in 1939, with the vision worth a year's waiting: "thinned to a fine radiance, spread like a great fan, and curved out into a curved rainbow." What comes before this also is extraordinary: Miranda at death's door with the influenza of 1918, afraid of her doctor just because he is her doctor, in charge of her death, and because he is a German doctor, and because it is 1918. Even in Denver, Colorado, where that story is set, a world war does not let one even die at peace. I think that, if the years to come winnow literary wheat from chaff as the past has done, this story may be valued as a unique record of that modern curse and ailment, horror of the German, which lapsed during the twenties, then began again; also as a prelude to *Ship of Fools.*

Miranda's beginning to recover from influenza is another extraordinary page; just less and less bitterness of pus in the naturally sweet flesh, up and up toward life, with a wink of consciousness more and more often. The strangest return, the way of the solitary ego, the opposite of the great legend—the Orpheus in Miranda keeping the Eurydice in her alive not by looking away but precisely by contemplating what was happening every instant.

Of the three nouvelles in that volume, indeed, of the five that she has published thus far, "Noon Wine" is the one that I love best. I may say, parenthetically, that Katherine Anne herself objects to my use of the borrowed French word and its several cognates, also European in origin, novella, novelle, and novelette. I see her point. As to vocabulary, whatever the problem, she is a purist, and it is vulgar to trick out one's writing about writing with this and that imported feather (though Poe did so a good deal). Also, as the author, to date, of only one large-scale work of fiction in an era when "novel, novel," is the word to conjure with, and when most of the praise as well as the pay goes to bulky productions, she must be glad of any nuance of one's criticism which will remind the reader that "Pale Horse, Pale Rider" and "Old Mortality" and "Noon Wine" and "Hacienda" and "The Leaning Tower" are major works. They are, indeed; and doubtless it took more skill, more time, and more creative strength to keep them to the length that, as it seemed to her (and as it sems to me), inspiration and subject matter in those five cases called for than it would have taken to amplify them, to swell them up with self-generating detail, to spin them out with extra passages of introductoriness and didacticism and suspense and consequences, as large-scale novelists ordinarily do.

But, for my part, I cannot wean myself from the use of the term "nouvelle," because it designates not just a certain length, let us say, twenty or thirty thousand words, but a scope and particular inspiration fundamentally differing from the several types of short story and the several variations of the novel. The nouvelle is an account of a limited number of characters in close connection, or in consequential or interesting contrast; and of their situation as a whole and their state of being in some detail and in depth, not just an incident or episode in their lives. It is a mode of narration in which the narrated time serves as a window to illuminate a remoter past and to reveal something of a foreseeable future; multum in parvo, but very multum and not too parvo. It often shows as many facets of meaning as a novel, but it does not apply to as many levels of experience and observation and significance. Along with Goethe's nouvelle which is called *Die Novelle* and Mann's *Death in Venice* and Benjamin Constant's *Adolphe* and Mérimée's *Carmen* and Colette's *Gigi* and Melville's *Billy Budd* and Forster's *The Eternal Moment*, Katherine Anne's "Noon Wine" is a model of the form, an example for the textbooks.

It has an epic quality despite its small scale and modern dress, with only two heroes, one heroine, and one significant villain, expressing themselves commonly, and in natural pitiful circumstances. The epic that it makes me think of, I may say, humorously but not insincerely, is *Paradise Lost*, because it has Lucifer in it, a very modern and American Lucifer named Mr. Hatch. Hatch, not exactly fat, "more like a man who has been fat recently"; Hatch, who goes to and fro "telling other people what kind of tobacco to chew"; Hatch, with the discovery and roundup of "twenty-odd escaped loonatics" to his credit. His prey this time is Olaf Helton, whose brother years before took away his harmonica, who therefore stabbed said brother with a pitchfork. He escaped, and since then has been working for lazy Mr. Thompson and his dear sickly wife. He has somewhat lightened their burden and much restored their prosperity. They have got in the habit of hearing what you might call his theme song, a drinking song, rendered over and over on a series of new harmonicas.

When Hatch appears on the scene it all goes like a charm, like a curse. To save Helton, as he thinks, Thompson kills Hatch. He is tried and acquitted; but the breach of the great taboo is too much for him to forgive himself. The Eumenides are in him, nagging, arguing; soon his state of mind is such that he frightens even his beloved wife. Therefore he condemns himself to death and executes himself. There is a most touching page toward the close which is like a song or an aria: Mrs. Thompson weeping to have Helton back, saying a sort of prayer against the violence of menfolk, kneeling before her icebox as if it were an altar; the icebox Helton had helped her to buy. This perfectly womanly woman, eternal bystander and born widow; and the typical hired man, the type of wrongdoer whom even the Eumenides might spare because there was no idea or idealism behind his wrong, whom everyone except the Hatches of this world must forgive; and the Thompsons' fine little boys, by the evolution of whose characters we are subtly made to feel time passing and humanity incessant: all these are exemplary, human and arch-human, in the grandest manner. Grand also, the way in which the murder of Hatch is made to epitomize our lesser losses of temper also, even the wielding of the jackknife of wit and of the little hatchet of righteous criticism, by which the psyche of the stupid man may be somewhat murdered and the heart of the murderous-minded man himself broken. Also it is a reminder of how evil may come of resistance to evil, of which the worldly man in this half-Germanized world needs to be reminded.

There is no end to the kinds of evil which Hatch typifies. You belittle him unfairly and unwisely if you assume that he has gone hunting his twenty-odd madmen just for the cash compensation. It has been chiefly to satisfy his clear sense of right and wrong; and to exercise the power to which he is entitled as a democratic citizen. There is some repression of the ego in our comfortable country, and therefore some perversion of it, therefore cruelty. Hatch has the legal mind, particularly what you might call the blue-legal mind.

Behold in him also political genius, which is psychopathic unless it is psychiatric, and in either case more oratorical than honest. At the start he positively woos Thompson, like a candidate for public office: Hatch "For Law and Order." And you might think that this hell-bent bullying technique would not get one vote; but you learn that it gets millions. In him also may be seen some evils of journalism, and some evils of the police, so worrisome and intimidating that one scarcely cares to comment on them.

Look at him as you like: he signifies always a little more than you have seen and seems larger than life-size; and you think that he must have more lives than a cat; and with facets like a diamond he throws bright, instructive flashes, on one thing and another. Thus I feel justified in having used that moot, incongruous word "epic." He is not only a man hunter, he is mankind as man hunter, sempiternal. He is not only a busybody, he is the great American busybody; godlike as only a devil can be. Lucifer! No wonder that Thompson at first is reminded of some-one he has seen before, somewhere. Katherine Anne just mentions this, without explanation. It is perhaps the only signal she gives that she meant Hatch to be a personification as well as a person. Thompson hates him long before there has been a peep out of him about his man hunt; and so does the reader, surely, upon instinct. Hatch-malevolence can often be felt previous to, and lies deeper than, Hatch-activity. It lies so deep indeed that one is half afraid to say simply that it is evil. I always particularly resent the fact that he has kept, as you might say, virtuous, in order to accumulate a good conscience, as one might pinch pennies half one's life to invest in a big business; and his air of friendliness with-out affection, curiosity without imagination, and the detached manner of his invasion of the others' privacy. Of course it is scarcely detachment to get chopped open by one's host's ax; but I feel that this is the least that could be expected to happen to him in the circumstances, an occu-pational hazard. I resent the fact that he manages—Katherine Anne lets him manage—not to deserve it.

A specific and unabashed (though somewhat mysterious) morality works through and through this whole tale, like a fat, like a yeast, like an antidote. Katherine Anne does not pity Hatch, but seemingly she would like to; she abstains from despising him. Perhaps suspicious of the very clarity of her hatred of hatchism, she compensates the individual Hatch for it by a kind of demi-deification and enlargement. She is as careful about him as if she were wearing his face as a mask for her face, and this were confession of a misdeed of hers. Do not forget that both Helton and Thompson commit murder; and the latter's plea of self-defense is specious or erroneous, if not dishonest. Hatch is not to blame for anything except his being, and his happening to be just there, in juxtaposition with these others. For many years he has been doing what he attempts that day; no one has ever objected before; what reason had he to suppose there was any law against it? The written law is a makeshift, and the unwritten law all double meaning. In entire civilization, every one of us is partly responsible for this darkness. Katherine Anne, mild even as she contemplates murder, assumes responsibility.

Let me say finally that it is a great factor in my admiration of this story that she has not pointed out any one of the significances I have seen in it and tried to list. There was no need to, I admiringly think. As critic, pro tem, it is my pleasure to point. The feeling of the good and evil in question doubtless accumulated in her heart in the abstract, for years; and the contrast of the two, no, three kinds of humanity, and eternal warfare of the two equally sincere schools of morality, must have come to her mind one day with such energy that there was no resisting the impulse to show them in action, in an ideal bout. Then, because of her humane and womanly humility, abstraction blushed; abstraction bowed to fate, the truest fate of all, that of circumstance and coincidence and dialogue; abstraction stooped to human nature, and dressed itself and embodied itself in this episode, whether fact or fancy or a mixture.

One could not ask for a more objective work of fiction than "Noon Wine." Everything that it tells is a question of its time and its place and its conjunction of characters, only four principals, with nothing of that darkling presence and involvement and purpose of the author behind the scenes, between the lines, which may be said to give a poetical quality or a fourth dimension to narrative. It is freestanding, with little or no pedestal, little or no matrix; and her important essay about the writing of it in the *Yale Review* in 1956 (twenty years after the fact), though richly reminiscent of the little experiences with which it began— the blast of a shotgun, a scream in death agony, "a fat bullying whining man," a poor wife perjuring herself, a curvetting horse, a doleful tune— made it seem an even more absolute creation or invention than I had supposed on first reading.

That essay begins with almost a formula: "By the time a writer has reached the end of a story, he has lived it at least three times over—first, in the series of actual events that, directly or indirectly, have combined to set up the commotion in his mind and senses that causes him to write the story; second, in memory; and third, in the re-creation of the chaotic stuff." And toward the close of it she arrives at a more profound statement: "I do know why I remembered them"—that is to say, the shot, the scream, the horse, the tune (as it were, spark, pollen, seed, yeast)—"and why in my memory they slowly took on their separate lives in a story. It is because there radiated from each of those glimpses of strangers some element, some quality that arrested my attention at a vital moment of my own growth, and caused me, a child, to stop short and look outward, away from myself; to look at another human being with that attention and wonder and speculation which ordinarily, and very naturally, I think, a child lavishes only on himself." To be noted for future textbooks, components and instrumentalities of creative writing—various accidental or incidental evidences of the senses, things the writer sees and hears and feels, and their timing and sequence in relation to the more general processes of his private and inner life; a childish or childlike mind, maturing by fits and starts in one way and another, peeping out of the hidey-hole of self, giving things a second look, thinking things over, and lavishing its curiosity and wonder.

Yeats said—did he not?—that certain of our nineteenth-century classics, notably Emerson's essays and *Leaves of Grass*, were somewhat vitiated by their not incorporating or reflecting any large and clear vision of evil. But certainly Hawthorne and Melville were not limited to optimism and fond ecstasy. "Noon Wine" is of that lineage, grandly and sorrowfully envisaging right and wrong, both on the personal level, where something can be done about it, and in the sense of the sublime, the insoluble. Let me call attention particularly to the power and the complexity of the characterization of the villain in it, Hatch, a veritable Lucifer; brilliantly signifying more, at every point, than the author actually tells us, faceted like a diamond, flashing instructively in many directions. "Noon Wine" would make a fine opera libretto for a composer able to write duets and trios and quartets, without which (I think) music drama never quite touches the heart.

It always pleases me to note how little continuousness, impingement, or repetition there is between one of Katherine Anne's stories and another. In the case of most specialists in short fiction, as in that of painters of easel pictures and composers of chamber music, one finds some new order of artistry every few years; and between, only variants of the same inspiration or the same method, efforts to perfect, or indeed a copying of themselves without much effort. Katherine Anne, when not hitting high spots, really has preferred not to hit anything at all, at least not anything fictitious. She just keeps turning the pages of her mind until she comes to one that is untouched, to which she then applies a new pen, silvery and needle-sharp. Line the stories up: "Flowering Judas," "He," "The Jilting of Granny Weatherall," "The Cracked Looking-Glass"; each advances a separate proposition in morals or psychology, solves an unfamiliar problem of form.

No theme except the given theme, one feels, could develop itself properly or transpire effectively in that particular setting and those circumstances. And yet she never forces the connection and congruity between the scene and the event. There is a minimum of anthropomorphism in her landscapes and changes of weather. Shapes and inanimate objects in her portrayal of the world are never geometrical or surrealistic or modernistic. Things are what they are; and what people do results directly from what *they* are. Everything is for the portraiture, inner portraiture mainly, and for the philosophy, which is almost entirely unspoken, and for the tale, the tale!

※ ※

Her most recent collection of stories was published in 1944. Recently four admirable short narratives, not portions of *Ship of Fools*, have appeared in magazines; one of them, "St. Augustine and the Bullfight," is (I think) a masterpiece, in a strange new form, a hybrid of essay and tale, of which I expect her to make further use. Also occasionally she has produced valuable pieces of expository prose. In every type of short work she is a ready writer, given a green light, and a little removal from sociability, and certain facilities in the way of board and keep.

But never a ready novelist! All that time, a third of a lifetime, her struggle with *Ship of Fools* has been going on. With the everlasting problem of her delicate health, and the other difficulties and jeopardies that I have tried to describe without making a melodrama and a sentimentality of her life, certainly she has not worked at the novel uninterruptedly; but she has kept up her dedication of herself to it, only it, and staked her reputation and her self-respect on it. "Even when I was a little child," she once said to me, "I knew that youth was not for me"—a sentence wonderfully expressive of her particular lifelong uneasiness, responsiveness to her fate up ahead, and great patience from start to finish, knowing or sensing that she was going to grow old at the appointed, self-appointed task.

Troubles, jeopardies, hardships; note that I do not say misfortunes. The perils and disorders, even the wounds of a war scarcely seem deplorable to the home-coming soldier (or to his grateful countrymen), unless his battle has been lost; not even then, if he has shown heroism and if his story has been nobly reported. The fearsomeness of child-bearing and the fatigues of parenthood are unhappy only if the children perish or turn out to be good for nothing. Likewise one cannot evaluate the experience of a literary genius unless and until one has perused all that has resulted from it. Obviously a great deal of heartbreak and travail has been Katherine Anne's lot. But, but, let us remind ourselves, no fortunate and facile youthful or even middle-aged person could have written *Ship of Fools*. It has required the better part of a lifetime of unshrinking participation in life and unshirking endeavor, of hardheadedness and heat of heart and almost fanaticism, and now we have the result; and surely it must seem to her, in her weariness and pride, cheap at the price.

So many writers of our generation brought forth novels in our twenties, immaturely. Often they were novels in name only, enlarged tales, family chronicles, disguised self-portraits. Some of us then hit upon a formula or worked out a method, so as to produce narrative reading matter wholesale; and some of us, on the other hand, simply got tired of the great form, or despaired of it. With lesser fish to fry, we let the white whale go. Not Katherine Anne! And when, twenty years ago, as a famed specialist in the short story, she let it be known that she had begun a novel, she meant precisely that: a large lifelike portrayal of a numerous and representative society, with contrasts of the classes and the masses and the generations and the ethnic groups, with causes and effects in the private psychology of one and all, and with their influences on one another—every man to some extent a part of every other man's fate—and all of this made manifest in behavior, action, plot! Despite destiny, unfavorable in some respects, despite passionate life and personal weakness and disadvantages in the day and age and in our present heterodox American culture, Katherine Anne would be a novelist, a novelist, or else! As the time passed, there arose in literary circles a murmur of skepticism or pessimism to which (I hope) she herself was deaf.

Let me confess that, at one point, when she had confided problems and despondencies to me, I began to write her a deplorable though well-meaning letter, advising her to give up the novel, as such; to salvage stories and sketches out of the incomplete manuscript; and to go on to whatever she had next on her agenda. Thank goodness, I was persuaded by my closest friend to consign this melancholy suggestion to the waste-basket, and presently I paid Katherine Anne a visit on her wooded hill in Connecticut, where, as she said, she lived "on guard and secretive and solitary as a woodchuck peeping out of its hidey-hole." And she read aloud several chapters that were new to me, and I suddenly caught sight of what was in her mind, the great novel structure; the whole so very much more than the sum of the parts. I came away repentant, exalted, and did not lose confidence in it or in her again.

Ship of Fools began with a sea voyage that she took in 1931, and specifically, she says, with an account of it in a letter to her friend and fellow writer, Caroline Gordon. Ten years later she began putting it in fiction form, and gradually, perhaps somewhat unintentionally, it ceased to be a reminiscence and a tale and became a true and full-length novel: The ship *Vera*, that is to say, Truth, but with no abstraction other than that, no symbolism, on its voyage from Veracruz in Mexico to Bremer-haven in Germany via four intermediate ports of call, a voyage only twenty-six days long in the narrated fact, but in the art of the telling, with reference to many of the passengers, lifelong, in that something of their past and something of their future is included in it all along, by means of great flashbacks and mirrorings of motive and fate, by means of a prophetic understanding of the patterns of their lives still to be lived; about three dozen of them clearly delineated and memorable, some un-forgettable: a lot of Germans and a Swede and three Swiss and four Americans, and some Mexicans and Cubans and Spaniards (a vague piti-ful collectivity of hundreds of the poorest Spaniards, deportees, in steerage); every age group; aristocrats and professional men and artists and various bourgeois and riffraff and merchant mariners (and that shadowy Spanish proletariat) diversely involved in love and lust and mortal illness and craziness and chauvinism and cruel intolerance and religiosity, actively involved, in brilliant incidents with hallucinating dialogue; all things motivating one another, all things illuminating one another.

What in the world made us so negative, Katherine Anne's friends and enemies, and all the literary gentry? With the long, solid, closely wrought, and polished work in hand, the grumpiness about it for so long seems strange. Occasionally, when publication had to be postponed again, and then again, did I not sometimes hear in certain voices, voices well-meaning enough as a rule, tones of what in psychoanalytical parlance used to be known as Schadenfreude, exhilaration-when-things-go-wrong? Have I ever been guilty of just that myself? I believe not. But who knows?

Though almost certainly she has had no notion of it, she has been enviable for years. Her fame has been out of proportion to the amount of her work, however highly one might think of it as to its excellence. At least in theory, a good many of us would willingly have experienced her sadnesses, shouldered her burdens, faced up to her disappointments, in order to have produced just those few volumes of her short fiction (even giving up hope of the legendary novel) and to have felt her satisfaction in consequence. How proudly she spoke of her vocation at times, almost as though she were a ruler or as though she were a saint! "I have tossed a good many things considered generally desirable over the windmill for that one intangible thing that money cannot buy, and I find to my joy that I was right. There is no describing what my life has been because of my one fixed desire to be a good artist, responsible to the last comma for what I write." Most of the time, at least much of the time, even when things have been in no wise flourishing for her, she has seemed somehow exultant, heroic, heroine-like.

Furthermore, she has a formidable wit, which may have troubled some people. Vide, if you have not taken cognizance of this, her satirical portrait of Gertrude Stein in *The Days Before,* or her more recent minority opinion of *Lady Chatterley's Lover,* by which some Lawrence admirers felt deflated as it were with beak and claw. I have tried to think of some sample of her humor in its briefer and sometimes even fiercer form, à vive voix or by mail, that it might be feasible to tell, naming no names. But hers is a type of humor that cannot be appreciated if the target is veiled. Of course in a way one is proud to be chastised with intellect and virtuosity like hers; at any rate one prides oneself on taking it stoically; but it may leave sorenesses of scar tissue, reflexes of spite. No matter.

It occurs to me that there is a minimum of laughter of any kind in *Ship of Fools*. George Moore maintained that humorousness always has a bad effect in a novel, disruptive of the illusion in it, drawing attention away from the characters in it to the humorous disposition of the author. I have never heard Katherine Anne say anything about this, but evidently her instinct has been in accord with that of the influential, half-forgotten Irish writer. Humor is one of the subjectivities, along with pathos and anger, powerful in her letters, distilled out of her fiction, for fiction's sake. . . .

Incidentally, I note this peculiarity of Katherine Anne's style: she rarely indulges in figures of speech. One evening in my family circle I read about thirty of these pages aloud, and only one simile caught my eye: little greenish-pale Hans has freckles "like spots of iodine." No one since Stendhal has written so plainly, so glass-clearly; and my author carries about three times as much evidence of the senses as the author of *Le Rouge et le Noir* ever did, and she is much less inclined to infatuation and spite and eccentric argument than he was.

For a while after I have been reading her, my own way of writing —with impulsive images, with effects of cadence and pace, harmoniousness and dissonance, based on my way of reading things aloud, with ideas that I sometimes let language itself provide, and with a certain impressionism due to my having a memory at once excitable and faulty, resuccumbing to emotions of the past when I should be just mustering up the details—puts me to shame.

Now, to give a recapitulation and a close to this rambling study of my friend's lifework, let me quote another of her letters, somber once more, but blended with some of her malicious spirit; showing also her great virtue of steadfastness. It was written in Liège, Belgium, where she had been given a Fulbright Fellowship to teach at the university. In a letter to her I had vexed her with a weak reference of some sort to *my* age, and she chose to take it personally and struck back with an expression of some pathos and acerbity.

"When you and others younger than I, by I forget how many years, but a good number, complain of getting old, I think with dismay: What must they be thinking of me?"

Truly, I had not been (in that letter) thinking of her at all.

"I have had such a struggle to survive," she wrote, "so many ill-
nesses that nearly crippled me when I was young, so many intimations
of mortality before my time; I felt more decrepit at twenty-four than
I have since; and now I do not have a proper sense of time. It does not
chop itself like stove wood into decades convenient for burning. It is a
vast drift in which I float, eddying back and forth, spinning round now
and then, moving always towards no fixed point; but one day it will
dissolve and drop me into the abyss."

In any case, she went on to say, she could never trust other people's
eyes or judgments in the matter. "When I was sixteen, a woman of
middle age, when told *my* age, said 'Ha, she'll never see eighteen again!'
And when I was twenty-eight, a man, not at all malicious, guessed my
age to be forty. Oddly enough, when I was fifty, another man, who
loved me, also thought me forty; and I told him about the other guess,
and wondered if I was never to escape from that particular decade."

Why, she asked me, should she worry about her visible years when
others were so happy to do that worrying for her? Though she did not
blame *me* for my worrisomeness, this sentence struck home.

She then told me her favorite story about age. She was lunching in
Hollywood with Charles Brackett, the distinguished screen writer (who
is an old friend of hers and of mine) and two important film directors;
a few tables away sat the then famous child actress, Margaret O'Brien,
with her mother, her governess, her director, and someone else. "And
the three men at my table looked her over as though she were a pony
they were thinking of buying, and one of them said, 'How old is she
now?' and another answered, 'Six years old,' and there was a pause, and
then Charlie said, 'She looks older than that.' There was a kind of nod-
around among them and the moment passed."

The concluding paragraph of this letter is a kind of prose poem:

"It is five o'clock, I am in a dowdy furnished apartment where the
keys don't turn, the gas cocks stick, the bathroom gadgets work half
way, the neighborhood is *tout-petit bourgeois,* the furnishings are from
the Belgian branch of Sears Roebuck, the place is suburban, the wild
yellow leaves are flying in a high bitter wind under a smoky sky, and I
have come to world's end, and what was my errand here? There is
nothing I wish to say to anyone here; does anybody want to listen? But
it does look as if here again, with all the unlikeliness, the place and the

time had met for me to sit at this table, three and one half feet square, and write something more of my own."

Amen to that, says her perennially grateful reader. She did not in fact write much in Liège. The autumn weather in that part of the world and the Fulbright schedule of lectures proved too much for her respiratory tract, and she had to come home. But it was not long afterward that she settled herself in Connecticut and began to see daylight as to her novel writing.

In that same letter of the dark night of her soul in Belgium, or, to be precise, teatime of her soul in Belgium, she declared that the only disturbing thing about the passage of time, for her, was the fact that she had four books all clearly conceived and partly begun and waiting to be finished. Now, three to go! And now perhaps not so many of us will care to bet against her.

II

Robert Penn Warren

Irony
with a
Center

THE FICTION of Katherine Anne Porter, despite widespread critical adulation, has never found the public which its distinction merits. Many of her stories are unsurpassed in modern fiction, and some are not often equaled. She belongs to the relatively small group of writers —extraordinarily small, when one considers the vast number of stories published every year in English and American magazines—who have done serious, consistent, original, and vital work in the form of short fiction—the group which would include James Joyce, Katherine Mansfield, Sherwood Anderson, and Ernest Hemingway. This list does not include a considerable number of other writers who, though often finding other forms more congenial—the novel or poetry—have scored occasional triumphs in the field of short fiction. Then, of course, there is a very large group of writers who have a great facility, a great mechanical competence, and sometimes moments of real perception, but who work from no fundamental and central conviction.

It was once fashionable to argue complacently that the popular magazine had created the short story—had provided the market and had cultivated an appetite for the product. It is true that the magazine did provide the market, but at the same time, and progressively, the magazine has corrupted the short story. What the magazine encourages is not so much the short story as a conscious or unconscious division of the artistic self of the writer. One can still discover (as in an address delivered by Mr. Frederick Lewis Allen to the American Philosophical Society) a genial self-congratulation in the face of "mass appreciation." But, writes Mr. R. P. Blackmur in reply:

> In fact, mass appreciation of the kind which Mr. Allen approves represents the constant danger to the artist of any serious sort: *the danger of popularization before creation....* The difference between great art and popular art is relatively small; but the difference between either and popularized art is radical, and absolute. Popular art is topical and natural, great art is deliberate and thematic. What can be popularized in either is only what can be sold ... a scheme which requires the constant replacement of the shoddy goods. He (Mr. Allen) does not mean to avow this; he no doubt means the contrary; but there it is. Until American or any other society is educated either up to the level or back to the level of art with standards, whether popular or great, it can be sold nothing but art without standards....

The fact that Miss Porter has not attempted a compromise may account for the relatively small body of her published fiction. There was the collection of stories published in 1931 under the title *Flowering Judas;* an enlarged collection, under the same title in 1935, which includes two novelettes, *The Cracked Looking-Glass* and *Hacienda*, the latter of which had been previously published by Harrison, in Paris; a collection of three novelettes under the title *Pale Horse, Pale Rider*, in 1939; the Modern Library edition of *Flowering Judas;* and a few pieces, not yet in book form, which have appeared in various magazines—for instance, sections of the uncompleted biography of Cotton Mather and the brilliant story "A Day's Work." [1]

Her method of composition does not, in itself, bend readily to the compromise. In many instances, a story or novelette has not been composed straight off. Instead, a section here and a section there have been written—little germinal scenes explored and developed. Or scenes or sketches of character which were never intended to be incorporated in

[1] Since included in the volume *The Leaning Tower*.

the finished work have been developed in the process of trying to understand the full potentiality of the material. One might guess at an approach something like this: a special, local excitement provoked by the material—character or incident; an attempt to define the nature of that local excitement, as local—to squeeze it and not lose a drop; an attempt to understand the relationships of the local excitements and to define the implications—to arrive at theme; the struggle to reduce theme to pattern. That would seem to be the natural history of the characteristic story. Certainly, it is a method which requires time, scrupulosity, and contemplation.

The method itself is an index to the characteristics of Miss Porter's fiction—the rich surface detail scattered with apparently casual profuseness and the close structure which makes such detail meaningful; the great compression and economy which one discovers upon analysis; the precision of psychology and observation, the texture of the style.

Most reviewers, commenting upon Miss Porter's distinction, refer to her "style"—struck, no doubt, by an exceptional felicity of phrase, a precision in the use of metaphor, and a subtlety of rhythm. It is not only the appreciation of the obviously poetical strain in Miss Porter's work that has tended to give her reputation some flavor of the special and exquisite, but also the appreciation of the exceptional precision of her language. When one eminent critic praises her for an "English of a purity and precision almost unique in contemporary American fiction," he is giving praise richly merited and praise for a most important quality, but this praise, sad to relate as a commentary on our times, is a kind that does encourage the special reputation. This same eminent critic also praises Miss Porter as an artist, which goes to say that he himself knows very well that her language is but one aspect of her creations; but even so, the word *artist* carries its own overtones of exquisiteness.

The heart of the potential reader may have been chilled—and I believe quite rightly—by the praise of "beautiful style." He is put off by a reviewer's easy abstracting of style for comment and praise; his innocence repudiates the fallacy of agreeable style. The famous common reader is not much concerned with English as such, pure or impure, precise or imprecise, and he is no more concerned with the artist as artist. He is concerned with what the English will say to him, and with what the artist will do for him, or to him.

It is, of course, just and proper for us to praise Miss Porter for her English and her artistry, but we should remind ourselves that we prize those things because she uses them to create vivid and significant images of life. All this is not to say that we are taking the easy moralistic, or easy Philistine, view of English or artistry. We know that the vividness and the significance of any literary work exist only in the proper medium, and that only because of a feeling for the medium and an understanding of artistry did the writer succeed, in the first place, in discovering vividness and significance. We hope that we shall never have to remind ourselves of that fact, and now we remind ourselves of the vividness and significance in which Miss Porter's English and artistry eventuate, only because we would balance praise for the special with praise for the general, praise for subtlety with praise for strength, praise for sensibility with praise for intellect.

But let us linger upon the matter of Miss Porter's style in the hope that it can be used as a point of departure. Take, for example, a paragraph from the title story of *Flowering Judas*, the description of Braggioni, the half-Italian, half-Indian revolutionist in Mexico, "a leader of men, skilled revolutionist, and his skin has been punctured in honorable warfare." His followers "warm themselves in his reflected glory and say to each other, 'He has a real nobility, a love of humanity raised above mere personal affections.' The excess of this self-love has flowed out, inconveniently for her, over Laura"—the puzzled American girl who has been lured to Mexico by revolutionary enthusiasm and before whom he sits with his guitar and sings sentimental songs, while his wife weeps at home. But here is the passage.

> Braggioni ... leans forward, balancing his paunch between his spread knees, and sings with tremendous emphasis, weighing his words. He has, the song relates, no father and no mother, nor even a friend to console him; lonely as a wave of the sea he comes and goes, lonely as a wave. His mouth opens round and yearns sideways, his balloon cheeks grow oily with the labor of song. He bulges marvelously in his expensive garments. Over his lavender collar, crushed upon a purple necktie, held by a diamond hoop: over his ammunition belt of tooled leather worked in silver, buckled cruelly around his gasping middle: over the tops of his glossy yellow shoes Braggioni swells with ominous ripeness, his mauve silk hose stretched taut, his ankles bound with the stout leather thongs of his shoes.

When he stretches his eyelids at Laura she notes again that his eyes are the true tawny yellow cat's eyes. He is rich, not in money, he tells her, but in power, and this power brings with it the blameless ownership of things, and the right to indulge his love of small luxuries. "I have a taste for the elegant refinements," he said once, flourishing a yellow silk handkerchief before her nose. "Smell that? It is Jockey Club, imported from New York." Nonetheless he is wounded by life. He will say so presently. "It is true everything turns to dust in the hand, to gall on the tongue." He sighs and his leather belt creaks like a saddle girth.

The passage is sharp and evocative. Its phrasing embodies a mixture, a fusion, of the shock of surprise and the satisfaction of precision—a resolved tension, which may do much to account for the resonance and vibration of the passage. We have in it the statement, "His mouth opens round and yearns sideways"—and we note the two words *yearns* and *sideways;* in the phrase, "labor of song"; in, "he bulges marvelously"; in, "Braggioni swells with ominous ripeness." But upon inspection it may be discovered that the effect of these details is not merely a local effect. The subtle local evocations really involve us in the center of the scene; we are taken to the core of the meaning of the scene, and thence to the central impulse of the story; and thence, possibly to the germinal idea of all of this author's fiction. All of these filaments cannot be pursued back through the web—the occasion does not permit; but perhaps a few can be traced to the meaning of the scene itself in the story.

What we have here is the revolutionist who loves luxury, who feels that power gives blameless justification to the love of elegant refinements, but whose skin has been punctured in "honorable warfare"; who is a competent leader of men, but who is vain and indolent; who is sentimental and self-pitying, but, at the same time, ruthless; who betrays his wife and yet, upon his return home, will weep with his wife as she washes his feet and weeps; who labors for the good of man, but is filled with self-love.

We have here a tissue of contradictions, and the very phraseology takes us to these contradictions. For instance, the word *yearns* involves the sentimental, blurred emotion, but immediately afterward the words *sideways* and *oily* remind us of the grossness, the brutality, the physical appetite. So with the implied paradox in the "labor of song." The ammunition belt, we recall, is buckled *cruelly* about his "gasping middle." The ammunition belt reminds us that this indolent, fat, apparently soft, vain man is capable of violent action, is a man of violent profession, and sets the stage for the word *cruelly*, which involves the paradox of the man who loves mankind and is capable of individual cruelties, and which, further, reminds us that he punishes himself out of physical vanity and punishes himself by defining himself in his calling—the only thing that belts in his sprawling, meaningless animality. He swells with "ominous ripeness"—and we sense the violent threat in the man as contrasted with his softness, a kind of great overripe plum as dangerous as a grenade, a feeling of corruption mixed with sentimental sweetness; and specifically we are reminded of the threat to Laura in the situation. We come to the phrase "wounded by life," and we pick up again the motif hinted at in the song and in the lingering rhythms: "He has, the song relates, no father and no mother, nor even a friend to console him; lonely as a wave of the sea he comes and goes, lonely as a wave." In nothing is there to be found a balm—not in revolution, in vanity, in love —for the "vast cureless wound of his self-esteem." Then, after the bit about the wound, we find the sentence: "He sighs and his leather belt creaks like a saddle girth." The defeated, sentimental sigh, the cureless wound, and the bestial creaking of the leather.

If this reading of the passage is acceptable, the passage itself is a rendering of the problem which the character of Braggioni poses to Laura. It is stated, in bare, synoptic form, elsewhere:

> The gluttonous bulk of Braggioni has become a symbol of her many disillusions, for a revolutionist should be lean, animated by heroic faith, a vessel of abstract virtues. This is nonsense, she knows it now and is ashamed of it. Revolution must have leaders, and leadership is a career for energetic men. She is, her comrades tell her, full of romantic error, for what she defines as a cynicism is to them merely a developed sense of reality.

What is the moral reality here? This question is, I should say, the theme of the story, which exists in an intricate tissue of paradox, and is posed only in the dream Laura has at the end, a dream which embodies but does not resolve the question.

With all the enchanting glitter of style and all the purity of language and all the flow and flicker of feeling, Miss Porter's imagination, as a matter of fact, is best appreciated if we appreciate its essential austerity, its devotion to the fact drenched in God's direct daylight, its concern with the inwardness of character, and its delight in the rigorous and discriminating deployment of a theme. Let us take another passage from her work, a passage from the novelette *Noon Wine*, the description of Mr. Thompson, a poor dirt-farmer in Texas, busy at his churning, a task that he, in his masculine pride and bitter incompetence, finds contemptible and demeaning:

> Mr. Thompson was a tough weather-beaten man with stiff black hair and a week's growth of black whiskers. He was a noisy proud man who held his neck so straight his whole face stood level with his Adam's apple, and the whiskers continued down his neck and disappeared into a black thatch under his open collar. The churn rumbled and swished like the belly of a trotting horse, and Mr. Thompson seemed somehow to be driving a horse with one hand, reining it in and urging it forward; and every now and then he turned halfway around and squirted a tremendous spit of tobacco juice out over the steps. The door stones were brown and gleaming with fresh tobacco juice.

This passage is simple and unpretending, a casual introductory description near the beginning of a story, but it succeeds in having its own kind of glitter and purity and flow. Here those things come, as in so much of Miss Porter's fiction, from the writer's rigorous repudiation of obvious literary resources, resources which, on other occasions, she can use so brilliantly. The things that stir our admiration in the passage from "Flowering Judas" are notably absent here, are notably eschewed. Here the style is of the utmost transparency, and our eye and ear are captivated by the very ordinariness of the ordinary items presented to us, the trotting motion of the churn, the swish of the milk, the tobacco juice glittering on the door stones. Miss Porter has the power of isolating common things, the power that Chekhov or Frost or Ibsen or, sometimes, Pound has, the power to make the common thing glow with an Eden-innocence by the mere fact of the isolation. It is a kind of indicative poetry.

Miss Porter's eye and ear, however, do not seize with merely random and innocent delight on the objects of the world, even though we may take that kind of delight in the objects she so lovingly places before us, transmuted in their ordinariness. If the fact drenched in daylight commands her unfaltering devotion, it is because such facts are in themselves a deep language, or can be made to utter a language of the deepest burden. What are the simple facts saying in the paragraph just quoted?

They are saying something about Mr. Thompson, poor Mr. Thompson who will die of a self-inflicted gunshot wound before many pages have passed, and will die of it because he is all the things we might have surmised of him if we had been able to understand beforehand the language of the simple facts of the scene at the churn. The pridefully stiff neck and the black whiskers, they tell us something. He is the sort of man who ought, or thinks he ought, to be holding the reins of a spanking horse and not the cord of a churn, and his very gesture has a kind of childish play acting. Somewhere in his deepest being, he is reminded of the spanking horse with the belly swishing in the trot, the horse such a fine manly man ought to have under his hand, if luck just weren't so ornery and unreasonable, and so he plays the game with himself. But he can't quite convince himself. It is only a poor old churn, after all, woman's work on a rundown and debt-bit shirt-tail farm, with kids and an ailing wife, and so he spits his tremendous spits of masculine protest against fate, and the brown juice gleams with its silly, innocent assertiveness on the stones the woman's broom has, so many times, swept clean of this and that. In the end, looking back, we can see that the story is the story of a noisy, proud, stiff-necked man whose pride has constantly suffered under failure, who salves his hurt pride by harmless bluster with his wife and children, and who, in the end, stumbles into a situation which takes the last prop of certainty from his life.

Our first glimpse of Mrs. Thompson is in the "front room," where she lies with the green shade down and a wet cloth over her poor weak eyes. But in spite of the weeping eyes, the longing for the cool dark, and all her sad incompetence, on the one hand, and Mr. Thompson's bluster and hurt pride on the other, there is a warm secret life between them:

"Tell *you* the truth, Ellie," said Mr. Thompson, picking his teeth with a fork and leaning back in the best of humors, "I always thought your granma was a ter'ble ole fool. She'd just say the first thing that popped into her head and call it God's wisdom."

"My granma wasn't anybody's fool. Nine times out of ten she knew what she was talking about. I always say, the first thing you think is the best thing you can say."

"Well," said Mr. Thompson, going into another shout, "you're so reefined about that goat story, you just try speaking out in mixed comp'ny sometime! You just try it. S'pose you happened to be thinking about a hen and a rooster, hey? I reckon you'd shock the Babtist preacher!" He gave her a good pinch on her thin little rump. "No more meat on you than a rabbit," he said, fondly. "Now I like 'em cornfed."

Mrs. Thompson looked at him open-eyed and blushed. She could see better by lamplight. "Why, Mr. Thompson, sometimes I think you're the evilest-minded man that ever lived." She took a handful of hair on the crown of his head and gave it a good, slow pull. "That's to show you how it feels, pinching so hard when you're supposed to be playing," she said, gently.

This little glimpse of their secret life, Mr. Thompson's masculine, affectionate bragging and bullying and teasing, and Mrs. Thompson's shy and embarrassed playfulness, comes as a surprise in the middle of their drab world, a sudden brightness and warmth. Without this episode we should never get the full force of Mr. Thompson's bafflement and anger when Mr. Hatch, the baleful stranger, misinterprets Mr. Thompson's prideful talk of his wife's ill health and says that he himself would get rid of a puny wife mighty quick. And without this episode we should never sense how that bafflement and anger flow, as one more component, into the moment when Mr. Thompson sees, or thinks he sees, the blade of Mr. Hatch's bowie knife go into the poor Swede's stomach, and he brings his axe down on Hatch's head, as though stunning a beef.

We are, however, getting ahead of ourselves. Let us summarize the apparently simple story. On Mr. Thompson's poverty-bit farm a stranger appears, a Swede, Mr. Helton, who takes work at a low wage, plays the harmonica in his off hours, and seems to inhabit some vague and lonely inner world. But Mr. Helton is a worker, and for the first time the farm begins to pay. Mr. Thompson can give up "woman's work," can do the big important things that become a man, and can bask in the new prosperity. Nine years later, to interrupt the new prosperity, another stranger appears, a Mr. Hatch, who reveals that the Swede is a murderer and a lunatic whom he will arrest and take back north to the asylum. When the Swede appears, Mr. Thompson sees, or thinks he sees, Mr. Hatch's knife going into his stomach. With his axe he kills Mr. Hatch, defending the Swede, defending what, he does not know.

After the deed, there isn't, strangely enough, a scratch on the Swede's stomach. This doesn't bother the jury, and Mr. Thompson is acquitted in no time at all. But it does bother Mr. Thompson. He simply can't understand things, how he could see the knife go in and then find it not true, and all the other things he can't understand. He had never intended to do it, he was just protecting the poor Swede. But we are aware that there had been the slow building up of the mysterious anger against Mr. Hatch, of the fear that Mr. Hatch threatened the new prosperity of the farm. And in the trial Mr. Thompson has been caught in a web of little lies, small distortions of fact, nothing serious, nothing needed to prove he wasn't guilty, just little twists to make everything clearer and simpler.

Is Mr. Thompson innocent or guilty? He doesn't really know. Caught in the mysteriousness of himself, caught in all the impulses which he had never been able to face, caught in all the little lies which had really meant no harm, he can't know the truth about anything. He can't stand the moral uncertainty of this situation, but he does not know what it is that most deeply he can't stand. He can't stand not knowing what he himself really is. His pride can't stand that kind of nothingness. Not knowing what it is he can't stand, he is under the compulsion to go, day after day, around the countryside, explaining himself, explaining how he had not meant to do it, how it was defense of the Swede, how it was self-defense, all the while plunging deeper and deeper into the morass of his fate. Then he finds that his own family have, all along, thought him guilty. So the proud man has to kill himself to prove, in his last pride, that he is really innocent.

That, however, is the one thing that can never be proved, for the story is about the difficult definition of guilt and innocence. Mr. Thompson, not able to trust his own innocence, or understand the nature of whatever guilt is his, has taken refuge in the lie, and the lie, in the end, kills him. The issue here, as in "Flowering Judas," is not to be decided simply. It is, in a sense, left suspended, the terms defined, but the argument left only at a provisional resolution. Poor Mr. Thompson—innocent and yet guilty, and in his pride unable to live by the provisional.

The Cracked Looking-Glass, too, is about guilt and innocence. It is the story of a high-spirited, pleasure-loving Irish girl, married to a much older man, faithful to him, yet needing the society of young fun-provoking men, to whom she takes a motherly or sisterly attitude. She lives a kind of lie—in fact, she can't tell anything without giving it a romantic embroidery. Then she is horrified to discover that her Connecticut neighbors think her a bad woman, suspect her of infidelities. At the end, sitting in her tight kitchen with Old Dennis, "while beyond were far off places full of life and gaiety . . . and beyond everything like a green field with morning sun on it lay youth and Ireland," she leans over and puts her hand on her husband's knee, and asks him, in an ordinary voice: "Whyever did ye marry a woman like me?"

Dennis says mind, she doesn't tip the chair over, and adds that he knew he could never do better. Then:

> She sat up and felt his sleeves carefully. "I want you to wrap up warm this bitter weather, Dennis," she told him. "With two pairs of socks and the chest protector, for if anything happened to you, whatever would become of me in this world?"
>
> "Let's not think of it," said Dennis, shuffling his feet.
>
> "Let's not, then," said Rosaleen. "For I could cry if you crooked a finger at me."

Again the provisional resolution of the forces of the story: not a solution which Rosaleen can live by with surety, but one which she must re-learn and re-earn every day.

With the theme of *The Cracked Looking-Glass* in mind, let us take another of the novelettes, *Old Mortality*.

To begin, *Old Mortality* is relatively short, some twenty thousand words, but it gives an impression of the mass of a novel. One factor contributing to this effect is the length of the time span; the novelette falls into three sections, dated 1885–1902, 1904, and 1912. Another factor is the considerable number of the characters, who, despite the brevity of the story, are sketched in with great precision; we know little about them, but that little means much. Another, and not quite so obvious but perhaps more important, factor is the rich circumstantiality and easy dis-cursiveness, especially in Part I, which sets the tone of the piece. The author lingers on anecdote, apparently just to relish the anecdote, to extract the humor or pathos—but in the end we discover that there has been no casual self-indulgence, or indulgence of the reader; the details of the easy anecdote, which seemed to exist at the moment for itself alone, have been working busily in the cellarage of our minds.

Part I, 1885–1902, introduces us to two little girls, Maria and Miranda, aged twelve and eight, through whose eyes we see the family. There is the grandmother, who takes no part in the action of the story, but whose brief characterization, we discover, is important—the old lady who, "twice a year compelled in her blood by the change of seasons, would sit nearly all day beside old trunks and boxes in the lumber room, unfolding layers of garments and small keepsakes . . . unwrapping locks of hair and dried flowers, crying gently and easily as if tears were the only pleasure she had left." (Her piety—stirred by the equinoxes, as unreflecting as tropism—provides the basic contrast for the end of the story; her piety does not achieve the form of legend—merely a compulsion of the blood, the focus of old affections.) There is the father, "a pleasant everyday sort of man"—who once shot to protect the family "honor" and had to run to Mexico. There is Cousin Eva, chinless and unbeautiful amidst the belles, who, when we first meet her, teaches Latin in a female seminary and tries to interest Maria and Miranda in that study by telling them the story of John Wilkes Booth, "who, handsomely garbed in a long black cloak"—so the story is recast by the little girls— "had leaped to the stage after assassinating President Lincoln. 'Sic semper tyrannis,' he had shouted superbly, in spite of his broken leg." There is Amy, dead, already a legend, a beautiful sad family story, the girl who almost had a duel fought over her in New Orleans, who drove her suitor, Cousin Gabriel, almost to distraction before she married him, and who died under mysterious circumstances a few weeks after her marriage. There is Gabriel himself, fond of the races, cut off by his grandfather without a penny, a victim of the bottle in his bereavement; he marries Miss Honey, who can never compete with the legend of the dead Amy. In this section, the little girls attempt to make the people they know and the stories they have heard fit together, make sense; and always at the center is the story of Amy.

Part II, in contrast with Part I with its discursiveness, its blurring of time, its anecdotal richness, gives a single fully developed scene, dated 1904. The father takes the little girls, on holiday from their convent school, to the races. There, out of family piety, they bet their dollar on Uncle Gabriel's horse—a poor hundred-to-one shot. (Piety and common sense—they know even at their tender years that a hundred-to-one bet is no bet at all—are in conflict, and piety wins only because of the father's pressure.) But Gabriel's horse comes in, and they see for the first time their romantic Uncle Gabriel—"a shabby fat man with bloodshot blue eyes . . . and a big melancholy laugh like a groan"—now drunk, and after his victory, weeping. But he takes them to meet Miss Honey, Amy's successor, in his shabby apartment, and the little girls know that Miss Honey hates them all.

Part III, 1912, shows us Miranda on a train going to the funeral of Uncle Gabriel, who has died in Lexington, Kentucky, but has been brought home to lie beside Amy—to whom he belongs. On the train Miranda, now a young lady recently married, meets Cousin Eva, whom she has not seen for many years, who has, since the days at the seminary, crusaded for woman suffrage and gone to jail for her convictions. The talk goes back to the family story, to Amy. "Everybody loved Amy," Miranda remarks, but Cousin Eva replies: "Not everybody by a long shot. . . . She had enemies. If she knew she pretended she didn't. . . . She was sweet as honeycomb to everybody. . . . That was the trouble. She went through life like a spoiled darling, doing as she pleased and letting other people suffer for it." Then: " 'I never believed for one moment,' says Cousin Eva, putting her mouth close to Miranda's ear and breathing peppermint hotly into it, 'that Amy was an impure woman. Never! But let me tell you there were plenty who did believe it.' " So Cousin Eva begins to reinterpret the past, all the romantic past, the legend of Amy, who, according to Cousin Eva, was not beautiful, just good-looking, whose illness hadn't been romantic, and who had, she says, committed suicide.

Cousin Eva defines the bitter rivalry under the gaiety of the legend, the vicious competition among the belles. And more:

> Cousin Eva wrung her hands. "It was just sex," she said in despair; [The word *despair*, caught in the frustrated and yet victorious old woman's casual gesture, is important—a resonance from her personal story which gives an echo to the theme of the story itself.] "their minds dwelt on nothing else. They didn't call it that, it was all smothered under pretty names, but that's all it was, sex."

So Cousin Eva, who has given her life to learning and a progressive cause, defines all the legend in terms of economics and biology. "They simply festered inside," she says of all the Amys, "they festered."

But Miranda, catching a Baudelairean vision of "corruption concealed under lace and flowers," thinks quite coldly: "Of course, it was not like that. This is no more true than what I was told before, it's every bit as romantic." And in revulsion from Cousin Eve, she wants to get home, though she is grown and married now, and see her father and sister, who are solid and alive, are not merely "definitions."

But when she arrives her father cannot take her in, in the old way. He turns to Cousin Eva. And the two old people, who represent the competing views of the past—love and poetry opposed to biology and economics—sit down together in a world, their world of the past, which excludes Miranda. Miranda thinks: "Where are my own people and my own time?" She thinks, and the thought concludes the story: "Let them go on explaining how things happened. I don't care. At least I can know the truth about what happens to me, she assured herself silently, making a promise to herself, in her hopefulness, her ignorance."

So much for the action of the story. We see immediately that it is a story about legend, and it is an easy extension to the symbol for tradition, the meaning of the past for the present. We gradually become acquainted with the particular legend through the little girls, but the little girls themselves, in their innocence, criticize the legend. Their father, speaking of Amy's slimness, for instance, says: "There were never any fat women in the family, thank God." But the little girls remember Aunt Keziah, in Kentucky, who was famous for her heft. (Such an anecdote is developed richly and humorously, with no obvious pointing to the theme, beyond the logic of the context.) Such details, in Part I, develop the first criticism of the legend, the criticism by innocent common sense. In Part II, the contrast between Gabriel as legend and Gabriel as real extends the same type of criticism, but more dramatically; but here another, a moral criticism, enters in, for we have the effect of Amy on other people's lives, on Gabriel and Miss Honey. This, however, is not specified it merely charges the scene of the meeting between Miranda and Cousin Eva on the way to Gabriel's funeral. Part III at first gives us, in Cousin Eva's words, the modern critical method applied to the legend —as if invoking Marx and Freud.

Up to this point, the line of the story has been developed fairly directly, though under a complicated surface. The story could end here, a story of repudiation, and some readers have interpreted it as such. But —and here comes the first reversal of the field—Miranda repudiates Cousin Eva's version, as romantic, too, in favor of the "reality" of her father, whom she is soon to see. But there is another shift. Miranda discovers that she is cut off from her father, who turns to Cousin Eva, whose "myth" contradicts his "myth," but whose world he can share. Miranda, cut off, determines to leave them to their own sterile pursuit of trying to understand the past. She will understand herself, the truth of what happens to her. This would provide another point of rest for the story—a story about the brave younger generation, their hope, courage, and honesty, and some readers have taken it thus. But—withheld cunningly until the end, until the last few words—there is a last reversal of the field. Miranda, makes her promise to herself in "her hopefulness, her ignorance." And those two words, *hopefulness, ignorance,* suddenly echo throughout the story.

Miranda will find *a* truth, as it were, but it, too, will be a myth, for it will not be translatable, or, finally, communicable. But it will be the only truth she can win, and for better or worse she will have to live by it. She must live by her own myth. But she must earn her myth in the process of living. Her myth will be a new myth, different from the mutually competing myths of her father and Cousin Eva, but stemming from that antinomy. Those competing myths will simply provide the terms of her own dialectic of living.

We remember that the heroine's name is Miranda, and we may remember Miranda of Shakespeare's *Tempest,* who exclaims, "O brave new world, that has such people in it!" Perhaps the identity of the name is not an accident. Miranda of *Old Mortality* has passed a step beyond that moment of that exclamation, but she, too, has seen the pageant raised by Prospero's wand—the pageant evoked by her father, the pleasant everyday sort of father, who, however, is a Prospero, though lacking the other Prospero's irony. For *Old Mortality,* like *The Tempest,* is about illusion and reality, and comes to rest upon a perilous irony.

In *Old Mortality* Miss Porter has used very conventional materials; the conventional materials, however, are revitalized by the intellectual scope of the interpretation and the precision and subtlety of structure. But Miss Porter has not committed herself to one type of material. The world of balls and horsemanship and romance is exchanged in *Noon Wine,* as we have seen, for a poverty-ridden Texas farm; in *Pale Horse, Pale Rider,* for a newspaper office and a rooming house at the time of World War I; in "Hacienda," "Flowering Judas" and "María Concepción," for Mexico. We may ask, What is the common denominator of these stories, aside from the obvious similarities of style (though the style itself is very flexible)? What is the central "view," the central intuition?

In these stories, and, as I believe, in many others, there is the same paradoxical problem of definition, the same delicate balancing of rival considerations, the same scrupulous development of competing claims to attention and action, the same interplay of the humorous and the serious, the same refusal to take the straight line, the formula, through the material at hand. This has implied for some readers that the underlying attitude is one of skepticism, negation, refusal to confront the need for immediate, watertight, foolproof solutions. The skeptical and ironical bias is, I think, important in Miss Porter's work, and it is true that her work wears an air of detachment and contemplation. But, I should say, her irony is an irony with a center, never an irony for irony's sake. It simply implies, I think, a refusal to accept the formula, the ready-made solution, the hand-me-down morality, the word for the spirit. It affirms, rather, the constant need for exercising discrimination, the arduous obligation of the intellect in the face of conflicting dogmas, the need for a dialectical approach to matters of definition, the need for exercising as much of the human faculty as possible.

This basic attitude finds its correlation in her work, in the delicacy of phrase, the close structure, the counterpoint of incident and implication. That is, a story must test its thematic line at every point against its total circumstantiality; the thematic considerations must, as it were, be validated in terms of circumstance and experience, and never be resolved in the poverty of statement.

In one sense, it is the intellectual rigor and discrimination that gives Miss Porter's work its classic distinction and control—that is, if any one quality can be said to be uniquely responsible. No, no single quality can take that credit, but where many writers have achieved stories of perception, feeling, sensibility, strength, or charm, few have been able to achieve stories of a deep philosophic urgency in the narrow space, and fewer still have been able to achieve the kind of thematic integration of a body of stories, the mark of the masters, the thing that makes us think first of the central significance of a writer rather than of some incidental and individual triumph. For Miss Porter's bright indicative poetry is, at long last, a literally metaphysical poetry, too. The luminosity is from inward.

Edward G. Schwartz

The Fictions
of Memory

O, wonder!
How many goodly creatures are there
here!
How beauteous mankind is! O brave
new world,
That has such people in't!
—THE TEMPEST (V, i)

BREATHLESS with admiration, Miranda hardly hears Prospero mildly admonish, " 'Tis new to thee." For in her eagerness to gaze on that new world unfolding before her, she looks with innocent wonder only at the human forms, and they are beautiful to her. But within the hearts and minds of the persons she sees (with the exception of Gonzalo) is another reality—a propensity to evil that has implicated them, in their times, in acts of treachery and malice. So Miranda's words are ironic: the "brave new world" she sees is deceiving; the beauty and nobility of mankind masks an inner truth, which Miranda, inexperienced and sheltered, cannot yet perceive.

Fated to emerge from that Arcadian dream, to lose those sweet illusions of safety, Katherine Anne Porter's Miranda begins her journey where Shakespeare's heroine ends hers. Miranda springs from a civilized Southern society rich in ceremony and ritual, quite certain that its pre-Civil War morality and manners will endure. Growing up compels her to enter a world of shifting values, of uncertainty, contradiction, and anxiety. She soon loses her innocence, recognizes herself to be in a country of immoderate wrath, learns what her earlier counterpart never had had to comprehend—the human need to fathom "the dark backward and abysm of time" (*The Tempest*, I, ii). Struggling to recover her lost freedom by discovering her burden and destiny, she enacts a profoundly moving drama.

That moral drama is the major theme of Katherine Anne Porter's stories.[1] She brings before us the emerging consciousness of the tender, perceptive mind suddenly made aware that its childhood dream of changelessness is false. Time's rheumatic touch blights all things. Order and continuity are restored only in the fictions of memory. Like the Old Man (in "The Charmed Life"), Miss Porter finds the meaning of the present in the past. While he unearths "whole skeletons, bushels of jade beads and obsidian knives, bronze bells and black clay whistles in the shape of birds," she comes upon bits of velvet and taffeta, faded photographs and forgotten keepsakes, wedding bands and casket screws. An old order in ruins is what she inevitably finds. Measuring human life in relation to a fixed point in time, she discovers a perspective for understanding man's fate. Our mortality circumscribes our lives, metes out freedom to those willing to earn it, ignores the cheat or fool who imagines himself beyond it. The new order is therefore internal, it terms the terms of consciousness, its relations those of time rather than of space, its value the freedom conferred by understanding, the grace of a pure awareness. In each story, it is a handful of chaos that Miss Porter takes up. The result is a perspective on chaos, a sensible pattern fitted up for the senseless, a virtue found for a deadly world.

Miss Porter's reality, then, defines itself through individual consciousness. Past and present are measured, as is the future, by memory. But conscious memory, particularly in the Miranda stories, is often thwarted. Between action and awareness, emotion and response, falls a shadow. Licensed by desire, awareness is curbed and response blunted. The inhibiting shadow cast by society, family, and self threatens to narrow Miranda's consciousness, to corrupt her innocence, to prevent

---

[1] The main body of Miss Porter's fiction consists of stories about the stable, orderly Southern world she knew as a child and the emerging new order of her own generation. The first six stories in *The Leaning Tower* and two short novels, *Old Mortality* and *Pale Horse, Pale Rider*, are about Miranda and her family. Nearly all of Miss Porter's fiction seems to me closely related in theme and treatment to the Miranda stories.

her from naming those magical words that might set her free. Given eyes to take this world's wonder with surprise, will Miranda, life's fortunate child, avoid the mortal sin of denying what her eyes have seen, her mind thought, her heart desired? Such a denial would be the final self-deception, "the last intolerable cheat of her heart"; for as we are creatures of sensation and intelligence, her denial would be a repudiation of life. But affirmation, not denial, is to become Miranda's fixed intent. Her initiation, conflict, and survival are described in "The Circus," *Old Mortality*, *Pale Horse, Pale Rider*, and "The Grave."

"The Circus" Miranda attends is her first. Her experience of it leads to nightmare and frightening vision.[2] Without understanding, she sees "the bold grinning stare" of dirty, ragged little boys peeping up from beneath the stands; hears the crowd's "roar of laughter like rage"; watches a clown blowing "sneering kisses from his cruel mouth." Ingenuous enough not to be surprised that the clown might be walking on air, she is "terrified" to see that he is on a wire. She hasn't yet learned the conventions that make the grotesque and the cruel funny. Horrified, she must be taken home. Later, when the family returns, the older children tell her what she missed. They mourn over Dicey, who had missed the circus on Miranda's account, "with their sad mouths, their malicious eyes watching Miranda squirm." Her father says, "You missed it, Baby, and what good did that do you?" The terrible irony of his remark, following as it does the conscious malice of the children, accents her vulnerability. The circus is certainly not the last organized and decorated joy that she will miss for being too completely there.

Only Miranda's Grandmother understands. Though she had been persuaded to go, she "never approved of circuses." The father tells her the children don't "seem to be much damaged" by their experience. But she thinks "the fruits of their present are in a future so far off, neither of us may live to know whether harm has been done or not." Her knowledge and the image used to express it are rather like Hawthorne's view (in *The House of the Seven Gables*) that

---

[2] Earlier, Huck Finn has much the same reaction to the feigned horrors of the circus. The apparent danger of "a drunk man" trying to ride a horse drives "the people just crazy" with laughter. Huck says, "It warn't funny to me, though; I was all of a tremble to see his danger." Mark Twain, *The Adventures of Huckleberry Finn* (New York: Charles L. Webster & Co., 1885), p. 193.

the act of the passing generation is the germ which must produce good or evil fruit in a far distant time; that, together with the seed of the merely temporary crop, which mortals term expedience, they inevitably sow the acorns of a more enduring growth, which may darkly over-shadow their posterity.

Possessing moral insight, this particular Grandmother is one of Miss Porter's heroines. She has taken upon herself the burden of conscious-ness, decision, responsibility. She is described in "The Source" as being for the family "the only reality . . . in a world otherwise without fixed authority."

The harm done Miranda haunts her evening reveries. In bed, she tries to imagine the charming performers, the sweet little furry ponies, the lovely pet monkeys that she had missed seeing at the circus. But, when she falls asleep, "her invented memories [give] way before her real ones, the bitter terrified face of the man in blowsy white falling to his death—ah, the cruel joke—and the terrible grimace of the unsmiling dwarf." Miranda's fears for her own safety in an indifferent world curb her earlier freedom. Awakening from her nightmare "completely sub-jugated by her fears," she wants no one, "not even Dicey, to be cross with her."

Brief as it is, "The Circus" raises problems that are basic to Miss Porter's art. The story must be seen through the eyes of an innocent child, yet what the child sees must have a symbolic value beyond her understanding. Miss Porter's solution is to allow the child no opinions: Miranda knows nothing about the ugliness or meanness of what she sees; she isn't permitted to rationalize about it. Her lack of preconcep-tions causes her to see the circus as dreadful and isolates her from family and society. Not understanding the conventions, she catches her first glimpse of the possible terrors and frustrations of human living. Though not come by intellectually, that glimpse is the real thing. The reader, recapturing the purity of childhood vision and seeing the truth that lurks beneath convention, discovers the meaning of Miranda's experience.

※　※

Consciousness is narrowed when a child, overwhelmed by a sense of guilt and inadequacy, becomes increasingly dependent upon the approval of family and society. As Miranda, taking fright, becomes amenable to the humanizing influences of the old folks, she falls under the sway of family legend and social taboo. She learns the conventions. She listens to the family's stories of the past. Her feelings and thoughts come to be shaped by the values of the old order. *Old Mortality* is about Miranda's struggle to be free in the present by going in search of the determining past. Unwilling to accept her family's legend of the past for a true account of it, to be permanently charmed by honored ways and family ties and the self-deceiving, sentimental romance of the South, Miranda resolves to "know the truth about what happens to me."

But the frailties of mortality impede her resolve. Rebellion against the old order deprives her of the illusions that give value to life. The family's grand legends had once confirmed for the child Miranda "the nobility of human feeling, the divinity of man's vision of the unseen, the importance of life and death, the depths of the human heart, the romantic value of tragedy." After the ancestral idols are broken, what remains? As she flees to marriage, the avenging furies of memory pursue her. She carries them within herself in the form of the ruinous expectations which were nurtured by the old order.

Child of that old order, Miranda cannot cut the past away nor can she render it powerless by story-telling. The latter puts one in the magical distance, where the colors of the view are luminous, the outlines still distinct, the major masses harmoniously composed. Yet remove that distance, approach more closely, and the scene becomes disordered, the colors dull, and objects invisible before dominate the composition. The landscape of her Uncle Gabriel's life can no longer be enjoyed by Miranda after the closer view she has of his actual manner of existence. Her clear vision of the past deepens her sense of isolation and moral chaos. More bitterly ironic, the freedom she may achieve is itself of limited value. As her mind "closed stubbornly against remembering, not the past but the legend of the past," Miranda had thought:

> I don't want any promises, I won't have false hopes, I won't be romantic about myself. . . . Let them go on explaining how things happened. I don't care. At least I can know the truth about what happens to me, she assured herself silently, making a promise to herself, in her hopefulness, her ignorance.

Those two words, *hopefulness, ignorance,* as Robert Penn Warren has written,

> suddenly echo throughout the story. Miranda will find *a* truth, as it were, but it, too, will be a myth, for it will not be translatable, or, finally,

communicable. But it will be the only truth she can win, and for better or worse she will have to live by it.

Such perilous ironies abound in Katherine Anne Porter's fiction, for her art is an art of remembering, its subject the artist's personal recollections. Miss Porter looks within, regards with steady eye the one reliable reality—the writer's self. Her artistic problem, then, is to see and understand that self precisely, to render her perceptions and understanding without abandoning the identity between the self that knows and sees and the self that's seen and known. Her style, unmannered as it is, is intensely personal, entirely an intimate thing. Irony, scrupulous objectivity, precision and subtlety of form—by these means, she fashions her mastery over the personal element and gives significance to action.

By the end of *Old Mortality*, Miranda has outgrown the brave platitudes of Longfellow's "Psalm of Life." She has repudiated the family's romantic interpretation of the Amy legend (a decadent legend that closely resembles Edgar Allan Poe's favorite theme). She has come to understand the moral implications of Uncle Gabriel's self-indulgent devotions. Limited by her mortality, she may yet have the fortitude to search the meaning of her life, unhampered by the conventional clichés, for some truth. If this hardly seems a positive resolution, it is really all Miss Porter allows her characters. Few of them can, like Miranda or the Grandmother in "The Source" and "The Circus," actually enlarge and purify their experience, recognize their true feelings, and keep their consciousness free.

Measuring the varying levels of consciousness of Miss Porter's characters, we discover their particular qualities. There are the opposites of Miranda and the Grandmother, those who, having no experience of their own, are unconcerned with the past. Then there are those who, struggling to be free, go down, their awareness closing and their tragedy contained in that. Finally, there are those who are ruined when the formulas fail: the sudden painful recognition that sometimes overtakes a man of the loss, in living, of his life; the action that follows an honest dim awareness and creates consequences that destroy the formulated mind unable to understand or ignore them.

The patriots who menace Miranda in *Pale Horse, Pale Rider* are nondescripts, incapable of thinking or feeling. Platitudes and slogans befoul their mouths. Their emotions have been manufactured for them, like their ready-made suits, their hats, their prosperous cigars. Their lives are so corrupt they have no sense of loss. Their evil is impersonal. God, Country, Home, Church, Law are in their keeping. In them they are secure. The Good is their argument, as it is of Mr. Hatch in *Noon Wine*. "Fact is, I'm for law and order, I don't like to see law-breakers and lunatics at large," he says. "The law is solidly behind me." Mr. Hatch is no mere angry poster, as the bond boosters are. He is alert about his business, shrewd, more than a match. His clichés are the same, but their intent is even more deadly. "When challenged he has his defense pat and ready, and there is nothing much wrong with it—it only lacks human decency, of which he has no conception beyond a faint hearsay," Miss Porter has written of him in *"Noon Wine:* The Sources." What free consciousness he has is thus misdirected.

Danny Dickerson, the "little drab man in a derby hat" whose vaude-ville act Miranda had panned, is a variation on the bond men. He has their belligerency; he runs through the whole routine of outrage. But now he is the victim of the formulas, and his ten-year-old clippings, his brilliantined curl, his lost side teeth are all symbolic of a day when he went smoothly along the main line. Miss Porter's handling of the temptations to Miranda by the corrupted mind is one of the triumphs of her art. After getting rid of the little man, Chuck tells Miranda how to avoid unpleasantness in the future. "All you have to do is play up the headliners, and you needn't even mention the also-rans. Try to keep in mind that Rypinsky has got show business cornered in this town; please Rypinsky and you'll please the advertising department; please them and you'll get a raise." Conventional satire becomes something more here, a serious condemnation of society, when the inference is drawn that then Miranda can please the bond men.

Chuck is willing to please them. His consciousness is in process of corruption. Dressed in sports clothing "to disguise the fact that he had a bad lung and didn't care for sports," he veils his slide into dishonest cynicism by shallow witticisms and mocking laughter. In him has be-gun that separation of act and judgment traditionally associated with hardened reporters. Miranda, aware of the danger, resists the separation.

The plague that crowds the hospitals and puts hearses in the streets, that attacks her and finally robs her of her love, is only incidentally a physical sickness. The true plague is spiritual, just as the war is, and

Adam and Miranda, Chuck and Towney are there, fighting it, losing it for the most part. The war is a sign of another, more brutal combat—quieter, crueler, quarterless.

> "Adam," she said, "the worst of war is the fear and suspicion and the awful expression in all the eyes you meet . . . as if they had pulled down the shutters over their minds and their hearts and were peering out at you, ready to leap if you make one gesture or say one word they do not understand instantly. It frightens me; I live in fear too, and no one should have to live in fear. . . . It's what war does to the mind and the heart, Adam, and you can't separate these two—what it does to them is worse than what it can do to the body."

Feelings arise in Miranda's consciousness and develop into ideas that are difficult to face. But when she goes with the Red Cross women in "a gay procession of high powered cars and brightly tinted faces to cheer the brave boys who already, you might very well say, had fallen in defense of their country," she brings her basket of sweets to a man who is the bitter embodiment of her own thoughts. " 'My own feelings about this whole thing, made flesh. Never again will I come here, this is no sort of thing to be doing. This is disgusting,' she told herself plainly." With this realization, she has moved toward the purity of consciousness that involves its unity with action.

※ ※

In her introduction to Eudora Welty's *A Curtain of Green*, Miss Porter admits to "a deeply personal preference" for the kind of story in which "external act and the internal voiceless life of the human imagination almost meet and mingle on the mysterious threshold between dream and waking, one reality refusing to admit or confirm the existence of the other, yet both conspiring toward the same end." At such times, the past and the present, the symbol and the surface, the orderly progress of the physical world and the phantom associations of the dream can all move together in the same sentences, establishing otherwise impossible relations with one another and, by means of these, unmasking the normal ones. Difficult to recapture by a deliberate effort of the will, the past is recovered spontaneously in reverie, dream, and delirium. Proceeding by association, recovery is largely irrational. It is founded not on health but on sickness, on a falling of the body and the mind toward death. This fall in Miss Porter's fiction nearly always is a fall into the past, toward the point of birth itself, toward the original free material, all the binding formulations of one's history scraping off in the descent.

Laura in "Flowering Judas" comes to an awareness of her own treason through dream. The dying grandmother in "The Jilting of Granny Weatherall" achieves a final awful illumination through her last confused reveries. And Miranda's glimpse at death in *Pale Horse, Pale Rider* is achieved through delirium and dream. Miss Porter's use of dreams is related to her attitude toward art. For her, art, in comparison to man's unconcluded relations, is "endlessly satisfactory" because

> the artist can choose his relations, and "draw, by a geometry of his own, the circle within which they shall happily *appear* to do so." While accomplishing this, one has the illusion that destiny is not absolute, it can be arranged, temporized with, persuaded, a little here and there. And once the circle is truly drawn around its contents, it too becomes truth.

The integrity of a work of art has its own peculiar and appropriate effects. The truth of fiction is thus defined functionally as being what must follow from what is given in the artist's created world.

Apply this view of art to the use of dreams and the dream sequences in her fiction are seen to have a subtle logic. The patterning of reverie, hallucination, and dream is formalized. In "The Jilting of Granny Weatherall," for example, poetic devices provide the structure for Granny's stream of consciousness. The unifying image of her final cloudy reveries is of the bride and groom. An elaborate analogy between her fitful memories of an early tragedy, when she had been jilted at the altar, and her final disillusionment, when again there was "no bridegroom and the priest in the house," provides the framework for the story. Besides this structural device, the poetic convention of free association is rigidly controlled by an intricate arrangement of word motifs which contain and develop the themes of the story. These word motifs are of three major kinds: the first—"a long day," "get a little rest" (pp. 123, 128, 129, 130) [3]—defines Granny's life; the second—"tomorrow," "plan of life" (pp. 123, 124, 126, 132, 135)—complicates the suggested definition by contrasting it with the clichéd morality of the old order; and the third—"bitter to lose things," "never more," "lighting the lamps," "thought you'd never come" (pp. 127, 128, 129, 131, 133, 136)—

---

[3] The page numbers in parentheses refer to "The Jilting of Granny Weatherall," *Flowering Judas and Other Stories* (New York: Modern Library, 1940).

extends the definition and the contrast by interfusing the themes of transience and decay, hope and disillusionment, illusion and reality, death and immortality.

Dream, the dumb show of the unconsious, reveals "the truth" Miranda is seeking in *Pale Horse, Pale Rider*. Her quest takes her into the "pit of sleep," back to the house of memory, that secret place of "storied dust" and "ancestral bones." As revelation is its object, the image of the pit appropriately suggests "the bottomless pit" in the book of Revelation (9:1–2, 20:3). Biblical allusions reinforce the ironic structure of the story: the plague, the war, the vision of the heavenly meadow, the pollution and the purification of waters appear in a quite different context in Revelation (16:1–21; 19:1–21; 20:11–14; 21:1–6; 22:1–3). Miranda's lover, Adam, "committed without any knowledge or act of his own to death," has an obvious biblical counterpart. (Miranda thinks of him as an innocent "sacrificial lamb" and, punning, compares him to a "fine healthy apple.") The title of the story, taken from a Negro spiritual about love and death, also has its biblical analogue (Revelation 6:8).

Death and guilt are the major ingredients of the dream, flight its major motion. Death is fond of the language of enchantment: come away, follow me. Like Death in the painting by Albert Pinkham Ryder, he is something gray and green beside you, a horseman on a pale horse, and it is difficult to know, while the race is being run, whether you are outrunning "Death and the Devil" or merely accompanying him. He has the customary smells, the customary shabby garments, the customary bearing. But the important thing is that his malice is "mindless." He regards Miranda "without meaning," with a "blank still stare." Principle envelops him. He, too, like his living prototype, Mr. Hatch, is well within the law. Unlike his lesser representatives, the bond men, he needs no threats. Time is his agent.

The "disturbing oppositions" of Miranda's daily existence invade her dreams. Awake, she resists the bond men's trite talk of "vile Huns," "glorious Belleau Woods," "Martyred Belgium," "atrocities, innocent babes hoisted on Boche bayonets." She knows the protective, "habitual, automatic" response, "*C'est la guerre.*" Ritualistic, casual, amused when they talk about the war, she and Adam feel they are taking it "properly" —"no teeth-gnashing, no hair-tearing." But in sleep Miranda is unprotected. She sees Dr. Hildesheim, "his face a skull beneath his German helmet, carrying a naked infant writhing on the point of his bayonet, and a huge stone pot marked Poison in Gothic letters." She hears herself scream, "Hildesheim is a Boche, a spy, a Hun, kill him, kill him before he kills you." This association of the insidious war jargon and the corruption of conscious action with the failures of love and the ensuing guilty conscience is nearly spectacular.

Because the approach to death is so much like an approach to birth, the experience can be liberating, for the grave and the womb are one in this sense (as in "The Grave," where they merge). Similarly, in these dreams, life and death become inverted. Miranda's dreams return her to the world of her childhood, a southwestern country of palm and cedar, of buzzards hovering overhead and the smell of crushed water herbs along river banks. Death and hell and evil are suggested by her dream of a jungle,

> ... a writhing, terribly alive and secret place of death, creeping with tangles of spotted serpents, rainbow-colored birds with malign eyes, leopards with humanly wise faces and extravagantly crested lions; screaming long-armed monkeys tumbling among broad fleshy leaves that glowed with sulphur-colored light and exuded the ichor of death, and rotting trunks of un-familiar trees sprawled in crawling slime....

Miranda's entry into this jungle symbolizes her journey into the unconscious. The end of her dream adventure appropriately is with the present danger, the war, the world's threat to life and consciousness and love.

In her next dream, the jungle becomes

> ... an angry dangerous wood full of inhuman concealed voices singing sharply like the whine of arrows and she saw Adam transfixed by a flight of these singing arrows that struck him in the heart and passed shrilly cutting their path through the leaves. Adam fell straight back before her eyes, and rose again unwounded and alive; another flight of arrows loosed from the invisible bow struck him again and he fell, and yet he was there before her untouched in a perpetual death and resur-rection. She threw herself before him, angrily and selfishly she interposed between him and the track of the arrow, crying, No, no, like a child cheated in a game, It's my turn now, why must you always be the one to die? and the arrows struck her cleanly through the heart and through

his body and he lay dead, and she still lived, and the wood whistled and sang and shouted, every branch and leaf and blade of grass had its own terrible accusing voice. . . .

This dream functions as foreboding of the future (satisfying a Jungian concept of dream as revelation), and is connected with the folk song, "Pale horse, pale rider, done taken my lover away." Images in the dream are drawn from Miranda's daily life. The simile, "inhuman concealed voices singing sharply like the whine of arrows," recalls Miranda's "O Apollo" prayer. God of light and poetry, Apollo also is the archer god whose singing arrows wreak pestilence upon a corrupted people (cf. *The Iliad*). The Dark Forest is an ancient almost universal symbol of lostness, of fear of the unknown, of the terrible uncertainty of human future. It recalls Dante's

> *Midway in our life's journey, I went astray*
> *from the straight road and woke to find myself*
> *alone in a dark wood. How shall I say*
>
> *what wood that was! I never saw so drear,*
> *so rank, so arduous a wilderness!*
> *Its very memory gives a shape to fear.*[4]

Miranda's dream takes in something of the Adonis legend too: he was transfixed by arrows to a tree in a wood; one of the origins of the Crucifixion legend.

Guilt is the constant emotion of Miranda's dreams. As she approaches death, "the barriers sink one by one, and no covering of the eyes shuts out the landscape of disaster, nor the sight of crimes committed there." But death itself is without attributes, without remorse, the blown-out light. What a comfort the grave is, for is there any point to life in all this pain? None, Miss Porter seems to say to the reader in *Pale Horse, Pale Rider*, but the burning point of life itself.[5] "This fiery particle set itself unaided to resist destruction, to survive and to be its

---

[4] Dante, *The Inferno*, tr. by John Ciardi (New York: New American Library, 1954), p. 28.

[5] In "The Jilting of Granny Weatherall," the attempt to give meaning to life by creating a stable objective order seems as futile as expecting permanence from bubbles or buildings in sand. For one thing, the task is never done, as Granny surmises. Tomorrow she resolves to do what remains. "It was good to be strong enough for everything, even if all you made melted and changed and slipped under

own madness of being, motiveless and planless beyond that one essential end. Trust me, the hard unwinking angry point of light said. Trust me. I stay." The desire for life is an instinctive thing, not to be reasoned with, for Miranda does not reason her way back to health. Nearest death, she is most utterly alive, a pure germ, and this germ rays out, expands into a vision that she later remembers as "a child's dream of the heavenly meadow." Her life is rising then. It is passing through the stages of its growth, getting thinner as it spreads out. She is in a company of pure identities—innocent, respectful, unencumbered.

Closer to consciousness, she becomes aware of the dead again. In a symbolic gesture of distaste, Miranda's complete return to sensation is filled with the smell of death and the contractions of pain. At that moment, the armistice is whistled. The war is over. Now death can begin in quiet earnest in its other way. The contrast between the bright atmosphere and people of her vision and the pallid objects around her is dreadful to her. But in some ways Miranda is free, for she remembers the vision she gained of her essential nature. Consequently, she can clearly see the world to which her own will to live has condemned her, "where the light seemed filmed over with cobwebs, all the bright surfaces corroded, the sharp planes melted and formless, all objects and beings meaningless, ah, dead and withered things that believed themselves alive!"

As it will not do "to betray the conspiracy," Miranda, smiling, tells the friends who visit her "how gay and what a pleasant surprise it [is] to find herself alive." She prepares a list of the things she needs to take up the challenge of life again: gray suede "gauntlets," gray sheer stockings, Bois d'Hiver perfume, lipstick, a fancy walking stick with a silver knob. Living will require that she "look properly to the art of the thing." Remembering herself as she had been in sickness and as she will be in health, she thinks: "Lazarus, come forth. Not unless you bring me my

---

your hands, so that by the time you finished you almost forgot what you were working for." Order, in Granny's mind, is clean folded linens, straight-lines of bottles, jugs and crocks and jelly glasses in splendid rows, well-fenced pastures, neatly furrowed fields, arranged affairs, a sensible will, and above all, weddings at which the groom appears. But the sudden guest always finds the house untidy, the family in disorder, and death is always sudden, permanently a surprise. There is never time enough to "spread out the plan of life and tuck in the edges." Her vision of a carefully planted, row-lined field is obscured by the dark smoke she identifies as from the stack of hell.

top hat and stick." The parallel between Miranda's restoration and Lazarus' suggests an ironic transformation of the biblical tale (John 11:1–44; 12:1–5). After four days in the tomb, Lazarus had been brought back to life by the faith of his sister Martha in the divinity of Jesus. But here Miranda is restored not by faith in a divinity, but by faith in a deluding dream concocted by the instinct of self-preservation. And her coming forth will be accompanied by "top hat and stick," symbols of human vanity and human pleasure.

Her own war won, can Miranda hope that the pain of her awareness will remain an honest pain, that her consciousness will continue pure, she free? Life is not that sort of easy thing. She begins to lie at once. To the memory of Adam, she tries to say that she returned for him, from love of him; but in that point of flame there was only herself, and the joy of the heavenly meadow was the joy that belongs to unentangled spirits. She came back out of sheer survival, as she, for the time being, remembers. But soon she will "cross back and be at home again," and the "cold light of tomorrow" will sometimes seem even warm, and indeed there will be time for everything. Now, at least, she is strong enough for everything too.

꽃 꽃

The purpose of Katherine Anne Porter's art is the recovery of order through consciousness. This sort of order has a great advantage over Granny Weatherall's. It can be completed. It can be made to endure. It can be honest and speak truly and recover the past. It can become an instrument of personal conquest and is itself a religious record. Completely apart from any autobiographical elements that may be there, to read Miss Porter's work is to be present at a moral struggle that swiftly and imperceptibly becomes one's own. Her stories not only record the effort of some of her characters to find freedom through awareness, they are themselves that effort and its success. Her art, like all great art, is about itself. The order, the understanding, the value it seeks, lies in its style, and as Miranda dwindles to an angry burning point of life, it, even more fiercely, swells, becoming lyrical in the presence of death. Miss Porter's is an art that can confidently say, as that same point says to Miranda: trust me, I stay.

It is the strategy of happenings to hide themselves in innocent surroundings, in old photographs and faded flowers, in yellowed letters wrapped with string and put past seeing away in trunks. Hidden thus, they wait like microscopic things, with all the oriental patience of disease, their opportunity to infect the present. The pattern of this action lies in Miranda's illumination in "The Grave." The meaning of "The Grave" derives from the epiphany Miranda obtains from her sudden recollection of "one burning day" twenty years earlier when she, a child of nine, and her brother Paul, aged twelve, found treasure in their family's discarded cemetery. The structure of the story consists of a series of analogies, the principal one being between the opened graves, where the children are united by a tacit, secret bond of knowledge and kinship, and the human mind as a burial place, which, when opened, yields secrets that restore the individual to communion and love. The sense, in the reading, is of a sun-drenched wholesome world, and Miranda's final epiphany of her brother, soberly smiling, the silver dove turning in his hands, is completely appropriate. The weight of the revelation is slowly felt, gradually increasing in the reader's mind, as it must have done in Miranda's. It is the revelation of true burial in this life, of irrevocable loss.

On that remembered day, the children began to play in the cemetery. They tried to simulate what they felt would be adult emotions and they failed. They experienced, instead, "an agreeable thrill of wonder." There was, in fact, "a small disappointment at the entire commonplaceness of the actual spectacle," for "when the coffin was gone a grave was just a hole in the ground." With no sense of horror, Miranda dropped "into the pit that had held her grandfather's bones." The time of such sight is short. They already understood what they ought to feel, even though they did not feel it, and of the two it was Paul, the elder, the less wise in being the wiser one, who was impressed by the dove's being the head of a coffin screw. Miranda calmly placed on her finger a ring that doubtless had slid from a bone when the bones were moved, and its curious effect was the desire in her to change her practical boyish clothes for the dress that local decorum had demanded. A dream of living grandly had stirred in her. The old myths were on her thumb.

They were hunting. Miranda asked idly, in their turns at shooting, if she might have the first snake. Snakes would not be frightening until later. Then Paul shot a rabbit and expertly skinned it. "The flayed flesh emerged dark and scarlet, sleek, firm; Miranda with thumb and finger felt the long fine muscles with the silvery flat strips binding them to the joints." The tone of this, the judgment in the language, would be appropriate for flowers or edible fruits. They discovered that the rabbit had unborn young:

> . . . there they were, dark gray, their sleek wet down lying in minute even ripples, like a baby's head just washed, their unbelievably small delicate ears folded close, their little blind faces almost featureless.

Writing like this is a triumph of recovery, of remembering. There is no adult horror or disgust. There is no sense, even, of these things overcome. The children walked from grave to grave wholly unconscious of the symbolism of their acts.

> Miranda said, "Oh, I want to *see*," under her breath. She looked and looked—excited but not frightened, for she was accustomed to the sight of animals killed in hunting—filled with pity and astonishment and a kind of shocked delight in the wonderful little creatures for their own sakes, they were so pretty. She touched one of them ever so carefully, "Ah, there's blood running over them," she said and began to tremble without knowing why. Yet she wanted most deeply to see and to know. . . .

In this way, Miranda penetrated one of the mysteries of life, for her not a mystery yet but something to be made one. It would no longer be possible then to see and to know. It was already difficult for Paul: "Don't you ever tell a living soul that you saw this. Don't tell a soul. Don't tell Dad because I'll get into trouble." Miranda, growing up, forgot. She had to. It was part of the price. Twenty years later, in Mexico, stimulated by a similar sun and the presence of similar odors, through a vendor's tray of sweets in the shapes of baby animals, she has a vision of that day, that sun, her brother. At first, she is horrified. The sensation is terribly real, and she sees the fetal rabbits in the candies. But when she thinks of the treasures she and her brother had found in the graves that day— the silver dove, the golden ring—her horror dies, and she takes joy in the picture of her brother's face. The scene is precisely worked. Her horror is adult. The commentary of the medium of her vision, sugar sweets, upon the content of that vision is macabre. Then she recovers her childhood sight. With it, she can still regain her brother, but could Miranda, even if it were in a flash as this, see those wonderful little gray creatures again? Miss Porter has. We easily see the art. We must not miss the moral achievement for which the art is testimony.

James William Johnson

Another Look at
Katherine Anne Porter

IN MODERN AMERICAN and British literature, there is no other writer
who occupies the position of Katherine Anne Porter. She has not published a volume of fiction since 1944, yet she is "among the most
distinguished masters of her craft in this country." Sporadic chapters
of a "novel in progress" are published in *Harper's* and the *Atlantic*,
yet this very novel has been heralded as forthcoming since 1941, when
it had another name. By her own admission, Miss Porter has burned
"literally trunksfull" of manuscripts of fiction, though she has steadily
produced reviews, essays, and translations in abundance. The frugal
but prolific writer, the exacting critic who can turn out articles for slick
magazines, the author who enjoys a peak reputation based on past and
anticipated work: such a paradox is Miss Porter.

That her reputation remains at a peak cannot be doubted. Since her
first story, published in 1930, Miss Porter has never gotten a completely
unfavorable review. She has been praised by *Time* and the *New York
Times* with equal enthusiasm. The *Saturday Review* has unequivocally
placed her in the category of Flaubert, Hawthorne, and James as a story

teller and artist. Her prose has been called "beautifully molded," "carefully wrought," "brilliant," and a masterpiece of "polish and lucidity." Even Edmund Wilson, voluble as he characteristically is, has confessed himself at a loss for critical terms laudatory enough to describe Miss Porter's stories. Before the phenomenon of her work, critics usually throw reserve aside and join the chorus of praise.

More important than verbal acclaim, however, in revealing Miss Porter's status in contemporary letters are the facts of her critical career. In 1941, she helped to launch the career of Eudora Welty on a wider sea with a critical preface to Miss Welty's stories. In 1942, she appeared on a radio broadcast dealing with Henry James's *The Turn of the Screw* which turned the Freudian critical tide and led to a revival of interest in James that is still going on. She was a member of the selection committee which gave the first Bollingen Foundation Award to Ezra Pound, thereby uncapping a reaction which must go down in literary history along with the Ossian controversy of the eighteenth century and the *Edinburgh Review* furor of the nineteenth. It was she, as a Fellow of the Library of Congress, who dropped by Robert Penn Warren's office one day with a newspaper clipping that became the genesis of Warren's novel, *World Enough and Time*. And it was Katherine Anne Porter who virtually single-handedly shattered the Gertrude Stein legend with an essay, "The Wooden Umbrella." Her effect on modern literature as a critic is inestimable: she has verbally shaken the widow of Dylan Thomas, castigated immature first novelists for their "self-love, self-pity, and self-preoccupation," and taken long, revealing second looks at such figures as Willa Cather, Ford Madox Ford, and most recently D. H. Lawrence.

It is in her versatility and achievement in a variety of rôles that the nature of Miss Porter's uniqueness in the world of letters is to be found. Creative artist, journalist, hired essayist, establisher of literary standards, arbiter of literary practice, she is in the truest guise a "professional writer." She is, morever, a woman and a Southerner. Herein lies her anomalous character. Although she shares the tradition and honor of Ellen Glasgow, Eudora Welty, and Carson McCullers, her critical activities give her a dimension which they do not possess. The obvious fact that she is first of all an original and dedicated writer of fictional literature separates her from such journalists turned novelist as Rebecca

West and Martha Gellhorn. Her very professionalism divides her from the women scholar-writers typified by Mary Ellen Chase. In short, Miss Porter is one of a very small group of professional women of letters whose undisputed literary merit is supplemented by journalistic and critical talent. As such, she stands in the company of George Sand, George Eliot, and Virginia Woolf. Perhaps her closest living counterpart is Elizabeth Bowen, whose work is unlike Miss Porter's in obvious ways. Even as a member of the *literatae,* Miss Porter has her differences. Her literary output is far less than that of her peers, and so far she has largely resisted the critical impulse to pontificate.

It is perhaps because of her admixture of abilities that Katherine Anne Porter as a writer of fiction has never been tellingly examined. The critic who attempts to isolate her fiction from the rest of her canon winds up rather self-consciously trying to evaluate her as a craftsman; hence the generalizations about her style. The critic who tries to correlate all of her work tends to misread her stories within the context of her topical essays and to find a totality and synthesis which do not exist. Harry J. Mooney's pamphlet, *The Fiction and Criticism of Katherine Anne Porter* (1957), is a case in point. Despite many perceptive comments, this study reads Miss Porter's fiction within an historical perspective which limits and distorts it. As a critic, Miss Porter possibly may be viewed in an historical context. As a craftsman, she must wait for time to place her in a tidily discernible literary milieu. But as a thinker and a writer of fiction—as a "witness to life," in her own phrase—she speaks to us today and we ought to be able to perceive some pattern of experience and meaning in what she says, if indeed she is the artist we all claim her to be.

Unfortunately, the task of criticizing her fiction has been more clearly delineated because of the gap of fifteen years dating from Miss Porter's last published work—"unfortunately" because it would appear that, except for her novel, she has now said fictionally all that she has to say. (Since this essay was written, Miss Porter has published a "new" story, "The Fig Tree," in *Harper's.* In truth, this story was written in 1934 along with the rest of the Miranda stories and the manuscript was misplaced until recently.) Miss Porter has indicated in the past that everything she has written has been "fragments of a much larger plan which I am still engaged in carrying out." Without hazarding too much of a guess, we may suppose that her novel, of which some half-dozen chapters have been published, will be her summarizing "testimony," her attempt at a total and transcendent view of life told with all the "truth and tenderness and severity" she is capable of. Yet even in the fragments (her stories and novelle), we can see the essence of Miss Porter's fiction: her themes, symbols, and underlying philosophical logos. Even without the published chapters of her novel and her hints on a television broadcast in the spring of 1959, we can comprehend her fictional world without waiting to read *Ship of Fools*.

꽃　꽃

First the themes. These are fewer in number than one might suspect from the variety of locales, subjects, and narrative methods that Miss Porter uses. In fact, much critical confusion has resulted from the effort to understand her stories in terms of their settings or personae (*i.e.*, the "Mexico" stories, the "Miranda" stories). When the fictional pieces are seen as assertions of a life perspective rather than as segments of experience, however—when they are viewed as expressions of theme rather than classified according to secondary resemblances—the stories group themselves in six units, each with a novella as its culmination and most complete thematic statement.

As a serious writer, Miss Porter is concerned, of course, with certain general and pervasive themes: the workings of the human heart; appearance and reality; the epiphanic apperception of truth; the subterranean rills of individual emotion which produce the emotional torrents of an historical era; self-delusion and its consequences. But she tends to use these broader topics to re-enforce more limited themes, which dramatize themselves in a variety of characters and places. Her specific themes are, as we have said, six in number.

Initially, there is the theme of the individual within his heritage, the relationship of past to present in the mind. "Old Mortality" is the novella which embodies this topic most tellingly, with its three stages of development in the mind of its child-heroine and its alteration of the legendary past through a series of clashes which it has with the factual present. There are four short stories illustrating the same theme, all of them coincidentally dealing with the same characters: "The Old Order," "The Source," "The Witness," "The Last Leaf." The two old ladies, one white and one black, in "The Old Order" talk always about the past, making it the very substance of the present and embalming the future with the dead. The Witness exists in the present but his mind dwells on what he believes happened long ago but actually did not. The Last Leaf, through her obdurant behavior in the present, gives the lie to sentimental memories of what the past was. And the Source is a farm which has become symbolic of a past stability and order which never existed except in golden retrospection.

These works treat what Miss Porter has recently called "the country of my heart." Autobiographical or not, they stand thematically with certain works of Faulkner, Mann, and Proust. Like Faulkner, Miss Porter is fascinated with the tragedy of the Old South and the effect of the legend on those who helped to create it. Like Mann, she sees the past as a wistfully perfect and stable order which is perfect only because it is completed, that is, dead. And like Proust, she emphasizes memories of human beings and the fragments of recollected days and ways as the bits which make up the mosaic of present thought. She never exaggerates the past by using it mythopoeically or giving it a transcendence over the present because of its historicity. Instead, she sees the past simply as a former time peopled by human beings living unheroic lives, for the most part. To her as to Homer, the generations of men are as leaves which wax green and then fall; and there is always one last leaf to remind the living of the human reality of the past.

A second theme is cultural displacement. Whether one is exiled willingly or unwillingly from his own heritage, he finds himself in an alien culture which often permits him to discover the inherent nature of human evil. "The Leaning Tower" takes this as its thesis, with its depiction of a young American artist in Nazi Germany in the days when the beast is beginning to emerge once more from its subconscious jungle. This novella is profitably compared with the final chapters of Thomas Wolfe's *You Can't Go Home Again* and Christopher Isherwood's *Goodbye to Berlin*, which utilize the same fictional situation. Both Wolfe and Isherwood are content to evoke a general mood of brutality and totalitarianism; Miss Porter clothes it in flesh in the persons of Hans, Otto, and Lutte. Where Wolfe editorializes, using such words as "evil," "brutal," and "stupid," Miss Porter simply and severely records the reactions of a decent, essentially unvocal young man to the revealing but unspectacular behavior of three young Germans, an Austrian, and a Pole. Thus embodied, Nazism is a tangibly, recognizably ugly aspect of humanity rather than the vaguely terrifying, whispered accounts of "those people" to be found in Wolfe's version.

"Flowering Judas" is a shorter statement of the theme of cultural displacement and the discovery of evil. This much-anthologized and criticized story anticipates "The Leaning Tower" in many ways: the idealistic young American protagonist, the removal to a remotely exotic culture, the militaristic background, the underlying tradition of violence and force in the strange culture, the final realization of evil by the protagonist. Unlike Charles Upton, who discovers that selfishness and a feeling of inferiority explain the megalomania of an unloved race, Laura of "Flowering Judas" finds herself guilty of a cold idealism which has cut her off from human beings and has blighted the growth of compassion in her heart. Charles is capable of compassion but is ineffectual; Laura is efficient but frigid. With these differences in protagonist, "Flowering Judas" and "The Leaning Tower" are thematically closely akin. Braggioni is the prototype of the Nazi pigs of the novella, and his nameless victims are finally personified in the hapless Otto.

The third group of stories deals with unhappy marriages and the self-delusion attendant upon them. "Rope," which serves as Miss Porter's version of the Battle of the Sexes, shows a violent squabble between a husband and wife over a trivial incident which reveals their deep-seated differences. "That Tree" explores a conflict of wills and temperaments between the male and female; and "A Day's Work" is a dreadfully sordid, if grotesquely funny, story about two mis-matched and long-married people. "The Cracked Looking-Glass" is the novella archetype of the theme, with its characterization of the fanciful Rosaleen, wed to the aging Dennis and trapped in rural New England. Similar in its external qualities to Eugene O'Neill's *Desire under the Elms,* the longer version of a mis-matched Irish immigrant couple ("A Day's Work" is the shorter) concerns itself with the wife's deficiencies in the marriage state. Rosaleen's unrealistic dreams of what her marriage should be have been so constantly eroded by the realities of her life that she has overworked her fancy almost to the point of dementedness.

Then there is the group of stories which have as their theme the death of love and the survival of individual integrity. "Pale Horse, Pale

Rider," the longest version, is a literal account of the death of love in the person of Adam, whose tragic death in the influenza epidemic of 1918 leaves Miranda, the "one singer," to mourn and to rebuild her life on the single principle of refusing to be comforted by a flight into religious illusion. "The Downward Path to Wisdom" is a study of the metaphoric death of love: at its conclusion the unwanted and rejected child discovers the core of his self in his little song of hatred. "Theft" shows a girl robbed of everything—things lost, borrowed books, unspoken words, "dying friendships and the dark inexplicable death of love"—until the theft of her purse reminds her that no loss but that of her hope in life and trust in others really matters. Other stories which ring variations on the same theme are "The Circus," "The Grave," and "The Fig Tree."

The fifth body of stories is those which deal with the theme of "Noon Wine": man's slavery to his own nature and subjugation to a human fate which dooms him to suffering and disappointment. The destiny which decrees that Mr. Thompson, the self-indulgent child of pride, will benefit from the lucky hiring of the insane farm hand also assures that he will finally be crushed under its grinding wheel. Miss Porter firmly insists that man's suffering is inextricably related to what he is, though she also suggests that certain destructive forces—disease, death—are inevitable and inescapable in spite of one's character and she implies strongly that the struggle of mankind goes on before an aloof and indifferent cosmos. In "María Concepción," for instance, the footloose and irresponsible Juan is drawn back to the life-pattern incorporated in his wife, who dispassionately murders her rival to possess her husband's child. In "Magic," the central figure, a young prostitute in a New Orleans bordello, struggles frantically to escape her enslaved existence, succeeding at last only to return voluntarily to the black tyranny of the madam. "He" shows the unavoidable tragedy of the abnormal child, the victim of a biological accident; but the suffering which His mother undergoes is compounded by her own foolish vanity and pride in refusing to accept the facts (her son's hopeless abnormality and her hatred of him). "The Jilting of Granny Weatherall" shows a dying old woman, stood up by the God she had supposed to exist, just as she had been jilted by an earthly fiancé and forced to live a life of disappointment and compensation. The violence and suffering, mental and physical, in these stories are denigrated by the ironic realization that man must face them with little choice, however senseless they may be.

Finally, there is "Hacienda," which is really too long to be a short story and too short, diffuse, and plotless to be a novella. Though it appears to stand alone, it is in fact an amalgam of all Miss Porter's themes. The hacienda is a timeless embodiment of the past way of life in the present. It is presently peopled by a number of aliens to Mexican culture, who react to their surroundings in various revealing ways. The master of the hacienda and his wife are the principals in an unhappy and futile marriage, and the husband has just undergone an ill-fated love affair with an actress. The complication of the story centers in a crime of passion committed by a Mexican serf, now hopelessly caught in a tangle of legal procedure.

Such are the recurrent themes of Katherine Anne Porter's seventeen short stories and six novelle. If the above summary is oversimplified, its categories can be defended with more details than space permits here. The important point is that thematically Miss Porter is working with a limited group of ideas which she presents with a uniformly superb style and a multiformly ingenious handling of symbols. It is this aspect of symbolism which must next occupy the attention of her would-be critic.

※ ※

During the 1940s, it was as symbolist that Miss Porter was most effusively praised by the totemist critics. In fact, criticism of her work became tantamount to an intellectual parlor game: "Let's see who can find the most abstruse symbols in 'Flowering Judas.'" Her work survived this craze, which was largely unnecessary, since the truth is that her symbols operate on the most direct level and where she intends a multiplicity of meaning, Miss Porter almost always tells the reader so.

Her titles, for example, almost invariably summarize symbolically the state of affairs she deals with in her story: "The Old Order," "The Circus," "Magic." If the story is more than an expository dissertation on its topic, it is always about that topic fundamentally. When her titles are literary or allusive, as with "Noon Wine," "Old Mortality," or "Pale Horse, Pale Rider," she works the substance of the quoted source into her own story: Mr. Helton, in "Noon Wine," plays the symbolic tune on his harmonica and the missing words are eventually supplied by the odious Mr. Hatch, or Adam and Miranda, of "Pale Horse, Pale Rider," chant the old slave tune while waiting for the ambulance to arrive. If Miss Porter uses an "objective correlative" as her title—"The Leaning Tower," "The Cracked Looking Glass"—it appears significantly in the story and someone comments on its connotations. Charles, of "The Leaning Tower," breaks the plaster replica of the Pisan landmark; and when it is returned, repaired, to its place, he mulls over its meaning for its owner and tries to understand how it typifies the unsound culture of Nazi Germany. Rosaleen is constantly distressed about the cracked mirror, which blurs her face so unrecognizably; but her imperfect and unsatisfactory marriage as mirrored in her "cracked" imagination cannot be replaced, and so the cracked looking glass remains hanging in the kitchen, after Rosaleen has fully pondered the consequences of its doing so. Even with such a title as "Rope," the primary meaning is an obvious one. It is a piece of rope that starts the quarrel; and though the "rope" may be seen as the uxorial quarrel woven out of a thousand threads of contention, or as the tie that binds the unfortunate combatants in marriage, or as the proverbial "enough rope" with which the wife in the story is likely eventually to hang herself, Miss Porter's title states clearly and directly the symbol of rope as the embodiment of contention.

The Porter symbolism also depends in obvious fashion on proper names. The masterful thing about the names of her characters is that they are appropriate for those people in those places. The names of real people are chosen from a cultural context which embodies certain values of the culture; thus when Miss Porter calls her heroine "Miranda," it is a suitable name for a little Southern girl of 1900, being Latinate and vaguely "literary." If as a fictional personage Miranda shares the innocence and optimism of Shakespeare's sheltered heroine, or if she literally becomes an "admirable" character because of her honesty and moral responsibility, Miss Porter's story is so much the richer. Miranda's last name, incidentally, is "Rhea," as we find from a close reading of "Old Mortality." "Rhea" is a fine old Southern name, thus appropriate; but Rhea was also the Greek Earth-Mother, and Miss Porter's Rheas live on the soil of a matriarchy run by a grandmother often described in divine terms. Such symbolism of nomenclature is not vital to the understanding of the stories, but it helps to reinforce characterization and theme.

Miss Porter's ingenuity with the symbolism of names is too extensive to treat except eclectically. "Old Mortality" alone provides numerous examples: the "beloved" Aunt Amy, the "divine" Uncle Gabriel shockingly gone to seed, the acid Miss Honey, Cousin Eva, who gives Miranda the apple of truth to eat. Then there is the indomitable Granny Weatherall, who has survived life's storms; Braggioni, the insufferable egoist; Mr. Hatch, the deviser of schemes; Mr. Helton, the inhabitant of a mental Hades, and so forth. In some stories, the thematic overtones are stated in the nature of the struggle between characters symbolically named. In "María Concepción," for example, the sterile "Mary of the Conception" kills the "Mary of the Rose"; *i.e.*, the principle of ritualistic propagation destroys the principle of love. We do not have to see this story as an allegorical history of Mariolatry, or as a primitive Aztec myth, to understand it as another of Miss Porter's explorations in the theme of the death of love as a part of man's destined suffering.

In the use of symbols other than in her titles and proper names, Miss Porter is equally adept. At times she deliberately uses mythic symbols, though she domesticates the myth to the level of reality. In "Pale Horse, Pale Rider," Adam is symbolically treated in an implicit way. Literally, Adam is a nice, handsome young man who dies. But he is an "Adam," a first man, a man in a state of innocence. He and Miranda are the inhabitants of the Paradise of Romantic Love and are so described. His fate, however, is worse than merely being exposed to sin (and it is significant that Miranda, like Eve, is the agent of the evil). He becomes a pagan god, whose beauty and love must be thematically divorced from the Christian tradition if Miranda's ultimate resolution is to have any meaning. Thus, Miranda offers to pray to Apollo; and finally in her dream, Adam becomes Baldur or Dionysos, the god perpetually slain and resurrected. Adam dies, like Baldur, forever; and Miranda's attempt to resurrect him through faith fails. Paradise thus is irrevocably lost, never to be regained; the utter despair of the death of love is subtly but clearly emphasized by Miss Porter's synthesis of Christian and pagan myths.

There are other "mythic" stories using traditional symbols. "María Concepción" is one, and the much discussed "Flowering Judas" is another, with its obvious reference to the Gospels as it studies the mind ot a budding traitor to a theoretically idealistic Cause. "The Circus" shows life as a noisy, three-ring spectacle under a flimsy Big Top, an image which Archibald MacLeish has used in a sonnet ("The End of the World") and a play (*J. B.*). No reader familiar with William Blake can miss the significance of the cry of "Weep, Weep" in "The Fig Tree." Within the Catholic context of many of the stories, "The Grave" has mythic undercurrents, with Miranda's yielding up of the Dove (Paraclete) for the wedding ring (Love) and her subsequent discovery that love means birth means death. But this interpretation reminds us again of how symbolic guessing games can get out of hand. "The Grave" is obviously, and simply, the story of a young girl's first realization of the nature of love and sex; and the ring and dove, as objects from the grave, underline the poignance of this emotional step toward maturity and death. Miss Porter, as ever, is concerned in this story with the human condition; and the human condition includes children who trespass in cemeteries and learn things prematurely.

Many of Miss Porter's symbols are the very stuff of her narrative and operate without calling up allusions or forming patterns of meaning. Mrs. Thompson's dark glasses in "Noon Wine" are symbolic in this fashion, as are the animal gravestones of "The Witness" and the patchwork of "The Old Order." A few individual symbols appear several times in the stories without any incremental repetition or external frame of reference. Miss Porter is apparently fond of these and they fulfill a self-renewing purpose for her. Chief of these is her death-image of a swirling cloud or whirlpool of darkness narrowing down to a pin point of light. The meadow is often a symbol of freedom, and a horseback ride expresses independence. A spring of fresh water symbolizes innocence, truth, or faith. Tangling and weaving images appear in her stories of the individual in his heritage; and weak or vicious people are figuratively animalistic: they are "penguins" or they have "rabbit teeth" or "skunk heads." Merely to list such images, however, gives them a commonplace quality which within their contexts they do not have.

A few basic themes, an adroit use of symbols, a limpid prose style—these combine in Miss Porter's stories to the propagation of a fictional point of view which is amazingly consistent and complete. The logos of her fictional attitude toward life is something like this:

The child is born into a world seemingly ordered and reasonable

but it is in fact chaotic, ridiculous, and doubt-ridden ("The Old Order").
He learns at an early age that he is an atomistic creature, often unloved
("The Downward Path"), and that the delightful spectacle of life masks
fear, hatred, and bitterness ("The Circus"). He discovers that life and
love must end in death ("The Grave," "The Fig Tree"). He must inevitably reject his heritage as lies and his family as hostile aliens ("Old
Mortality"); but when he tries to substitute something else in their
place, he is driven back by his own weaknesses to what he has been
conditioned to ("María Concepción," "Magic"). If he makes the break
with the past and tries to replace the lost old love with a new, he is
doomed to despair ("Pale Horse, Pale Rider"). If he tries to substitute
another heritage for his own, he finds it full of evil ("The Leaning
Tower"); or he discovers that he has lost his power to love through
denying his own tradition ("Flowering Judas"). There is nothing for him
to cling to but his desperate belief in his own courage and integrity
("Theft") and what little of love and certainty he has in life ("The
Cracked Looking-Glass"). But life is senselessly cruel ("He"), full of
frustration and contention ("Rope," "That Tree," "A Day's Work");
and it ends in annihilation and the extinction of all hope ("The Jilting of
Granny Weatherall"). Such is Miss Porter's fictional philosophy.

Katherine Anne Porter is conventionally praised for her humanity
and warmth and for the stoic virtues which her people show in the face
of life's hardships. It is true that she sets up the stoic as the best sort
of behavior. It is also true that the dignity and compassion of her characters are strikingly apparent. But Miss Porter's world is a black and
tragic one, filled with disaster, heartbreak, and soul-wrecking disillusionment. The most noble of her characters—the Grandmother, Charles
Upton, Miranda, Granny Weatherall—must submit in the nature of
things to sorrows which are not ennobling but destructively abrasive of
joy, love, and hope; all of them end with a bleak realization of the
Everlasting Nay. They are confronted by the thing "most cruel of all,"
which in its enormity transcends all other sorrows—the obliteration of
hope. The tiny particle of light must always be snuffed out in the depths
of the whirlpool.

This despair-filled vision is not the one which Miss Porter presents
in the non-fiction she has written on subjects corresponding to those of
her fiction. In her essays, hope remains in spite of human error and

human history. Love need not die and life can have order and meaning. But the essays are topical and temporary; they deal with the merely ethical. The stories concern the ultimately moral and realistic, and they are completely negative in their final perception of truth. It is unlikely that Miss Porter's novel will alter this view. Once there was a "Promised Land"; then, "No Safe Harbor"; now it is a "Ship of Fools." To Miss Porter's severely truthful eyes, we are all in the same boat and the waters are rising.

If we accept the foregoing interpretation of her fiction, we then have grounds for estimating the stature of Katherine Anne Porter as an artist. In penetration, her ultimate vision of reality is equal to that of any modern writer, Mann and Faulkner included. Her tragic sense is as keen as Hardy's or Virginia Woolf's; and her knowledge of human feeling is as incisive and compassionate as Conrad's. Yet even her most dedicated admirers hesitate to place her among these titans, the general feeling being that she lacks their volume, their comprehensiveness, their "scope."

Had Miss Porter left those trunksfull of manuscripts unburned, the objection based on volume could have been met. Yet this very act of selectivity is an indication of the guiding principle which has made her unique. Her critical judgment, as accurate and impartial as a carpenter's level, has limited her artistry in several ways. It has not permitted her to universalize but has confined her to being a "witness to life." Consequently, her fiction has been closely tied to what she herself has experienced firsthand. The fact that Miss Porter's essays parallel her stories in theme—love, marriage, alien cultures—is significant in this light. Her artistic preoccupation with "truth" has prevented the fictional generalizations often thought of as scope.

Moreover, Miss Porter's "truth" is the truth of feeling and behavior rather than that of ideas. Her emphasis is always on her characters, and her stories are about people rather than humanity or concepts. Because she narrows her attention to specific individuals, extending their dimensions only by the subtle use of the mythic technique noted before, her stories give the impression of constriction. In addition, her people are in no way exceptional, even in their most flamboyant actions: they are grandmothers, farmers, career girls, and artists acting like grandmothers, farmers, career girls, and artists. If fate involves them in exceptional situations, it is their ordinary or average qualities which are illuminated, not their superhuman or heroic. One has but to compare Mr. Thompson of "Noon Wine" and Raskolnikov of *Crime and Punishment*—both of them ax murderers—to see the literary effects. One is real and the other surpasses reality. It is always reality that concerns Miss Porter.

Finally, Miss Porter's self-criticism has prevented her from publishing, or even preserving, anything less than perfect by her own severe standards. As a result, she has no magnificent failures; and the magnificent failure is often the writer's masterpiece. *Ship of Fools*, now "in progress" for twenty years, may turn out to be a success. If it does not, Miss Porter's admirers may justly fear it will never be published, her principles being what they are. All of her fiction published so far has been perfect—limited but perfect. Her readers can be thankful that Katherine Anne Porter has pleased herself sufficiently to permit three volumes of fiction to appear, though they must regret, with the aesthetic theorists of the eighteenth century, that perfection is often bought at the cost of greatness.

John W. Aldridge

Art and Passion in
Katherine Anne Porter

EVER SINCE the publication of *Flowering Judas,* her first volu
stories, in 1930, Katherine Anne Porter has enjoyed a reputati
excellence that criticism has done little to confirm or deny. ¹
not to say that criticism has neglected her. Over the years a
but respectable amount of commentary has grown up around her
and individual stories of hers have so long been the standard s
of undergraduate explication that it is now possible to mistake th
hieroglyphs belonging to the archaeology department. Yet the b
this criticism has failed to establish for Miss Porter the clear cl
distinction that everyone seems to agree she possesses. It has
always approached her with the highest admiration, yet been singularly
unable to say exactly what is admirable about her. It has sounded her
symbols, plumbed her metaphors, prodded and poked among her ironies
and ambiguities, and come up with very little that would distinguish
her writing from a newly excavated Babylonian grocery list.

As a result, Miss Porter occupies today a most peculiar position. She
is widely recognized as a creative artist of almost awesome fastidious-

ness, whose very paucity of production has come to be regarded as the mark of a talent so fine that it can scarcely bring itself to function. Her stories are considered to be distinguished examples of their type and have undoubtedly had enormous influence on the contemporary development of the form. Yet the precise nature of her artistic qualities continues to be one of the great unsolved mysteries of modern literature. She remains the symbol and custodian of an excellence that is almost everywhere appreciated but almost nowhere clearly understood.

In his review of her third volume of stories, *The Leaning Tower*, in 1944, Edmund Wilson described some of the problems that Miss Porter poses for the critic. "Miss Porter is baffling," he said, "because one cannot take hold of her work in any of the obvious ways. She makes none of the melodramatic or ironic points that are the stock in trade of ordinary short story writers; she falls into none of the usual patterns and she does not show anyone's influence. She does not exploit her personality either inside or outside her work, and her writing itself makes a surface so smooth that the critic has little opportunity to point out peculiarities of color or weave. If he is tempted to say that the effect is pale, he is prevented by the realization that Miss Porter writes English of a purity and precision almost unique in contemporary American fiction. If he tries to demur that some given piece fails to mount with the accelerating pace or arrive at the final intensity that he is in the habit of expecting in short stories, he is deterred by a nibbling suspicion that he may not have grasped its meaning and have it hit him with a sudden impact some minutes after he has closed the book."[1]

The appearance of Miss Porter's *Collected Stories* would seem, on the face of it, to do nothing to simplify these problems. It merely confronts the critic with more material to puzzle over and be baffled by, and the initial effect of reading it is rather like having to eat through a large plateful of hors d'oeuvres while wondering if dinner will ever come or whether perhaps this *is* dinner. The book brings together all the shorter fiction Miss Porter has ever published: the entire contents of the three previous collections—*Flowering Judas; Pale Horse, Pale Rider;* and *The Leaning Tower*—as well as four stories never before published in book form. It is thus, with the necessary omission of her one book

[1] From *Classics and Commercials* by Edmund Wilson (New York: Farrar, Strauss, 1950). By permission of the publisher.

of essays, *The Days Before,* and her one novel, *Ship of Fools,* a complete representation of the literary achievement of her long lifetime. And what strikes one with dismaying force is how much less impressive this achievement seems than, given her reputation and obvious stature, it ought to seem.

The scope of the volume enables one to recognize and appreciate the variety of Miss Porter's imaginative interests and the range of her technical skills, but it also throws into rather harsh perspective certain qualities of hers that were less noticeable in the various earlier volumes when one read them separately. The effect, for example, of a good deal of her writing does indeed seem pale. At times it seems downright colorless. And the explanation is scarcely that she writes such a pure English, but rather that all contradictions and discords appear to have been sacrificed to the purity of the English. If Miss Porter ever faced a choice between creating colorfully and dangerously and preserving the fine veneer of her style, she obviously decided in favor of her style. She has been most careful to take no imaginative risks that she could not easily and gracefully put into words. As a result, the purity of her English— and there can be no doubt that it *is* pure—is at once a tribute to her verbal fastidiousness and testimony to the existence within her of psychic and artistic limitations that have prevented her from producing work of the first magnitude.

These same limitations have also, to my mind, been responsible for the failure of certain of Miss Porter's stories to arrive at the final intensity that Mr. Wilson was deterred by his nibbling suspicion from expecting, but which I see no reason not to insist upon. But then Mr. Wilson was much too eager to give Miss Porter the benefit of every doubt, presumably because he took it for granted that she is too good not to know at all times exactly what she is doing. I incline toward the opposite view. I think she is not quite good enough always to know, that she is frequently uncertain of her meanings, and that at times she is even downright baffled by the direction in which her work is taking her. It simply does not seem to me true that one is justified in withholding criticism of her lapses from intensity on the ground that the meaning of the stories in which they occur will very probably hit one some minutes after closing the book. This, to be sure, can happen, and when it does, the sensation is most agreeable. But one would be foolish to live in hope of this kind of tardy revelation, for too often one is not hit at all, after no matter how long a wait.

Of course this may indicate only that one is stupid. But it may also indicate that the meaning is too obscure or ambiguous to be apprehended. Certainly, there are moments when such seems to be the case, when inspiration evidently failed and the original idea was not conceived with sufficient force to be fully embodied in materials best suited to its expression. In fact, one often has the sense of a low creative vitality at work in Miss Porter's stories, a vitality capable of only intermittent flashes of real intensity and coherence, even though the pressure of discipline, of sheer will power and craft, may be enormous behind it. The discipline frequently gives to even her most uninspired productions a surface effect of elegance and stylistic finish, but it cannot compensate for the lack of true imaginative strength and originality of vision.

Yet however true this may seem to be, one is forced to admit that it is a fair judgment of only certain of Miss Porter's stories. About others one's judgment is necessarily very different. Actually, a good many of both her admirers and her detractors have made the mistake of looking in the wrong place for evidence of her most characteristic achievement. They have too often focused their attention on those of her stories that are popularly supposed to be her best, and have either been baffled by much that they found in them and said so as Mr. Wilson did, or they have adopted the less courageous course of praising the profundity of what they did not always understand. The virtue of *The Collected Stories* is that, in addition to providing insight into Miss Porter's limitations, it enables one to see that she does not stand or fall on the basis of her best known or merely fashionable work, but that there is an abundance of much more interesting material that is rarely given the attention it deserves. The book also makes clear what Mr. Wilson by the end of his review had come to suspect: that although Miss Porter is known chiefly for her stories of delicate and oftentime overly subtle psychological complication, in which everything is tightly packed in the manner of a symbolist poem, her best work has not been done in this form at all, but in the form of the loosely organized, leisurely developed, semifictional reminiscence, in which people and places are more meditated upon than evoked, the meaning is simple and plain, and there is no overt attempt to create an effect of art.

This is to say that Miss Porter's important achievement appears to be represented not by such a story as her famous "Flowering Judas" or any of her other stories about Mexico that have attracted and merited so much attention, but by her longer stories and short novels about childhood, wartime romance, and family life such as "Old Mortality," "Pale Horse, Pale Rider," and "The Old Order." In comparison with these works, "Flowering Judas," though beautifully formed, seems self-conscious and coldly, effortfully inward, full of straining for symbolic effect, while they have about them an air of relaxation and warmth, as well as a seemingly natural richness of texture, which gives them such a very different quality one might almost suppose them to have been written by another person altogether.

The difference makes two things clear about Miss Porter: first, that she is at her best in the short novel rather than in the short story, and second, that although she is usually considered to be an international writer who is equally at home in Mexico, Germany, and the various other places that have provided settings for her fiction, she is actually a regionalist writer who is truly at home in only one place, the American Southwest of her childhood. The Southwest, along with her ancestral Old South, is the source of her most potent imaginative material, and it is significant that she seems obliged to imagine it least of all her materials. It is simply part of her personal and cultural inheritance, as Faulkner's Mississippi was part of his, and she writes about it so well and with such apparent ease because she remembers it both as experience she lived through and in the form of stories about her family's history that she grew up learning by heart. Miss Porter tells some of these stories in her essay, "Portrait: Old South," and reveals not only the depth of her emotional involvement with Southern culture but how extensively and literally she has used her own and her family's experience in her fiction.

It seems to be a particular pity that she has not chosen to make even more extensive use of it than she has. But this has all along been her problem. More than anything else, she appears by talent and emotional inclination to be a Southern story-teller and memoirist in the Faulknerian or even the Wolfean tradition. And these materials dealing with her native region suggest the vitality she has occasionally allowed herself to bring to this tradition. Yet some perverse fastidiousness or shyness has always compelled her to turn away in the main body of her work from the Southern experience, to repress her feelings of intense personal connection with it, and to try to serve an ideal of complete artistic objectivity. In the process she has written many flawlessly executed stories about other people and places, stories that so often seem to possess all the admirable virtues except the warm responsiveness to life that distinguishes her Southern writings, and that final intensity of meaning to which Mr. Wilson referred. There exists, in short, a great distance between the work in which Miss Porter's art seems purest and the imaginative materials about which she evidently feels most passionately. Somewhere along that distance lies a possible point of reconciliation, where art and passion might have joined to produce a great writer and did not.

Eudora Welty

The Eye
of the
Story

IN "OLD MORTALITY" how stirring the horse race is! At the finish the crowd breaks into its long roar "like the falling walls of Jericho." This we hear, and it is almost like seeing, and we know Miss Lucy has won. But beyond a fleeting glimpse—the "mahogany streak" of Miss Lucy on the track—we never get much sight of the race with our eyes. What we see comes afterward. Then we have it up close: Miss Lucy bleeding at the nose. For Miranda has got to say "That's winning too." The race would never have got into the story except that Miranda's heart is being prepared to reject victory, to reject the glamor of the race and the cheering grandstand; to distrust from now on all evidence except what she, out of her own experience, can testify to. By the time we *see* Miss Lucy, she is a sight for Miranda's eyes alone: as much symbol as horse.

Most good stories are about the interior of our lives, but Katherine Anne Porter's stories take place there; they show surface only at her choosing. Her use of the physical world is enough to meet her needs and no more; she is not wasteful with anything. This artist, writing her stories with a power that stamps them to their last detail on the memory, does so to an extraordinary degree without sensory imagery.

I have the most common type of mind, the visual, and when first I began to read her stories it stood in the way of my trust in my own certainty of what was there that, for all my being bowled over by them, I couldn't see them happening. This was a very good thing for me. As her work has done in many other respects, it has shown me a thing or two about the eye of fiction, about fiction's visibility and invisibility, about its clarity, its radiance.

Heaven knows she can see. Katherine Anne Porter has seen all her life, sees today, most intimately, most specifically, and down to the bones, and she could date the bones. There is, above all, "Noon Wine" to establish it forever that when she wants a story to be visible, it is. "Noon Wine" is visible all the way through, full of scenes charged with dramatic energy; everything is brought forth into movement, dialogue; the title itself is Mr. Helton's tune on the harmonica. "Noon Wine" is the most beautifully objective work she has done. And nothing has been sacrificed to its being so (or she wouldn't have done it); to the contrary. I find Mr. Hatch the scariest character she ever made, and he's just set down there in Texas, like a chair. There he stands, part of the everyday furniture of living. He's opaque, and he's the devil. Walking in at Mr. Thompson's gate—the same gate by which his tracked-down victim walked in first—he is that much more horrifying, almost too solid to the eyes to be countenanced. (So much for the visual mind.)

Katherine Anne Porter has not in general chosen to cast her stories in scenes. Her sense of human encounter is profound, is fundamental to her work, I believe, but she has not often allowed it the dramatic character it takes in "Noon Wine." We may not see the significant moment happen within the story's present; we may not watch it occur between the two characters it joins. Instead, a silent blow falls while one character is alone—the most alone in his life, perhaps. (And this is the case in "Noon Wine" too.) Often the revelation that pierces a character's mind and heart and shows him his life or his death comes in a dream, in retrospect, in illness or in utter defeat, the moment of vanishing hope, the moment of dying. What Miss Porter makes us see are those subjective worlds of hallucination, obsession, fever, guilt. The presence of death hovering about Granny Weatherall she makes as real and brings as near as Granny's own familiar room that stands about her bed—realer, nearer, for we recognize not only death's presence but the character death has come in for Granny Weatherall.

The flash of revelation is revelation but is unshared. But how unsuspecting we are to imagine so for a moment—it *is* shared, and by ourselves, her readers, who must share it feeling the doubled anguish of knowing this fact, doubled still again when it is borne in upon us how close to life this is, to *our* lives.

It is to be remembered that the world of fiction is not of itself visible. A story may or may not be born in sensory images in a given writer's mind. Experience itself is stored in no telling how many ways in a writer's memory. (It was "the sound of the sea, and Beryl fanning her hair at the window" that years later and thousands of miles away brought Katherine Mansfield to writing "At the Bay.") But if the physical world *is* visible or audible in the story, it has to be made so. Its materialization is as much a created thing as are the story's characters and what they think or do or say.

Katherine Anne Porter shows us that we do not have to see a story happen to know what is taking place. For all we are to know, she is not looking at it happen herself when she writes it; for her eyes are always looking through the gauze of the passing scene, not distracted by the immediate and transistory; her vision is reflective.

Her imagery is as likely as not to belong to a time other than the story's present, and beyond that it always differs from it in nature; it is *memory* imagery, coming into the story from memory's remove. It is a distilled, a re-formed imagery, for it is part of a language made to speak directly of premonition, warning, surmise, anger, despair.

It was soon borne in upon me that Katherine Anne Porter's moral convictions have given her readers another way to see. Surely these convictions represent the fixed points about which her work has turned, and not only that but they govern her stories down to the smallest detail. Her work has formed a constellation, with its own North Star.

Is the writer who does not give us the pictures and bring us the sounds of a story as it unfolds shutting out part of life? In Katherine Anne Porter's stories the effect has surely been never to diminish life but always to intensify life in the part significant to her story. It is a darkening of the house as the curtain goes up on this stage of her own.

Her stories of Mexico, Germany, Texas all happen there: where love and hate, trust and betrayal happen. And so their author's gaze is turned not outward but inward, and has confronted the mysterious dark from her work's beginning.

Since her subject is what lies beneath the surface, her way—quite direct—is to penetrate, brush the stuff away. It is the writer like Chekhov whose way of working is indirect. He moved indeed toward the same heart and core but by building up some corresponding illusion of life. Writers of Chekhov's side of the family are themselves illusionists and have necessarily a certain fondness for, lenience toward, the whole shimmering fabric as such. Here we have the professional scientist, the good doctor, working with illusion and the born romantic artist—is she not? —working without it. Perhaps it is always the lyrical spirit that takes on instantaneous color, shape, pattern of motion in work, while the meditative spirit must fly as quickly as possible out of the shell.

All the stories she has written are moral stories about love and the hate that is love's twin, love's impostor and enemy and death. Rejection, betrayal, desertion, theft roam the pages of her stories as they roam the world. The madam kicking the girl in "Magic" and the rest of the brutality in the characters' treatment of one another; the thieving that in one form or another infects their relationships; the protests they make, from the weakness of false dreams or of lying down with a cold cloth over the eyes, on up to towering rages: all this is a way of showing to the inward eye: Look at what you are doing to human love.

We hear in how many more stories than the one the litany of the little boy at the end of "The Downward Path to Wisdom," his "comfortable, sleepy song": "I hate Papa, I hate Mama, I hate Grandma, I hate Uncle David, I hate Old Janet, I hate Marjory, I hate Papa, I hate Mama. . . ." It is like the long list of remembered losses in the story "Theft" made vocal, and we remember how that loser's decision to go on and let herself be robbed coincides with the rising "in her blood" of "a deep almost murderous anger."

"If one is afraid of looking into a face one hits the face," remarked W. B. Yeats, and I think we must conclude that to Katherine Anne Porter's characters this face is the challenging face of love itself. And I think it is the faces—the inner, secret faces—of her characters, in their self-delusion, their venom and pain, that their author herself is contemplating. More than either looking at the face or hitting it, she has made a story out of her anger.

If outrage is the emotion she has most strongly expressed, she is using outrage as her cool instrument. She uses it with precision to show what monstrosities of feeling come about not from the lack of the existence of love but from love's repudiation, betrayal. From which there is no safety anywhere. Granny Weatherall, eighty, wise, affectionate and good, and now after a full life dying in her bed with the priest beside her, "knew hell when she saw it."

The anger that speaks everywhere in the stories would trouble the heart for their author whom we love except that her anger is pure, the reason for it evident and clear, and the effect exhilarating. She has made it the tool of her work; what we do is rejoice in it. We are aware of the compassion that guides it, as well. Only compassion could have looked where she looks, could have seen and probed what she sees. Real compassion is perhaps always in the end unsparing; it must make itself a part of knowing. Self-pity does not exist here; these stories come out trenchant, bold, defying; they are tough as sanity, unrelinquished sanity, is tough.

Despair is here, as well described as if it were Mexico. It is a despair, however, that is robust and sane, open to negotiation by the light of day. Life seen as a savage ordeal has been investigated by a straightforward courage, unshaken nerve, a rescuing wit, and above all with the searching intelligence that is quite plainly not to be daunted. In the end the stories move us not to despair ourselves but to an emotion quite opposite because they are so seriously and clear-sightedly pointing out what they have been formed to show: that which is true under the skin, that which will remain a fact of the spirit.

Miranda, by the end of "Old Mortality" rebelling against the ties of the blood, resenting their very existence, planning to run away now from these and as soon as she can from her own escape into marriage, Miranda saying "I hate loving and being loved," is hating what destroys loving and what prevents being loved. She is, in her own particular and her own right, fighting back at the cheat she has discovered in all that's been handed down to her as gospel truth.

Seeing what is not there, putting trust in a false picture of life, has been one of the worst nightmares that assail her characters. "My dreams never renege on me, Mr. Richards. They're all I have to go by," says Rosaleen. (The Irish are no better than the Southerners in this respect.) Not only in the comic and touching Rosaleen, the lovely and sentient and tragic Miranda, but in many other characters throughout the stories we watch the romantic and the anti-romantic pulling each other to pieces. Is the romantic ever scotched? I believe not. Even if there rises a new refrain, even if the most ecstatic words ever spoken turn out to be "I hate you," the battle is not over for good. That battle is in itself a romance.

Nothing is so naturally subject to false interpretation as the romantic, and in furnishing that interpretation the Old South can beat all the rest. Yet some romantic things happen also to be true. Miss Porter's stories are not so much a stand against the romantic as such, as a repudiation of the false. What alone can instruct the heart is the experience of living, experience which can be vile; but what can never do it any good, what harms it more than vileness, are those tales, those legends of more than any South, those universal false dreams, the hopes sentimental and ubiquitous, which are not on any account to be gone by.

For there comes a confrontation. It is then that Miss Porter's characters, behaving so entirely like ourselves, make the fatally wrong choice. Enter betrayal. Again and again, enter betrayal. We meet the betrayal that lies in rejection, in saying No to others or No to the self, or that lies with still more cunning in saying Yes when this time it should have been No.

And though we are all but sure what will happen, we are possessed by suspense.

It appears to me irrelevant whether or not the story is conceived and put down in sensory images, whether or not it is dramatic in construction, so long as its hold is a death-grip. In my own belief, the suspense— so acute and so real—in Katherine Anne Porter's work never did depend for its life on disclosure of the happenings of the narrative (nothing is going to turn out very well) but in the writing of the story, which becomes one single long sustained moment for the reader. Its suspense is one with its meaning. It must arise, then, from the mind, heart, spirit by which it moves and breathes.

It is a current like a strand of quicksilver through the serenity of her prose. In fiction of any substance, serenity can only be an achievement of the work itself, for any sentence that is alive with meaning is speaking out of passion. Serenity never belonged to the *now* of writing; it belongs to the later *now* offered its readers. In Katherine Anne Porter's work the forces of passion and self-possession seem equal, holding each other in balance from one moment to the next. The suspense born of the writing abides there in its own character, using the story for its realm, a quiet and well-commanded suspense, but a genie.

There was an instinct I had, trustworthy or not, that the matter of visibility in her stories had something to do with time. Time permeates them. It is a grave and formidable force.

Ask what time it is in her stories and you are certain to get the answer: the hour is fateful. It is not necessary to see the hands of the clock in her work. It is a time of racing urgency, and it is already too late. And then recall how many of her characters are surviving today only for the sake of tomorrow, are living on tomorrow's coming; think how we see them clearest in reference to tomorrow. Granny Weatherall, up to the last—when God gives her no sign acceptable to her and jilts her Himself—is thinking: "There was always so much to be done, let me see: tomorrow." Laura in "Flowering Judas" is "waiting for tomorrow with a bitter anxiety as if tomorrow may not come." Ordinary, self-respecting, and—up to a certain August day—fairly well blessed Mr. Thompson, because he has been the one to kill the abominable Mr. Hatch, is self-tried, self-pleaded for, and self-condemned to no tomorrow; neither does he leave his sons much of a tomorrow, and certainly he leaves still less of one to poor, red-eyed Mrs. Thompson, who had "so wanted to believe that tomorrow, or at least the day after, life, such a battle at best, was going to be better." In "Old Mortality" time takes Miranda by the hand and leads her into promising herself "in her hopefulness, her ignorance": "At least I can know the truth about what happens to me." In "Pale Horse, Pale Rider" the older Miranda asks Adam, out of her suffering, "Why can we not save each other?" and the straight answer is that there is no time. The story ends with the unforgettable words "Now there would be time for everything" because tomorrow has turned into oblivion, the ultimate betrayer is death itself.

But time, one of the main actors in her stories—teacher, fake healer, conspirator in betrayal, ally of death—is also, within the complete control of Miss Porter, with his inimical powers made use of, one of the

movers of her writing, a friend to her work. It occurred to me that what
is *seeing* the story is the dispassionate eye of time. Her passionate mind
has asked itself, schooled itself, to use Time's eye. Perhaps Time is the
genie's name.

Laura is stuck in time, we are told in "Flowering Judas"—and told
in the timeless present tense of dreaming, a brilliant working upon our
very nerves to let us know precisely Laura's dilemma. There is in all
Katherine Anne Porter's work the strongest sense of unity in all the
parts; and if it is in any degree a sound guess that an important dramatic element in the story has another role, a working role, in the writing
of the story, might this not be one source of a unity so deeply felt? Such
a thing in the practice of an art is unsurprising. Who can separate a
story from the story's writing?

And there is too, in all the stories, a sense of long, learning life, the
life that is the story's own, beginning from a long way back, extending
somewhere into the future. As we read, the initial spark is not being
struck before our eyes; the fire we see has already purified its nature
and burns steadied by purpose, unwavering in meaning. It is no longer
impulse, it is a signal, a beacon.

To me, it is the image of the eye of time that remains the longest
in the mind at her story's end. There is a judgment to be passed. A moral
judgment has to be, in all reason, what she has been getting at. But in a
still further act of judiciousness, I feel, she lets Time pass that judgment.

Above all, I feel that what we are responding to in Katherine Anne
Porter's work is the intensity of its life, which is more powerful and
more profound than even its cry for justice.

They are excoriating stories. Does she have any hope for us at all?
Well, do we not feel its implication everywhere—a desperate hope for
the understanding that may come, if we use great effort, out of tomorrow, or if not then, maybe the day after? Clearly it has to become at
some point an act of faith. It is toward this that her stories all point:
here, it seems to me, is the North Star.

And how calm is the surface, the invisible surface of it all! In a style
as invisible as the rhythm of a voice, and as much her own as her own
voice, she tells her stories of horror and humiliation and in the doing
fills her readers with a rising joy. The exemplary prose that is without
waste or extravagance of self-indulgence or display, without any claim

for its triumph, is full of pride. And her reader shares in that pride, as well he might: it is pride in the language, pride in using the language to search out human meanings, pride in the making of a good piece of work. A personal spell is about the stories, the something of her own that we refer to most often, perhaps, when we mention its beauty, and I think this comes from the *making* of the stories.

Readers have long been in the habit of praising (or could it be at times reproaching?) Katherine Anne Porter by calling her a perfectionist. I do not agree that this is the highest praise, and I would think the word misleading, suggesting as it does in the author a personal vanity in technique and a rigidity, even a deadness, in her prose. To me she is something more serious than a perfectionist. I celebrate her for being a blessed achiever. First she is an artist, of course, and as an artist she is an achiever.

That she hasn't wasted precious time repeating herself in her stories is sign enough, if it were needed, that she was never interested in doing the thing she knew already that she was able to bring off, that she hasn't been showing off for the sake of high marks (from whom?), but has patiently done what was to her her born necessity, quietly and in her own time, and each time the way she saw fit.

We are left with a sense of statement. Virginia Woolf set down in her diary, on the day when she felt she had seen that great brave difficult novel *The Waves* past a certain point in the writing: "But I think it possible that I have got my statues against the sky." It is the achieving of this crucial, this monumental moment in the work itself that we feel has mattered to Katherine Anne Porter. The reader who looks for the flawless result can find it, but looking for that alone he misses the true excitement, exhilaration, of reading, of re-reading. It is the achieving— in a constant present tense—of the work that shines in the mind when we think of her name; and in that achieving lies, it seems to me, the radiance of the work and our recognition of it as unmistakably her own.

And unmistakable is its source. Katherine Anne Porter's deep sense of fairness and justice, her ardent conviction that we need to give and to receive in loving kindness all the human warmth we can make—here is where her stories come from. If they are made by the mind and address the mind, they draw their eloquence from a passionate heart. And for all their pain, they draw their wit, do they not, from a reserve of natural gayety? I have wondered before now if it isn't those who were born gay who can devote themselves most wholeheartedly in their work to seriousness, who have seriousness to burn. The gay are the rich in feeling, and don't need to save any of it back.

Unmistakable, too, is what this artist has made. Order and form no more spring out of order and form than they come riding in to us upon seashells through the spray. In fiction they have to be made out of their very antithesis, life. The art of making is the thing that has meaning, and I think beauty is likely to be something that has for a time lain under good, patient hands. Whether the finished work of art was easy or hard to make, whether it demanded a few hours or many years, concerns nobody but the maker, but the making itself has shaped that work for good and all. In Katherine Anne Porter's stories we feel their making as a bestowal of grace.

It is out of the response to her particular order and form that I believe I may have learned the simplest and surest reason for why I cannot see her stories in their every passing minute, and why it was never necessary or intended that a reader should. Katherine Anne Porter is writing stories of the spirit, and the time that fills those moments is eternity.

III

Cleanth Brooks

On 'The Grave'

IF I HAD to choose a particular short story of Katherine Anne Porter's to illustrate her genius as a writer—the choice is not an easy one—I think that I should choose "The Grave." I did choose it some months ago for a lecture in Athens, where the special nature of the audience, whose English ranged from excellent to moderately competent, provided a severe test. The ability of such an audience to understand and appreciate this story underlines some of Miss Porter's special virtues as a writer. Hers is an art of apparent simplicity, with nothing forced or mannered, and yet the simplicity is rich, not thin, full of subtleties and sensitive insights. Her work is compact and almost unbelievably economical.

The story has to do with a young brother and sister on a Texas farm in the year 1903. Their grandmother, who in some sense had dominated the family, had survived her husband for many years. He had died in the neighboring state of Louisiana, but she had removed his body to Texas. Later, when her Texas farm was sold and with it the small family cemetery, she had once more moved her husband's body, and those of the other members of the family, to a plot in the big new public cemetery. One day the two grandchildren, out rabbit hunting with their small rifles, find themselves in the old abandoned family cemetery.

> Miranda leaped into the pit that had held her grandfather's bones. Scratching round aimlessly and pleasurably as any young animal, she scooped up a lump of earth and weighed it in her palm. It had a pleasantly sweet, corrupt smell, being mixed with cedar needles and small leaves, and as the crumbs fell apart, she saw a silver dove no larger than a hazel nut, with spread wings and a neat fan-shaped tail.

Miranda's brother recognizes what the curious little ornament is—the screw-head for a coffin. Paul has found something too—a small gold ring—and the children soon make an exchange of their treasures, Miranda fitting the gold ring onto her thumb.

Paul soon becomes interested in hunting again, and looks about for rabbits, but the ring,

> shining with the serene purity of fine gold on [the little girl's] rather grubby thumb, turned her feelings against her overalls and sockless feet. . . . She wanted to go back to the farm house, take a good cold bath, dust herself with plenty of Maria's violet talcum powder . . . put on the thinnest, most becoming dress she ever owned, with a big sash, and sit in the wicker chair under the trees.

The little girl is thoroughly feminine, and though she has enjoyed knocking about with her brother, wearing her summer roughing outfit, the world of boys and sports and hunting and all that goes with it is beginning to pall.

Then something happens. Paul starts up a rabbit, kills it with one shot, and skins it expertly as Miranda watches admiringly. "Brother lifted the oddly bloated belly. 'Look,' he said, in a low amazed voice. 'It was going to have young ones.'" Seeing the baby rabbits in all their perfection, "their sleek wet down lying in minute even ripples like a baby's head just washed, their unbelievably small delicate ears folded close," Miranda is "excited but not frightened." Then she touches one of them, and exclaims, "Ah, there's blood running over them!" and begins to tremble. "She had wanted most deeply to see and to know. Having seen, she felt at once as if she had known all along."

The meaning of life and fertility and of her own body begin to take shape in the little girl's mind as she sees the tiny creatures just taken from their mother's womb. The little boy says to her "cautiously, as if he were talking about something forbidden: 'They were just about ready to be born.' 'I know,' said Miranda, 'like kittens. I know, like babies.' She was quietly and terribly agitated, standing again with her rifle under her arm, looking down at the bloody heap." Paul buries the rabbits and cautions his sister "with an eager friendliness, a confidential tone quite unusual in him, as if he were taking her into an important secret on equal terms: Listen now. . . . Don't tell a soul."

The story ends with one more paragraph, and because the ending is told with such beautiful economy and such care for the disposition of incidents and even the choice of words, one dares not paraphrase it.

> Miranda never told, she did not even wish to tell anybody. She thought about the whole worrisome affair with confused unhappiness for a few days. Then it sank quietly into her mind and was heaped over by accumulated thousands of impressions, for nearly twenty years. One day she was picking her path among the puddles and crushed refuse of a market street in a strange city of a strange country, when without warning, plain and clear in its true colors as if she looked through a frame upon a scene that had not stirred nor changed since the moment it happened, the episode of that far-off day leaped from its burial place before her mind's eye. She was so reasonlessly horrified she halted suddenly staring, the scene before her eyes dimmed by the vision back of them. An Indian vendor had held up before her a tray of dyed sugar sweets, in the shapes of all kinds of small creatures: birds, baby chicks, baby rabbits, lambs, baby pigs. They were in gay colors and smelled of vanilla, maybe. . . . It was a very hot day and the smell in the market, with its piles of raw flesh and wilting flowers, was like the mingled sweetness and corruption she had smelled that other day in the empty cemetery at home: the day she had remembered always until now vaguely as the time she and her brother had found treasure in the opened graves. Instantly upon this thought the dreadful vision faded, and she saw clearly her brother, whose childhood face she had forgotten, standing again in the blazing sunshine, again twelve years old, a pleased sober smile in his eyes, turning the silver dove over and over in his hands.

The story is so rich, it has so many meanings that bear close and subtle relations to each other, that a brief summary of what the story means will oversimplify it and fail to do justice to its depth, but I shall venture a few comments.

Obviously the story is about growing up and going through a kind of initiation into the mysteries of adult life. It is thus the story of the discovery of truth. Miranda learns about birth and her own destiny as a woman; she learns these things suddenly, unexpectedly, in circumstances that connect birth with death. Extending this comment a litttle further, one might say that the story is about the paradoxical nature of truth: truth wears a double face—it is not simple but complex. The secret of birth is revealed in the place of death and through a kind of bloody sacrifice. If there is beauty in the discovery, there is also awe and even terror.

These meanings are dramatized by their presentation through a particular action, which takes place in a particular setting. Something more than illustration of a statement is involved—something more than mere vividness or the presentation of a generalization in a form to catch the reader's eye. One notices, for example, how important is the fact of the grandmother's anxiety to keep the family together, even the bodies of the family dead. And the grandmother's solicitude is not mentioned merely to account for the physical fact of the abandoned cemetery in which Miranda makes her discovery about life and death. Throughout this story, birth and death are seen through a family perspective.

Miranda is, for example, thoroughly conscious of how her family is regarded in the community. We are told that her father had been criticized for letting his girls dress like boys and career "around astride barebacked horses." Miranda herself had encountered such criticism from old women whom she met on the road—women who smoked corncob pipes. They had always "treated her grandmother with most sincere respect," but they ask her "What yo Pappy thinkin about?" This matter of clothes, and the social sense, and the role of women in the society are brought into the story unobtrusively, but they powerfully influence its meaning. For if the story is about a rite of initiation, an initiation into the meaning of sex, the subject is not treated in a doctrinaire polemical way. In this story sex is considered in a much larger context, in a social and even a philosophical context.

How important the special context is will become apparent if we ask ourselves why the story ends as it does. Years later, in the hot tropical sunlight of a Mexican city, Miranda sees a tray of dyed sugar sweets, moulded in the form of baby pigs and baby rabbits. They smell of vanilla, but this smell mingles with the other odors of the marketplace, including that of raw flesh, and Miranda is suddenly reminded of the "sweetness and corruption" that she had smelled long before as she stood in the empty grave in the family burial plot. What is it that makes the experience not finally horrifying or nauseating? What steadies Miranda and redeems the experience for her? I quote again the concluding sentence:

> Instantly upon this thought the dreadful vision faded, and she saw clearly her brother, whose childhood face she had forgotten, standing again in the blazing sunshine, again twelve years old, a pleased sober smile in his eyes, turning the silver dove over and over in his hands.

I mentioned earlier the richness and subtlety of this beautiful story. It needs no further illustration; yet one can hardly forbear reminding oneself how skilfully, and apparently almost effortlessly, the author has rendered the physical and social context that gives point to Miranda's discovery of truth and has effected the modulation of her shifting attitudes—toward the grave, the buried ring, her hunting clothes, the dead rabbit—reconciling these various and conflicting attitudes and, in the closing sentences, bringing into precise focus the underlying theme.

Ray B. West, Jr.

Symbol and Theme in 'Flowering Judas'

KATHERINE ANNE PORTER, in writing of Katherine Mansfield's fictional method in 1937, said that she "states no belief, gives no motive, airs no theories, but simply presents to the reader a situation, a place and a character, and there it is; and the emotional content is present as implicitly as the germ in the grain of wheat." Of her own method she has written: "Now and again thousands of memories converge, harmonize, arrange themselves around a central idea in a coherent form, and I write a story."

Enlightening though these statements are concerning Miss Porter's concept of a short story, true as they appear to be of her own fiction and of the creative process, they still leave the reader with his own problem of "understanding" when he is confronted with the individual story. If we disregard the fact that the first statement was made about a fellow artist (it is still descriptive of Miss Porter's own stories), we must yet discover the "germ" which produced the emotion and which flowers into the final form of the story. Though we might say that the converging, the harmonizing, and the arranging constitute a logical, though partly subconscious, activity which serves to bring the objects of

memory into some kind of order, still it is the nature of this synthesis—
particularly in the predominantly social themes from *Flowering Judas*
(1930) to *The Leaning Tower* (1944)—which puzzles most readers.

That Miss Porter herself was aware of the nature of her sensibility
is clear from her comments concerning Miranda in a late story, who
had, she says, "a powerful social sense, which was like a fine set of
antennae radiating from every pore of her skin." Miss Porter's own social
sense is most obvious (perhaps too obvious) in her latest long story,
"The Leaning Tower," but it is not with the most obvious examples that
the reader wishes to concern himself; rather, with the seemingly obscure;
and since I have nowhere seen published or heard expounded an examination of "Flowering Judas," and since it is perhaps Miss Porter's best
known story (to my mind, her most successful single work of fiction),
let us examine that with the aim of understanding just what the author
means by social sensibility—how it operates within the story itself.

※ ※

The surface detail in "Flowering Judas" is relatively simple. An
American girl who has been educated in a Southern convent is in Mexico
teaching school and aiding a group of revolutionaries under Braggioni,
a sensual hulk of a man, formerly a starving poet, but who is now in a
position to indulge even his appetite for the most expensive of small
luxuries. The girl (Laura) teaches her children in the daytime and at
night runs errands for Braggioni, acting as go-between for him and the
foreign revolutionaries, delivering messages and narcotics to members
of the party who are in jail. At the point where the story opens, Braggioni has come to Laura's apartment to discover, if possible, whether it
would be worth the effort to attempt an assault upon her "notorious
virginity," which he, like the others, cannot understand. Laura is
physically attractive, and this is not the first time that she has been
courted by the Mexicans. Her first suitor was a young captain whom she
evaded by spurring her horse when he attempted to take her into his
arms, pretending that the horse had suddenly shied. The second was a
young organizer of the typographers' union who had serenaded her and
written her bad poetry which he tacked to her door. She had unwittingly
encouraged him by tossing a flower from her balcony as he sang to her

from the patio. A third person, Eugenio, is unknown to the reader until near the end of the story, when it turns out that he is expected to die of a self-imposed overdose of the narcotics which Laura had delivered to him at the prison. He is, however, the principal figure in a dream which ends the story, a dream in which Laura imagines him to have accused her of murdering him and in which he forces her to eat of the blossoms of the Judas tree which grows in the courtyard below her window.

All of the immediate action takes place in Laura's apartment after she has returned and found Braggioni awaiting her. He sings to her in a voice "passionately off key," talks about their curious relationship, about the revolution, and finally leaves after having Laura clean his pistol for use in a May-day disturbance between the revolutionaries and the Catholics of a near-by town. Braggioni returns to his wife, whom he has deserted for a month to pay attention to Laura, and who, despite the fact that she has been weeping over his absence, accepts his return gratefully and washes his feet. Laura goes to bed and has her dream of Eugenio.

It will be seen, even from this brief summary, that there are a great many details unexplained by the course of the action. There is the concern with revolutionary activities running throughout; there are the comments concerning Laura's religious training: the nun-like clothing, her slipping away into a small church to pray, the May-day demonstration. Obviously, a great many details have symbolic references, not least of which is the title itself.

If we turn to any standard encyclopedia, we discover that the Flowering Judas is a tree commonly known as the Judas tree or Red-bud. We learn further that a popular legend relates that it is from this tree that Judas Iscariot hanged himself. A second fact is that the exact title appears in a line from T. S. Eliot's poem "Gerontion":

> In the juvescence of the year
> Came Christ the tiger
>
> In depraved May, dogwood and chestnut, flowering judas,
> To be eaten, to be divided, to be drunk
> Among whispers.

This is scarcely a coincidence, since Eliot's passage so clearly suggests Laura's activity at the end of the story. Our first question is:

what use is made of this symbol? The dividing, the eating and drinking among whispers suggests the Christian sacrament, but it is a particular kind of sacrament. "Christ the tiger" refers to the pagan ritual in which the blood of a slain tiger is drunk in order to engender in the participants the courage of the tiger heart. In a sense this is only a more primitive form of sacrament, one which presupposes a *direct* rather than symbolic transfer of virtues from the animal to man. In the Christian ritual, the symbolic blood of Christ is drunk in remembrance of atonement; that is, symbolically to engender the virtues of Christ in the participant.

If the Judas tree, then, is a symbol for the betrayer of Christ (the legend says that its buds are red because it actually became the body of Judas, who is said to have had red hair), then the sacrament in which Laura participated—the eating of the buds of the Flowering Judas—is a sacrament, not of remembrance, but of betrayal.

This leads us to other uses of the Saviour-symbol in the story. The first is Braggioni, who, at one point, is even called a "world-saviour." It is said that "his skin has been punctured in honorable warfare"; "He has a great nobility, a love of humanity raised above mere personal affection"; finally, he is depicted, like Christ, undergoing the final purification, the foot-washing. But there are important reservations in the use of this symbol: (1) the note of irony with which Braggioni is depicted and which suggests the attitude the reader should take toward him; (2) each time the Christ-like epithet is used, it is accompanied by other, non-Christian characteristics: "His skin has been *punctured* in honorable warfare, but *he is a skilled revolutionary*"; he is a *professional* lover of humanity, a *hungry* world-saviour. It is the use of the religious symbols alongside the secular which makes Braggioni the complex and interesting character that he is.

The second use of the Christ-symbol is present in the character of Eugenio, who is seen first as one of the revolutionary workers languishing in jail, but who figures most prominently as the person in Laura's dream. His name contains the clue to his symbolic meaning—well-born. As Christ is the Son of God, he is well-born. He is, likewise, a symbol of all mankind—Man. We say he is the "Son of Man." In this respect, Eugenio is also Christ-like, for he is well-born without the reservations noted in the character of Braggioni—in the highest sense. And as Judas was the direct cause of Christ's crucifixion, so Laura becomes the murderer of Eugenio (of Man) by carrying narcotics to his prison cell, the narcotics through which he (Christ-like) surrendered himself up to death.

We can say, then, that the use of religious symbolism by Miss Porter might suggest that her story be taken as a kind of religious allegory. But there are other, complicating symbols. There is, for instance, Laura's fear of machines such as the *automobile;* there is her dislike for things made on *machines;* and finally there is the statement that *the machine is sacred* to the workers. In the last instance, we may see how the word "machine" is coupled with the religious word "sacred," thus bringing the two kinds of symbols into juxtaposition, just as the same thing is implied in the descriptions we have had of Braggioni. For instance, "His skin has been punctured in honorable warfare" suggests the act of crucifixion, but "puncture" is not a word which we would ordinarily use in describing either the nailing of Christ to the cross or the piercing of his flesh by the spear of the Roman soldier. The most common use of "puncture" now is its reference to automobile tires (of which Laura is afraid). Likewise, the word "professional" used to modify "a lover of humanity" brings the modern idea of business efficiency into conjunction with the image of Christ, as though one were to say, explicitly: "Braggioni is an impersonal, cold-blooded Christ."

A third type of symbols is composed of love-symbols (erotic, secular, and divine). The story shows Laura unable to participate in love upon any of the levels suggested: (1) as a divine lover in the Christian sense, for it is clear that she is incapable of divine passion when she occasionally sneaks into a small church to pray; (2) as a professional lover in the sense that Braggioni is one, for she cannot participate in the revolutionary fervor of the workers, which might be stated as an activity expressive of secular love for their fellow men; she cannot even feel the proper emotion for the children who scribble on their blackboards, "We lov ar ticher"; (3) as an erotic lover, for she responds to none of her three suitors, though she thoughtlessly throws one of them a rose (the symbol of erotic love), an act of profanation, since the boy wears it in his hat until it withers and dies.

Having located these symbols, it is now our problem to examine the use that is made of them. More specifically, we can say that the religious symbols represent the Christian ideology, while the secular are symbols most readily identified with the attitudes of Marxism. As philosophy,

7,12, 30, 34, 136

they would seem to represent the two most extreme positions possible; yet both claim as their aim the betterment of mankind. If we consider them as areas within which man may act, we might represent them as two circles.

The third field (love) is not so much an area within which man performs as it is an attitude toward his actions. The fact that we refer to "divine love" and "secular love" will illustrate this distinction. On the other hand, if we speak of a "code of love," then love comes to resemble a kind of philosophy and is similar to Christianity and Marxism. As there is evidence in the relationship of Laura to the young captain and to her suitor from the typographers' union that Miss Porter had this relationship in mind as well as the other, we might represent our third symbolic field as a circle overlapping the other two, but also existing as a separate area.

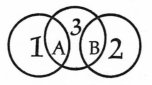

At this point, we must remember the relationship between "Flowering Judas" and Eliot's "Gerontion." The poem is concerned with a wasteland image; that is, with a view of life as a wasteland, sterile and barren as old-age, because of the absence of any fructifying element. Eliot's old man in the poem says:

> I have lost my passion: why should I need to keep it
> Since what is kept must be adulterated?
> I have lost my sight, smell, hearing, taste, and touch:
> How should I use them for your closer contact?

In "Flowering Judas" Laura has lost the use of her senses: when the children scribble their message of love, she can feel nothing for them.

They are only "wise, innocent, clay-colored faces," just as the revolutionists have become "clay masks with the power of human speech." She is like the prisoners, shut off from human contact, who, when they complain to her, " 'Dear little Laura, time doesn't pass in this infernal hole, and I won't know when it is time to sleep unless I have a reminder,' she brings them their favorite narcotics, and says in a tone that does not wound them with pity, 'Tonight will be really night for you.' " Seeing the colored flowers the children have painted, she remembers the young captain who has made love to her and thinks, "I must send him a box of colored crayons." She confuses the children with the prisoners, "the poor prisoners who come every day bringing flowers to their jailor." "It is monstrous," she thinks with sudden insight, "to confuse love with revolution, night with day, life with death." Laura, like the figure in Eliot's poem, has lost her passion, she has lost her sight, smell, hearing, taste, and touch. She cannot use them for closer contact.

Now, if we return to our circles, perhaps this can be made clear. The philosophical systems represented by each circle (1. religion. 2. revolution. 3. love) represent a means of dealing with the wasteland. That is, faith in any one of the systems will provide a kind of signpost, which is the first step in transforming the wilderness of modern social living. By observing the signposts, we at least know where we are going or what we are doing there. Yet—it is still the wasteland. However, when we superimpose circle 3 upon either of the other two, the sterility disappears. In other words, either orthodox religion or socialism is a wasteland until transformed by the fructifying power of love; obversely, love is impossible without the object provided by either. In terms of our diagram, all is sterility outside the circles or at any point within the circles where 3 does not overlap either 1 or 2—that is, within the areas A or B.

Laura may be said to be outside any of the circles. Because of her early training, she is pulled away from a belief in the revolutionary cause of Braggioni. Because of her desire to accept the principles of revolution, she is unable to accept the principles of her religious education. Without either Christianity or Marxism, it is impossible for her to respond to her suitors or to the children. She cannot even feel pity for the prisoners; she can only supply them with narcotics, which likens their condition to hers, for her life seems to be a sense-less kind of existence similar to the drugged sleep of the prisoners.

Braggioni's condition is likened to Laura's ("We are more alike than you realize in some things," he tells her), but there are two important differences: (1) he has the revolutionary ideal as a guide; (2) he is capable of redemption, as the final, footwashing scene with his wife ("whose sense of reality is beyond criticism") shows. We can say, then, that Braggioni is not, as Laura is, outside the circles. He is within one of them, but it is not until he is touched with pity that he is brought wholly within the area of redemption (either A or B). Laura is not redeemed, even though she desires it, as the eating of the buds of the Judas tree suggests. Her sacrament is a devouring gesture and Eugenio calls her a cannibal, because she is devouring him (Man). She is, like Judas, the betrayer; and her betrayal, like his, consisted in an inability to believe. Without faith she is incapable of passion, thence of love, finally of life itself. Reduced to the inadequacy of statement, we might say that the theme, lacking all of the story's subtle comment, might be rendered as: Man cannot live divided by materialistic and spiritual values, nor can he live in the modern world by either without faith and love.

As the Nazi landlady in "The Leaning Tower" is made to say when overcharging the American student who wishes to cancel his lease: "Indecision is a very expensive luxury."

Laura's world, then, is as barren and sterile as the world of Eliot's "Gerontion"; it is a living death. Said another way, the living world exists only in our sensory perception of it, and any deadening of the senses (through a denial of traditional human values) constitutes a relinquishing of moral responsibility—the betrayal of mankind into the hands of the Braggionis or, as in "The Leaning Tower," into the hands of the Nazis.

This is, I suspect, what one reviewer discovered as early as 1938, when, in a review of the volume *Flowering Judas*, he wrote: "Miss Porter, I feel, is one of the most 'socially conscious' of our writers." But one might also fear that this reviewer was thinking in terms of the predominant Marxist movements of the thirties, into none of which Miss

Porter could, obviously, be made to fit. "I do not mean," he continued, "simply that she is conscious of the physical suffering of her impoverished people; I mean rather that she understands the impoverishment of mind and spirit which accompanies the physical fact, and she sees too that some native goodness in these minds and spirits still lives."

But if "some native goodness" were all Miss Porter's characters had to recommend themselves to us as resolutions of our social dilemma, then every author who does not allegorize good and evil is still "socially conscious," and the reviewer's remarks represent a somewhat dubious compliment. The fact is, however, that he was right perceptually. Behind Miss Porter's elaborate structure of symbol and myth lies the psychological motivation which produces the theme. The germ which lies implicit in the grain of wheat is the central idea about which her memories cluster. An idea does not constitute her "meaning" in the usual sense of the word, but it represents a concept which makes the surface detail available to meaning. To put it another way, the very rightness of the *ideological* fact (the myth or symbol) charges the *particular* fact (the object as it exists in nature) with a meaning that is presented as an experiential whole, but which is available in all its complex relationships only when we have become aware of the entire field of reference.

Sarah Youngblood

Structure and Imagery in 'Pale Horse, Pale Rider'

KATHERINE ANNE PORTER has long been regarded as one of the finest writers of contemporary fiction, and the justice of this respect is felt by most readers familiar with her work. A consideration of structure and imagery in one of her major works may, by explicating its richnesses, serve to show more specifically the reasons for Miss Porter's place in contemporary fiction. This is one of the functions which explicative criticism may perform, not only the unfolding of a work for our widest contemplation but also the establishing or affirming of canons of respect. An examination of *Pale Horse, Pale Rider* illuminates the dimensions of both her work and her reputation.

Structurally, this short novel can be viewed as three units or sections of action, each section presenting action of an increasingly psychological kind, in a setting generally different from the others. The first section introduces Miranda and extends to her collapse from illness; the second describes her night of delirium in the room of the boarding-house; the third presents her hospital experience. It will be noted that the first section opens with Miranda in the isolation of a dream, but this isolation is immediately intruded upon when she wakes to the reality of her room and the world she must enter for survival. Thereafter, the first section can be said to present Miranda-in-the-world, as, in the narrowing psychological focus of the story, the succeeding sections present Miranda-and-Adam, and Miranda alone. The last section would seem to be a reverse reflection of the first, since it concludes with Miranda's preparation to move back into the world.

In terms of spatial movement, the opening section is thus the largest and most inclusive. This spatial inclusiveness is appropriate to the initiation of themes in the novel, and all of the themes stated here in image or action figure in the later sections as motivation and explanation. The themes—political, social, psychological, and moral in their implications—require a certain largeness of stage for postulation, and this is available in the shifting scenes of the opening section: the room, the newspaper office, the theater, the dance-hall, the streets of the city. Also available is a necessarily large cast of characters, by which we follow Miranda's reaction to her world: the newspaper staff, the bond salesmen, the Junior League girls, the lovers in the dance hall, the soldiers in the hospital, the has-been vaudeville actor. And over all this stage and its actors, and conditioning it all, is the state of war, which provides a prime mover for all of the issues, since war is examined not only in its political and social implications, but particularly in its psychological or moral implications: ". . . the worst of war is the fear and suspicion. . . . It's the skulking about and the lying. It's what war does to the mind and the heart. . . ." The presence of war is a conditioning factor in the action and themes of the novel. War is the "gong of warning" which wakes Miranda from sleep and beats the rhythm of the day for her. It focuses in the day-to-day world of Miranda the theme of death which haunts her dream, since war has unreined the "pale horse" of destruction. War posits, in the relationship of Adam and Miranda, the conflict of the individual's obligations to society, and to himself, since in a state of war, in the non-life that war creates (Miranda speaks of peacetime or pre-war time as "in life," making the distinction in time a distinction in being), Adam and Miranda are bound by obligations to society which prevent their unity, even though, ironically, the only dedications which could have value for them now in a war-world would be those based upon love for each other. They are compelled to fulfill obligations created by a society operating upon hatred, not love.

A corollary of this theme is the confusion of appearance and reality which so disturbs Miranda's equilibruim in the world. The war creates fear and suspicion, distrust and hypocrisy, which transforms daily reality into a disturbing set of distorting mirrors. "Towney" may, in the cloakroom, privately despair of the pressures placed upon her by flag-waving tyrants acting as patriots, but in the office later she can summon her "most complacent patriotic voice" to praise the idea of Hut Service. Miranda's wondering reaction to this is repeated in her later, rather terrified, reaction to the theater-crowd, which enthusiastically responds, in a kind of conditioned reflex, to the patriotic jargon of the bond salesman: "There must be a great many of them here who think as I do, and we dare not say a word to each other of our desperation, we are speechless animals letting ourselves be destroyed, and why? Does anybody here believe the things we say to each other?" These contradictions in apparent reality, "the disturbing oppositions in her day-to-day existence," find pervasive expression in the general pattern of hypocrisy which the cautious citizen in war must assume. It is noteworthy, therefore, that everything in Miranda's experience of the daily world that rightly should have been an act of love has degenerated to an act of duty done out of fear: the buying of bonds, the comforting of soldiers. This is a part of what she calls the "disturbing oppositions" in her existence, and one illustration of the appearance/reality theme. (Note, for example, the specific irony of the title of the bonds she is compelled to buy.) The theme is operative at the minor levels of the story, as in the reference to Chuck's father, who "beamed upon him with the bleared eye of paternal affection while he took his last nickel," as well as within the larger plot-development of the novel wherein the golden health of Adam and the sickliness of Miranda conceal the ultimate conclusion of Adam's death and Miranda's survival.

War conditions the action in other ways. It creates the necessity for a "code" or "system" among the younger generation, much like the code of Hemingway's characters, which makes possible for them a "proper view" of chaos, a proper existentialist formula of casualness and flippancy for maintaining cynical control: because the situation is absurd, behave as if it were amusing. When the bond-salesmen accuse Miranda of ignoring the war, she meets the absurdity of the accusation with her formal system:

> "Oh, the war," Miranda had echoed on a rising note and she almost smiled at him. It was habitual, automatic, to give that solemn, mystically uplifted grin when you spoke the words or heard them spoken. "*C'est la guerre*," whether you could pronounce it or not, was even better, and always, always, you shrugged.

Miranda's conversations with Adam in this section of the novel make use of "the kind of patter going the rounds" as a way of suppressing the sense of the chaotic which informs both characters. "Their smiles approved of each other, they felt they had got the right tone, they were taking the war properly." Above all, thought Miranda, "no tooth-gnashing, no hair-tearing, it's noisy and unbecoming and it doesn't get you anywhere." This is, finally, only another of the masks of reality war has forced them to assume. The system of attitudes is so rigidly adhered to that only delirium can finally compel Miranda to admit in speech to Adam the reality of her terror and her love.

The result of all these interacting implications of war is to assure the isolation of each individual. Since Miranda is the point-of-view character whose reactions are the strict concern of the reader, her isolation and her lucid awareness of it require some examination. Enough has been said of the effect of war in her world to indicate her response to that external condition; the war-theme is, besides, the most obvious nucleus of implication in the story, and other elements demand more explication.

At the psychological level *Pale Horse, Pale Rider* is the dramatization of Miranda's death-wish, a dramatization presented in the ironical form of a reversal, and taking the metaphorical form of a journey. The title of the novel indicates the primacy of the death-theme (of which the war is only, for Miranda, a kind of specific vehicle; one feels that in a situation devoid of war conditions, another vehicle would have been present for her). The title also presents the major symbol of the story, which appears in Miranda's first dream in a kind of double vision. Miranda is pursued by the pale rider, "that lank greenish stranger," but she is also herself the pale rider on Graylie, the pale horse, since she carries the seeds of death within her. This dream foreshadows the final outcome of the story, since "the stranger rode on." Almost all of the images of the dream suggest images in the later dreams: the journey is reiterated in varying forms later (the ship on the river; the journey toward and back from the seashore paradise). The "daylight" images are here, as later, associated with vision, clarity, the ability to distinguish reality from illusion: "Early morning is best for me because trees are trees in one stroke . . . there are no false shapes or surmises. . . ." The memory-laden house is clearly a symbol of the past, and of stranglingly close human relationships which Miranda desires to escape from, and she both seeks death as an escape, and yet flees from it; it is "this journey I do not mean to take," and her attitude toward death is here ambivalent. She desires isolation, and freedom from the past ("I'll take Graylie because he is not afraid of bridges"), but she also cries to the stranger, "I'm not going with you this time—ride on!" As the dream fades, and before Miranda is completely conscious, she draws herself "out of the pit of sleep, waited in a daze for life to begin again." This image of sleep as a pit, and synonymous with death, anticipates the later dream in which death itself is the pit. This image also, by suggesting the bottomless pit described in Revelation, forms part of the pattern of religious imagery in the story.

The pale rider allusion of the title is the most obvious, but others can be remarked in this first section of the novel. Adam's name is symbolic since he is "committed without any knowledge or act of his own to death," and since he is a vessel of innocence, golden "purity," as Miranda calls it: "Pure, she thought, all the way through, flawless, complete, as the sacrificial lamb must be." In this remark, she views him simultaneously as Adam, Unfallen Man, and Isaac, the victim, offered to propitiate the wrath of God. As the latter he shares with all the young soldiers the role of sacrificial victim. To increase the symbolic value of his character, his health is emphasized (in a symbolic pun he is compared to a "fine healthy apple"), and his golden, glowing appearance is repeatedly described, suggesting not only his health and handsomeness but also a certain "man of the Golden Age" quality which his physical perfection connotes and Miranda's idealism confirms. Adam himself, far from being a romantic, is a very stable and normal person, which Miranda senses, and she clings to a strength in him which she lacks. That she realizes the idealism of her view of him is made clear in the irony of the line immediately following her thought of him as a sacrificial lamb: "The sacrificial lamb strode along casually, accommodating his long pace to hers, keeping her on the inside of the walk in the good American style...."

Related to this religious imagery associated with Adam is Miranda's remark about the epidemic of influenza: "It seems to be a plague... something out of the Middle Ages," since this calls into focus two sets of religious associations: the plague as a sign of God's wrath, and the danse macabre (in which the "lank stranger" symbol of death is also operative). The influenza epidemic is also, of course, the physical counterpart of the illness of society at war.

The second section of the novel opens, as does the first, with Miranda in sleep, waking to discover that a day has passed. In her illness her memory "turned and roved after another place she had known first and loved best," a place clearly Southern, which merges into a dream in which death is represented as a tropical jungle of vivid colors, sulphur-colored light, and the "hoarse bellow of voices." As in the first dream, Miranda commits herself to the journey but does not complete it: she boards the ship, but does not arrive at the jungle, the "secret place of death," before she wakes. Nevertheless, in her talk with Adam afterwards, she speaks as if she were already dead: "Let's tell each other what we meant to do," and her review of her life and attitudes is carefully kept in the past tense, except for her impulsive outburst about the sensuous delights of being alive: her love of weather, colors, sounds. In this conversation the religious theme again occurs, here introduced in an explicit discussion of religion between the characters. Miranda is revealed to be a Catholic, and her preoccupation with religion, anticipated by her earlier allusions, is emphasized here and will recur in later crises. The Negro spiritual which she and Adam try to sing (there are "about forty verses" and they can't remember the third line) gives another element of meaning to the title of the novel since it combines the religious and the love themes.

The scene is followed by another dream, in which Adam figures, and which repeats many of the images of the second dream: the jungle is here an "angry dangerous wood," the voices of the second dream recur, their sound compared to arrows which pierce Adam and Miranda. This curious simile, although its phallic symbolism is apparent, seems also to be a subconscious extension of Miranda's earlier remark, "I even know a prayer beginning O Apollo," since Apollo is associated with pestilence and plagues, which in Greek drama are often referred to as the darts or arrows of an angry Apollo. This is a pagan analogy of the medieval Christian view of plagues; and within the dream, the arrows which finally kill Adam but not Miranda symbolize the disease and its actual final results. In Miranda's mind the arrows are also associated with the everydayness of valentines and arrows, a symbolism she is later able to explain rationally. The attitude of Miranda reflected in the dream is also significantly changed from that of her first dream. The ambivalence of her desire for death is absent. "Like a child cheated in a game," she demands her right to die, and "selfishly" attempts to die and save Adam's life. He dies only because of her intervened presence, having before undergone "a perpetual death and resurrection," and this also foreshadows the actual outcome of the plot.

᛭ ᛭

The time of the third section extends over a month; yet Miranda's experience in the hospital telescopes this time into a series of dreams. Her illness is enough advanced that even in the passages of time in which she is relatively conscious, her surroundings impinge upon her mind in the dimensions of dream-experience. For example, the incident of the two internes, hidden by a screen, removing a dead body from the bed next to hers, is to Miranda a "dance of tall deliberate shadows" (an image suggesting again the danse macabre theme, like churchwall paintings) whose significance she does not fully comprehend—the shroud of the corpse she describes as "a large stiff bow like merry rabbit ears dangled at the crown of his head." Likewise the incident of the filthy old man being dragged down the hall between "two executioners" may be a dream but is more likely a half-conscious, half-dream interpretation of an actual sight in the hall where Miranda's bed is placed. The sight is distorted in her own half-conscious mind by her own sense of guilt, which had been the dominating emotion of her last dream, and by her idea of the plague as a punishment of the guilty, in which the persons society regards as saviours (the doctors) become the executioners. Here again, the earlier allusion to Apollo is relevant, in his dual function as saviour (god of healing) and destroyer (sender of plagues).

To Miranda the whiteness of her hospital environment is its most impressive feature. Beds, shadows, persons, walls, lights are white; even the fog which rises around everything, as her mind loses its rational grasp of experience, is "pallid white." This is to be contrasted with the lush colors of the earlier dream, particularly since the whiteness seems to her to represent not death but oblivion, the road to death, "the landscape of disaster." In the first section of the novel, Miranda had at one point "held her hands together palms up, gazing at them and trying to understand oblivion," which she there identified with her future loneliness without Adam. Later in this section she speaks of oblivion as a "whirlpool of gray water." The images of whiteness seem to be a general symbol of negation; the passage recalls Melville's chapter on the whiteness of the whale; here there is the same element of terror in response to the whiteness.

Miranda's dream of Dr. Hildesheim, who becomes, like the Hun torturer in her nightmare, a variant of the pale rider figure and almost a parody of it, indicates how deeply her mind has absorbed the jargon of the current propoganda which she hates. The dream, by verging on the ridiculous (he carries "a huge stone pot marked Poison in Gothic letters"), is like a poetic-justice punishment vaguely threatened by the bond salesmen to those who don't buy bonds. Besides being a revealing comment on the insidious corruption wrought by propaganda, the brief nightmare contains two images which, in her later dream of paradise, reappear as transfigured symbols: the "pasture of her father's farm" and "a well once dry" with the "violated water" of the poison. The dream also reveals her present fear of death, a fear both conscious and subconscious:

> The road to death is a long march beset with all evils, and the heart fails little by little at each new terror, the bones rebel at each step, the mind sets up its own bitter resistance and to what end? The barriers sink one by one, and no covering of the eyes shuts out the landscape of disaster. . . .

Her dreams in this period have the duality of her earlier daily experience: "Her mind, split in two, acknowledged and denied what she saw in the one instant," and this anticipates the final conflict between her rational will to die and her irrational instinct to live. It is ironic that the "angry point of light" symbolizing her will to live is the ultimate source of the radiance which spreads and curves into the rainbow of her paradise. This has a metaphorical logic also in that she has earlier desired death as escape but feared it as a dark jungle of evil things and of guilt. Here in her dream of paradise her mind postulates what death ideally should be (all that actual life is not), and its features are the opposite of those associated with death in the earlier nightmares. The jungle, the angry wood, becomes the meadow, the darkness becomes radiance, the incessant voices become silence and "no sound," the serpents and exotic evil animals become human beings transfigured in beauty who "cast no shadows"—that is, who no longer have any duality or ambivalence of being, but are "pure identities." In this paradise there is solitude for everyone (what Miranda desired in her dream-escape from her childhood home) but not loneliness or isolation: "each figure was alone but not solitary." The distinctive features of the paradise are silence, radiance, joy. In its features this paradise suggests the traditional mystical experience, and Miranda's later revulsion to the colorless sunlight and pain of the actual world suggests the disillusioned "stage of experience" which a mystic undergoes after his return to the world of a tangible reality. This suggestion of the mystical experience is strengthened by the variety of religious imagery elsewhere in the story, and by the presence within the paradise of the rainbow-symbol. The paradise is Miranda's personal interpretation of the apocalyptical revelation alluded to in the title.

She is drawn back from this paradise by the awareness that "something, somebody was missing . . . she had left something valuable in another country," and her remark that "there are no trees here" seems to be the form her memory of Adam, by association, takes (as in her earlier comparison of him to "a healthy apple"). The dead are absent, and she has consistently viewed Adam as committed to death, so that she is forced back through the wasteland of her march, "the strange stony place of bitter cold," to find him. There is also here the implication that all of the real world is the world of the "dead." The imagery of the world she returns to is dominantly that of violent noise, and gray colorless light, "where the sound of rejoicing was a clamor of pain" and "it is always twilight or just before morning, a promise of day that is never kept." To Miranda now "the body is a curious monster, no place to live in," as the flesh is alien to the returned mystic, and she is like "an alien who does not like the country in which he finds himself, does not understand the language." But the conspiracy must not be betrayed, the illusion that life is preferable must be maintained out of courtesy to the living. The irony of Miranda's situation is overwhelming: the "humane conviction and custom of society" insist that life is best, and will force her to pay twice for the gift of death, making her endure again at some future date the painful journey to the blue sea and tranquil meadow of her paradise. It is a part of this irony that Adam, for whom she returned, is already dead. The casual understatement with which she and the reader are informed of his death is consistent with her situation: since she has lost paradise, the other loss is inevitable and even unsurprising. It doesn't touch her because her heart is "hardened, indifferent. . . ."

She makes symbolic preparation for re-entrance into the world of "dead and withered beings that believed themselves alive," by requesting a number of significant things. They are her symbolic armor and mask, and they include cosmetics (". . . no one need pity this corpse if we look properly to the art of the thing" applies not only to her physical mask of cosmetics but to her mask of future behavior); a pair of gloves, which she calls *gauntlets*; and a walking stick. The last object is richly connotative. Its silvery wood and silver knob suggest Miranda's emphasis upon "the art of the thing," the appearance she must maintain. Its purpose is to help her, a kind of cripple, through her journey back again to death. When Towney warns against its expensiveness and comments that walking is hardly worth it, Miranda's "You're right" is an assured and cynical answer which arises out of her awareness of the symbolic act implied. Her mental image of herself as Lazarus come forth with "top hat and stick" is a dual vision of herself as he has been and as she will be in the world where appearances must be maintained; imagistically, we have come full circle again to the "disturbing oppositions" of that world of appearances. She is, with her walking stick, herself the pale rider, unhorsed and alone now, crippled by her first journey and preparing for her next: "Now there would be time for everything."

Brother Joseph Wiesenfarth, F. S. C.

Reflections in 'The Cracked Looking-Glass'

HENRY JAMES'S *nouvelle* "The Beast in the Jungle" is the story of an opportunity missed; it is the story of the fate of John Marcher, who spends his life waiting for something to happen to him and who, when it does happen, fails to notice it. James's "In the Cage" presents the little drama of a very imaginative and vibrant young woman's easing the ache of the actual in a Cinderella world, but ultimately finding that world so dangerous that she scurries back to reality before the coach becomes a pumpkin. In Katherine Anne Porter's "The Cracked Looking-Glass," which parallels elements of both of James's tales, Rosaleen O'Toole passes from the world of the man's waiting to that of the girl's scurrying as she rescues herself from the dream and accepts reality. It is the story of a dreamer whose every day is spent in anticipation of "something great . . . going to happen," but who must finally admit that each of her days has been a "straying from one terrible disappointment to another." It projects the complex action of a woman's making her life meaningful almost at the moment she realizes how much of it has been otherwise, and in so doing "The Cracked

Looking-Glass" dramatizes the accommodation of her illusions to reality.[1]

Rosaleen and Dennis O'Toole are two very different persons. Dennis, about seventy-five, is no longer robust: "He clacked his teeth together and felt how they didn't fit anymore, and his feet and hands seemed tied on him with strings." To him the past is something upon which the present is built, and as the foundation of the present, it is static and dead. "His past lay like a great lump within him; there it was, he knew it all at once . . ." Life for Dennis is a peaceful existence in the present: the quiet life of a soft chair, a warm kitchen fire, a comfortable pipe, and a young and handsome wife. Rosaleen carries her forty-five years very well; after twenty-five years of marriage she "didn't look to be a year older." To Rosaleen the past is exciting and alive; it holds for her more of what life seems to be meant for than does the present. It is the storehouse of stories, dreams, and sundry unrealities. The past contrasts violently with the present, which is a round of farm chores, unpleasant neighbors, and caring for Dennis: "She said to the cow: 'It's no life, no life at all. A man of his years is no comfort to a woman'. . ." The contrast of their lives in these and other ways creates a problem for Rosaleen: "It wasn't being a wife at all to wrap a man in flannels like a baby and put hot water bottles on him." At the heart of Rosaleen's discontent lies the problem of the meaning of her marriage to Dennis. "The Cracked Looking-Glass" is a dramatization of her groping toward a realization of that meaning.

The answer to the question of the meaning of Rosaleen's marriage may be thought of as evolving in three movements, which—while ultimately interdependent—can be quite accurately described as involving faith in the past, hope in the future, and love in the present.

The object of faith in the past is the dream—a form of illusion readily available to Rosaleen, who unconsciously uses it to mollify the impact of reality upon herself. At one time, "The world is a wilderness"; at another, "Life is a dream." Rosaleen's mechanism for dealing with

---

[1] Critics have given very little attention to "The Cracked Looking-Glass"; in fact no extensive commentary exists. For brief notes see Harry John Mooney, *The Fiction and Criticism of Katherine Anne Porter* (Pittsburgh, 1957), pp. 44–46; Robert Penn Warren, "Katherine Anne Porter (Irony with a Center)," *Kenyon Review*, IV (Winter 1942), 41ff.; Charles A. Allen, "Katherine Anne Porter: Psychology as Art," *Southwest Review*, XLI (Summer 1956), 224ff.

reality as wilderness is to metamorphose it into "reality" as dream. As "The Cracked Looking-Glass" begins, Rosaleen is doing precisely this for Mr. Pendleton, to whom she is relating the story of the Billy-cat:

> "It was the strangest thing happened to the Billy-cat, Mr. Pendleton. He sometimes didn't come in for his supper till after dark, he was so taken up with the hunting, and then one night he didn't come at all, nor the next day neither, nor the next, and me with him on my mind so I didn't get a wink of sleep. Then at midnight on the third night I did go to sleep, and the Billy-cat came into my room and lep upon my pillow and said: 'Up beyond the north field there's a maple tree with a great scar where the branch was taken away by the storm, and near to it is a flat stone, and there you'll find me. I was caught in a trap,' he says; 'wasn't set for me,' he says, 'but it got me all the same. And now be easy in your mind about me,' he says, 'for it's all over.' Then he went away, giving me a look over his shoulder like a human creature, and I woke up Dennis and told him. Surely as we live, Mr. Pendleton, it was all true. So Dennis went beyond the north field and brought him home and we buried him in the garden and cried over him."

Dennis however, is not partial to this imaginative construct:

> "Always something, now," he commanded, putting his head in at the kitchen door. "Always telling a tall tale."
> "Well," said Rosaleen, without the least shame, "he wanted a story so I gave him a good one. That's the Irish in me."

Dennis, in striking contrast with his wife, has an alternate interpretation of what it means to be Irish:

> To be Irish, he felt, was to be like him, a sober, practical, thinking man, a lover of truth. Rosaleen couldn't see it at all. "It's just your head is like a stone!" she said to him once, pretending she was joking, but she meant it.

The action of the story subsequent to this event develops through an interplay between reality and the illusion until the point is reached when Rosaleen is able to accommodate herself to the truth that Dennis invariably sees so clearly.

The neat and orderly solution to the death of the Billy-cat that Rosaleen uses to assuage Mr. Pendleton's curiosity—and quite probably her loss of the cat as well—is similar to the dreams she has dreamed and will dream to accommodate herself to reality. The story of great-grandfather is typical.

Rosaleen and her sister Honora, when they were girls, were ordered to keep a watch over their dying great-grandfather. Their giddiness, however, so provoked the old man that "great-grandfather opened the one eye full of rage and says, '. . . To hell with ye.'" The disturbing effects of this incident were made benign for Rosaleen through the mediation of a dream in which the old man ordered his great-granddaughter to have a mass said for his soul, now in Purgatory. The reality was accommodated to the dream and Rosaleen was able to live with it.

This pattern repeats itself again and again: first the painful reality presents itself, and then the dream that assuages the pain occurs. During her youth in Ireland Rosaleen missed marrying a young Irish boy. The chance missed has a particular poignancy at this trying time in Rosaleen's married life, but a dream has intervened and softened the impact of reality:

> Rosaleen nodded her head. "Ah, Dennis, if I'd set my heart on that boy I need never have left Ireland. And when I think how it all came out with him. With me so far away, him struck on the head and left for dead in a ditch."
> "You dreamed that," said Dennis.
> "Surely I dreamed it, and it is so. When I was crying and crying over him—" Rosaleen was proud of her crying—"I didn't know then what good luck I would find here."

Again, when the young Irishman Kevin left the O'Tooles after having lived with them for a year, he wrote to them only once. His obvious ingratitude is argued away by Rosaleen's dream. She dreams that Kevin is dead. He did not write because "he hadn't the power any more."

The central adventure in this phase of Rosaleen's life of illusion is her dream that Honora lies dying in Boston. The dream comes in the dead of winter and at a time when things seem so bad that they cannot get worse. Dennis has even come to think that "there would come a day when she would say outright, 'It's no life here, I won't stay here any longer. . . .'" Reality has become bitter; Rosaleen's dream comes to sweeten it. Obviously, she must go to Boston to see Honora. The trip is made by way of New York, where a few hours are allocated for two romantic movies: "The Prince of Love" and "The Lover King." Then Rosaleen proceeds to Boston, only to find that Boston is the point of no return. Rosaleen has literally allowed her imagination to take her too far this time: in leaving her Connecticut home she has left the place where the dream can safely be believed in. Her attempt to live the dream in Boston is an utter failure. Honora is not only not sick, but she has moved from her old address without ever having notified Rosaleen. Faith in the dream is no longer possible (as Rosaleen later tells Dennis: "I don't put the respect on dreams I once did"). But reality is still too difficult for Rosaleen to accept; her substitute for both it and the belief she has lost becomes an unfounded hope in the future.

Here with the Honora episode the patterning of meaning can be seen in a transitional phase. With the Billy-cat, great-grandfather, the young Irish boy, and Kevin, the reality appeared first and then the dream which made that irksome reality acceptable. The Honora sequence initiates a change in this pattern as it moves from reality (the difficult life in Connecticut) to dream (the dying Honora) to reality (Honora's having moved). Subsequent to this episode the movement *reality-illusion* (as dream) gives place to the movement *illusion-reality*. Since the illusions that Rosaleen nurtures for a comfortable future are intended to transform from uncongeniality certain aspects of that future, the illusions that will effect the transformation appear initially; and then reality makes its incursion to destroy those illusions. Just as the story changes at this point—when *reality-illusion* is replaced by *illusion-reality*—it will change again when this new system disintegrates and *reality* alone remains. At that point the story will end. In outline, then, the entire configuration of central meanings may be shown as follows:

> *reality-illusion*
>> Billy-cat episode
>> Great-grandfather episode
>> Irish boy episode
>> Kevin episode
>
> *reality-illusion-reality*
>> Honora episode
>
> *illusion-reality*
>> Hugh Sullivan episode
>> Neighbor episode
>> Kevin episode
>> Guy Richards episode
>
> *reality*
>> Rosaleen-Dennis tableau
>> at the end of the story

The *illusion-reality* segment of this development is shaped by Rosaleen's making the object of hope in the future one or another illusion on which will depend the possibility of a comfortable life with Dennis in Connecticut. She seeks first to create a substitute for Kevin when she happens upon Hugh Sullivan, the down-and-out Irish immigrant whom she meets in Boston. She befriends the young man, feeds him, and offers him a job on the Connecticut farm. Hugh, however, takes her generosity to be a solicitation of another kind: "It's not safe at all," said Hugh, "I was caught at it once in Dublin, and there was a holy row!" With this misinterpretation, hope for the future as it relates to Sullivan is destroyed for Rosaleen: "The *cheek* of ye," said she, "insulting a woman could be your mother."

Rosaleen loses the support of another illusion almost immediately after her return to Connecticut. She finds that her neighbor thinks of her in the same way that Hugh Sullivan did: "So that's the way it is here, is it? That's what my life has come to, I'm a woman of bad fame with the neighbors.'"

Rosaleen, urgently in need of comfort, thinks again about Kevin; if the dream about Honora was wrong, the dream about Kevin becomes, by analogy, just as incorrect: " 'All day long I've been thinking Kevin isn't dead at all, and we shall see him in this very house before long.' " Dennis, however, remains an adamant realist: "That's no sign at all," he said. Rosaleen thinks no more about Kevin. Guy Richards becomes the next object of her hope.

The Guy Richards case has an element of complexity about it.[2] Throughout most of the story Rosaleen denies his attractive features. He has loomed as a danger to her: "If ever he lays a finger on me; I'll shoot him dead." But Rosaleen is obviously on the defensive here because Guy—with his "voice like the power of scrap-iron falling"—is all that Dennis is not. Toward the end of the story she admits the part that

---

[2] It is noteworthy that Richards at one point in the story begins to recite Fitz-Greene Halleck's "Marco Bozzaris," a ballad in which a Turkish chieftain awakens from a dream of conquest to find that Bozzaris and his Grecian followers have surrounded and all but defeated his army. Through this brief allusion, Richards is associated with the dream world which Rosaleen has already renounced and with her expectations for the future, which subsequently prove to be as unfounded as those of the Turkish leader.

Richards plays in making reality a little more endurable. She waits for him to stop in and exchange a word of greeting:

> Rosaleen didn't know what to expect, then, and then: surely he couldn't be stopping? Ah, surely he *couldn't* be going on? She sat down again with her heart just nowhere, and took up the tablecloth, but for a long time she couldn't see the stitches. She was wondering what had become of her life; every day she had thought something great was going to happen, and it was all just straying from one terrible disappointment to another.

As Guy Richards goes rattling down the road, Rosaleen's hope is shattered. Just as the ordering mechanism of the past collapsed when her dream was confronted with the reality of Honora's absence, the promise of the future—already minimized by Hugh Sullivan's cynicism and her neighbor's uncharity—is destroyed by Richards' failure to stop. The failure of the visions of faith and hope to substantiate themselves has made meaningless that past and that future which were structured on them. Only love and the present remain for Rosaleen, and these she accepts as she makes her whole-hearted return to reality:

> Ah, what was there to remember, or to look forward to now? Without thinking at all, she leaned over and put her head on Dennis's knee. "Whyever," she asked him, in an ordinary voice, "did ye marry a woman like me?"
>
> "Mind you don't tip over in that chair now," said Dennis. "I knew well I could never do better." His bosom began to thaw and simmer. It was going to be all right with everything, he could see that.
>
> She sat up and felt his sleeves carefully. "I want you to wrap up warm this bitter weather, Dennis," she told him. "With two pairs of socks and the chest protector, for if anything happened to you, whatever would become of me in this world?"
>
> "Let's not think of it," said Dennis, shuffling his feet.
>
> "Let's not, then," said Rosaleen. "For I could cry if you crooked a finger at me."

Here at the story's end Rosaleen breaks the pattern of her life. She frees reality from the dreams and illusions that she used formerly to disguise it. Thus, paradoxically enough, order is reestablished by attention to a reality which until this time has constituted disorder. The appearance of order in the dream and the illusion, in the objects of faith and hope, gives place to the truth of Dennis's old age and the reality of love in the present.

Besides this linear, diachronic movement—structured in a pattern which repeats basic meanings associated with the softening of reality by some form of an illusion until the point is reached where the illusion can no longer withstand the demands of reality—the story has another kind of movement in relation to its central symbol. That movement might best be called centripetal and centrifugal—rather than linear—since it has a center in the cracked looking-glass, toward which meanings continually move and from which they are tangentially released. These meanings, too, it would seem, are very complex and give to the linear movement new dimensions to the degree that the complexity of the cracked looking-glass as a central symbol is understood.

I suggested at the beginning of this essay that the plot structure of "The Cracked Looking-Glass," parallels in part that of two of Henry James's *nouvelles:* "The Beast in the Jungle" and "In the Cage," and I briefly demonstrated some similarities between it and these tales. In relation to them "The Cracked Looking-Glass" takes on a more profound significance—in the same manner that any story does when its relation to a basic myth or archetype is understood. The fact, for instance, that Rosaleen is in danger of suffering the same fate as Marcher makes her predicament more meaningful to the reader who knows something about Marcher. The facts, too, that Dennis has a pipe that is carved with a "crested lion glaring out of jungle," and that he sets aside this pipe when Rosaleen is on the verge of rejecting her last chance to return to reality, suggest Katherine Anne Porter's interest in extending the boundaries of meaning in her story to those of James's. Miss Porter employs a similar technique to create connotations for her central symbol.

The cracked looking-glass provides some immediately available meanings. Obviously, as its description shows, Rosaleen does not see clearly when she looks into it. Also Rosaleen consults the glass on special occasions only; when Kevin *leaves,* when she *leaves* Guy Richards, when Guy *leaves,* and when she *leaves* to visit Honora. It has nothing to do with *staying* with Dennis. This is so, probably, because the glass is certainly a symbol of their marriage, which does not reflect the romantic love of the New York movies that Rosaleen relishes. And, of course, there is a thirty-year gap in their ages. But in the light of other literary works in which this symbol appears, Katherine Anne Porter's mirror symbol takes on other meanings as well.

In the Telemachus section of Joyce's *Ulysses*,[3] "Stephen bent forward and peered at the mirror held out to him, cleft by a crooked crack, hair on end." It is a mirror that Buck Mulligan stole from the room of an Irish maid-servant.

> Drawing back and pointing, Stephen said with bitterness:
> —It is a symbol of Irish art. The cracked lookingglass of a servant.

The relevance of this excerpt to the story is immediately obvious. Rosaleen was formerly a "chambermaid in a rich woman's home." The glass is hers. If for Stephen the cracked mirror is a symbol of Irish art, for the reader—as he refers it to Rosaleen—it is the symbol of her imagination. Her view of the world, like that of Irish artists' for Daedalus, is distorted. Through Joyce, then, this new dimension is added to the symbol's complex of meanings, and by reference to Joyce the defective mirror symbolizes Rosaleen's involvment with an unreal world.

The cracked looking-glass also suggests a relation to Tennyson that explores a dimension of the symbol's meaning different from the one suggested by Joyce. The Lady of Shalott spends her days weaving a "magic web with colours gay," while observing through a mirror the reality of life outside her tower. She looks out directly on life, though, when attracted by the figure of Sir Lancelot, whom she follows to Camelot and her death. She leaves behind her, as a symbol of the end of her isolation from reality, "the mirror crack'd from side to side." The incidental and otherwise irrelevant note that Rosaleen has been sewing a never-to-be-finished tablecloth for fifteen years suggests a connection with the Lady of Shalott. Less tenuous is the fact that to both women reality is mediated: to one through a mirror and to the other through illusions. Rosaleen goes to Boston, just as the Lady went to Camelot, and her confrontation with reality deals a death blow to the dream and spells the beginning of the end for her illusions. The symbol of reality for both, then, is the cracked looking-glass; and as a symbol of reality the mirror is, as Dennis twice tells Rosaleen, "a good enough glass."

The last extension of meaning for this symbol that I should like to

---

[3] I am indebted to Professor James Hafley of The Catholic University of America for directing me to *Ulysses* for an instance of the mirror symbol and for further suggesting an investigation of symbol's possible relation to Tennyson's "Lady of Shalott."

suggest is *in a way* Pauline: "We see now through a mirror in an obscure manner, but then face to face." The inadequate looking-glasses of the ancients, which Paul refers to here, were as unsatisfactory as Rosaleen's cracked mirror when like that mirror they literally attempted to reflect reality. The crack in Rosaleen's glass and the inadequacy of the one referred to in I Corinthians 13:12 require an eventual face-to-face confrontation. For Paul that confrontation takes place when charity is perfected in heaven; for Rosaleen and Dennis it occurs when she abjures her faith in the dream and her hope in the illusion and recognizes that for her the only reality is love in the present. Husband and wife then meet face to face in the final tableau without even the suggestion of the defective glass (which Joyce had referred to as "crooked"): "I could cry if ye crooked your finger at me." If for St. Paul in one sense faith and hope pass away, so for Rosaleen faith in the dream and hope in the illusion represent, in a non-theological way, ultimately unsatisfactory answers for human fulfillment; and for both—again in their own sense of the word—*love* abides in its sustaining greatness.

The function and meaning of the mirror symbol in "The Cracked Looking-Glass," then, as I have attempted to demonstrate, are very complex. The symbol derives its dimensions from the meanings that accrete to it in the course of the action of the story and those that it has in relation to the sources from which I have suggested it may spring. It stands at the center of the story in a chameleon-like fashion, meaning one thing now and one thing later while still being the same thing and having all the possibilities of its meaning simultaneously. In the cracked looking-glass the imagination of Rosaleen, the imperfection of human love, the necessity of accepting that love as it is, the marriage of Rosaleen and Dennis, reality, the difficulty of knowing reality, and many other meanings that the story incorporates are symbolized. Thus, along with the linear organization of the meanings patterned by the interplay of reality with the dream and the illusion, the centrifugal and centripetal action of this symbol testifies to the craftsmanship of Katherine Anne Porter as it shapes the esthetically satisfying form assumed by those illusions and allusions that are so carefully reflected in "The Cracked Looking-Glass."

George Core

'Holiday'
A Version
of Pastoral

FOR HENRY JAMES the ideal form of fiction on the "dimensional ground" is the "beautiful and blest *nouvelle,*" that indeterminate measure which falls between the short story and the novel, a genre which is his favorite and of which he is master. The same can be said of Katherine Anne Porter who would agree with James that the "forms of wrought things" are "all exquisitely and effectively, the things; so that, for the delight of mankind, form might compete with form and might correspond to fitness; might . . . have an inevitability, a marked felicity." James, in his magisterial way, does not often bother with matters of precise definition, and in this instance he makes no distinction between the longer short story and the short novel. Miss Porter, herself a great admirer of James and the most deliberate and severe perfectionist writing American fiction since his death, has noted that difference in the Preface to her *Collected Stories.* For her there are four forms of fiction: short stories, long stories, short novels, and novels. Miss Porter's best work is in the short novel: "Pale Horse, Pale Rider," "Old Mortality," and "Noon Wine"; of these (all fine works) the last is the best—and a masterpiece. Her long stories—"The Cracked Looking-Glass," "Ha-cienda," "The Leaning Tower," and "Holiday"—are not so good on the whole as the short novels—or the short stories. Of these "Holiday" is easily the finest: it is a story which will endure because form and idea are one—technique provides a window to a fable of universal propor-tions—and because the action in its totality—in its confluence of language, metaphor, theme, movement: in short, in its life—carries with it an absolute inevitability.

It is easy enough to stake out the preliminary ground on which this story should be examined: it is a narrative which dramatizes what William Empson calls a version of pastoral, that subject which finds its archetypal lineage in man's impulse to return to the Garden, to a prelapsarian world forever green and innocent. "Holiday" is characteristic of Miss Porter's art in that it is faultlessly written, closely wrought, and economically presented through a sharp, clear perspective and a gradually and firmly-evolving focus which narrows to a view that is at once tentative and final, innocent and ironic, luminous and dark. The center of composition is here, but beyond this the mystery of the art remains almost inviolate.

The total configuration of "Holiday" possesses a self-sufficient order and achieves a symmetrical unity even though the life it describes, ren-ders, and embodies is far from neat and orderly, being rife with the terri-ble stresses and disrelations which are typical of the human lot even at its best. In many respects this story is a celebration of the soil which is tilled by those who know and understand it deeply and intuitively. Yet at the same time "Holiday" contains a tragic dimension which moves the reader to awe, regret, and finally acceptance, as the narrator herself is moved in the course of the action. It is a double story of sorts in which the two lines of action meet. On the one hand it is the narrator's story of a chapter in her life, involving a real but unexplained crisis—a psychic turning point; on the other it is almost a typical episode in the Müllers' lives from which they do not attempt to wrest a philosophic and re-ligious meaning: a spring which brings birth, marriage, and death. The element of death brings a uniqueness to an action which is otherwise typical of the Müllers' lives, and it gives the plot a necessary and mov-ing dramatic context.

At the beginning the narrator is haunted by troubles of her own, and she runs to the home of the Müllers to lose and to find herself.

Through the persona Miss Porter states in the opening paragraph what might appear to be the "moral" of the story:

> But this story I am about to tell you happened before this great truth impressed itself upon me—that we do not run from the troubles and dangers which are truly ours, and it is better to learn what they are earlier than later, and if we don't run from the others, we are fools.

The obvious theme of individual responsibility versus common obligation is soon joined to the governing theme—the fools of life motif which appears in St. Paul. So this *apparently* artless tale begins—as a simple story, not a polished literary artifice, told much in the manner of the lyric or ballad; and the tone of some naïveté and undeniable humility is in perfect accord.

It is at this point—the outset of "Holiday"—that the story stands a chance of foundering, for the narrator's unexplained troubles and her removal to the country are a bit disingenuous and forced, and the reader may feel that he is getting bogged down in merely referential narrative. All, however, comes right in short order, and the drama unfolds steadily and surely as the plot moves towards complication. The action must be viewed and reported by a stranger—an articulate, compassionate reflector who in this case represents the vantage point of the larger, cosmopolitan world. Her general attitude and particular frame of mind are important, and they must be identified early in the story as indeed they are. Therefore the reader is all the more impressed with the narrator's sympathetic portrayal of the Müller family. The stranger's narrative voice contributes in no small part to the unfolding design of "Holiday." The unnamed persona certainly reminds us of Miranda, a Miranda living sometime between the period of "Old Mortality" and "Pale Horse, Pale Rider"; but there is no reason to suppose once and for all that she is, for unlike Miranda in "Pale Horse, Pale Rider" and many stories in *The Old Order*, she is on the periphery of the action, and she interprets as well as reports the events, as does the nameless narrator of "Hacienda."

On any level "Holiday" is about the Müller family. The larger frame of the story, the enveloping action, deals with the family as a whole and the archetypal experiences that affect all families; whereas the particular instance of this larger pattern that provides the main action involves one member of the family. All the Müllers work unceasingly to increase the already-abundant store of the Müller dynasty. They are German peasants who toil with great reward in East Texas: the crops abound and the livestock multiply while the Müllers marry and increase. In the course of the story the youngest daughter, Hatsy, is married; and another daughter, Gretchen, bears one of many third-generation Müllers. All live under the same roof. All are curiously alike, save one:

> I got a powerful impression that they were all, even the sons-in-law, one human being divided into several separate appearances. The crippled servant girl brought in more food and gathered up plates and went away in her limping run, and she seemed to me the only individual in the house. . . . She was whole, and belonged nowhere.

The narrator gradually realizes that the servant, Ottilie, is an older sister of Hatsy, Gretchen, and a third sister, Annetje. Ottilie has been terribly and hopelessly transfigured by a nameless childhood accident, and what remains is a grotesque distortion of humanity. She is pictured as a frenzied automaton, "a mere machine of torture," working in "aimless, driven haste," preparing and serving "that endless food that represented all her life's labors." Yet paradoxically Ottilie is the most human and sympathetic character in the story (and it is her story): she ironically achieves humanity in inhumanity, whereas the remainder of her family do not. The mystery of this paradox is at the heart of the story, and here Miss Porter's irony finds its true center in "Holiday."

Despite the success of the Müllers there are deficiencies which the narrator does not articulate so much as sense, and we, through her deepening consciousness, perceive the terrible shortcomings of the Müllers—and of humanity. We see the typical contradiction of the German character: Father Müller reads *Das Kapital* religiously every evening and knows whole passages by heart:

> And here was this respectable old farmer who accepted its dogma as a religion—that is to say, its legendary inapplicable precepts were just, right, proper, one must believe in them, of course, but life, everyday living, was another unrelated thing.

The dimension of satire is coming into play. The "natural man" is bemused by the sophisticated life of the outside world to the extent that he reads Marx; but sensing that Marx's abstractions have nothing whatever to do with his essential life, he therefore ignores them. The obvious satiric motif directed towards a national type—the phlegmatic German —and the concomitant irony quickly deepen as the conflict of the story develops and the lines of action gather.

These same respectable Müllers have forgotten that Ottilie is a member of their family. We want to be indignant, but the matter is not so simple as that, because the narrator sympathizes in large part with the Müllers:

> It is not a society or a class that pampered its invalids and the unfit. So long as one lived one did one's share. This was her place, in this family she had been born and must die; did she suffer? No one asked, no one looked to see. Suffering went with life, suffering and labor. While one lived one worked, and that was all, and without complaints, for no one had time to listen, and everybody had his own troubles. So, what else could they have done with Ottilie? As for me, I could do nothing but promise myself that I would forget her, too; and to remember her for the rest of my life.

The last sentence reminds one of Robert Penn Warren's line: "Forgetting is just another kind of remembering." In this patriarchial world Ottilie has lost her original place as child, wife, and mother—functions which are fulfilled by all her sisters, but she is assigned another place, and in and through it she works out her own salvation, while at once remembering her past.

In the simplest sense the story is about suffering and labor, about the labor of the farm, the labor of childbirth, the labor of life, and the labor of death. For there is not only marriage and childbirth, but death. Mother Müller dies as the result of her struggles in a storm which ravages the countryside and blights the land. The order of nature is thrown into discord, and so is the order of the family when Mother Müller is stricken: "The family crowded into the room, unnerved in panic, lost unless the sick woman should come to herself and tell them what to do for her." Father Müller cries, " 'Ach, Gott, Gott. A hundret tousand tollars in the bank . . . and tell me, tell, what goot des it do?' " With the understatement and directness of her creator the narrator tells us:

> This frightened them, and all at once, together, they screamed and called and implored her in a tumult utterly beyond control. The noise of

their grief and terror filled the place. In the midst of this, Mother Müller died.

The death is the turning point of "Holiday" and the author deftly works out the complications in the remaining few pages of the story. We are concerned with the reactions of the Müllers to the death, of Ottilie on the one hand and the remainder of the family on the other. There is finally no one right attitude, any more than there is a clearly wrong one. The resolution comes in the bringing of the conflicting attitudes and tensions to a sharp and dramatic but deliberately ambiguous focus.

Only moments before Hatsy, accompanied by her shy new husband, has shouted at Ottilie who is apparently afraid and frightened by the storm "in a high, penetrating voice as if to a deaf person or one at a great distance, 'Ottilie! Suppertime. We are hungry!' " Hatsy and her husband then go on to care for a sick lamb. Ottilie, the human lamb, is sacrificed to the needs of the family. This implicit comparison of animal life to human life is one of the most striking aspects of the story. Shortly after she arrives at the farm the narrator watches Hatsy and Mother Müller separate nursing calves from their mothers so the dams can be milked. When Gretchen's child is born, she nurses like "a young calf." One is reminded of "The Grave" when Miranda and her brother discover the tiny unborn litter in the dead mother rabbit, and Miranda begins to understand the mystery of life and death. Later in "Holiday," immediately after Ottilie has appeared to clear the table, Annetje expresses fear that her brother will trap Kuno, a German shepherd. The narrator observes that "Annetje was full of silent, tender solicitudes.... Still, she seemed to have forgotten that Ottilie was her sister. So had all the others.... She moved among them as invisible to their imaginations as a ghost." For the family Ottilie is a ghost from the past, preserved only in the photograph she keeps. Theirs is a cruel, practical, and necessary accommodation. On the day of Mother Müller's funeral the narrator dreams that she hears the howls of Kuno who is caught in a 'possum trap. But it is not Kuno the narrator hears: it is Ottilie, caught in a far more vicious trap, and nightmare becomes waking life. Ottilie, like Benjy Compson, bellows against disorder in her world. She howls "with a great wrench of her body, an upward reach of the neck, without tears."

The persona thinks that Ottilie wants to join the funeral procession and they start out together in the ludicrous spring wagon that has brought the narrator to the farm. The story here is coming full circle, as spring, which had just begun when the narrator arrived at the farm, is coming into full bloom against the "peacock green of the heavens," with its "sun westering gently." Time and life go on in the same ways despite death. Suddenly Ottilie laughs, "a kind of yelp, but unmistakable laughter." The speaker then sees her "ironical mistake":

> There was nothing I could do for Ottilie, selfishly as I wished to ease my heart of her; she was beyond my reach as well as any other human reach, and yet, had I not come nearer to her than I had to anyone else in my attempt to deny and bridge the distance between us, or rather, her distance from me? Well, we were both equally fools of life, equally fellow fugitives from death. We had escaped for one day more at least. We would celebrate our good luck, we would have a little stolen holiday, a breath of spring air and freedom on this lovely, festive afternoon.

We do not know why Ottilie laughs. It may be a triumphant laugh since she is still among the living. She is perhaps once again trying to affirm her humanity as she has done so poignantly earlier when she has shown to the speaker her picture as a normal, healthy child. Here is one of the most compassionate and compelling scenes in all literature: its tenderness and pathos are unforgettable. Ottilie's entire predicament is brilliantly rendered and starkly portrayed in this vignette. Her joy seems blasphemous on the funeral day, the family holy day with which the holiday is ended. Yet is not the family's treatment of her equally blasphemous, and why is the afternoon "festive"? Ottilie's laughter is best regarded as an affirmation amidst almost unbearable suffering and sorrow; and Ottilie celebrates the triumphant return of spring and the continuance of life amidst grief and death, even as the other Müllers turn their thoughts toward the future while they are fashioning the coffin for Mother Müller and preparing her body for burial. "For a while they would visit the grave and remember, and then life would arrange itself in another order, yet it would be the same."

So Ottilie assumes life in our minds which the other Müllers do not assume in their "mystical inertia" of mind and "muscular life." Ottilie, the caricature who is once described as unreal, is more human and real than the remainder of the family. As Father Müller has realized for them, they are the fools of life. Ottilie, physically and mentally and psychically wrenched by fate, is still less a fool and more a person, and she celebrates her "good luck," her "stolen holiday," even while returning to the kitchen to continue her suffering. It is a final irony that Ottilie is able to steal a holiday only when her mother has died.

One should note that Miss Porter is unafraid of coming dangerously close to telling the reader what the themes of "Holiday" are as the story comes to an end. She does this elsewhere with equal facility, especially in "Old Mortality." There are the old themes revolving around the life-cycle and its fundamental rhythms, but the answer is not so easy as it looks on the surface, for there is also the question of appearance, illusion, and reality. The fools of life theme is both Christian and existential, and Miss Porter uses it in a darker sense in "Pale Horse, Pale Rider" and *Ship of Fools*. Miranda returns from her sojourn with the Pale Rider to feel that she has been tricked, and it is ironical to her that she has been placed "once more safely in the road that would lead her again to death." Throughout her fiction Miss Porter shows us the truth of St. Paul's statement: "Let no man deceive himself. If any man among you seemeth to be wise in this world, let him become a fool, that he may be wise." Miranda, the narrator of "Holiday," and Ottilie achieve wisdom thus, although they come to it in radically different ways, and Ottilie's perception, like her howl and her laugh, is of a very special and finally unknowable order.

The life of "Holiday" demands our attention a moment longer. This microcosm of the human community is a bountiful world with a shared simple life, but it is also "a house of perpetual exile," as the narrator says. Its people are "solid, practical, hard-bitten, land-holding German peasants, who struck their mattocks into the earth deep and held fast wherever they were, because to them life and the land were one indivisible thing; but never in any wise did they confuse nationality with habitation." So the Müllers are typical plain (if wealthy) folk of an agrarian world and characteristic Germans; they are of the land and yet are alienated from its principle inhabitants. Here is revealed another deep irony in the story, and through touches such as these (which are deliberate and which count significantly in the ultimate meaning of the fable) the author is able to suggest a spreading field of meaning and value. Miss Porter triumphantly explores what Empson calls one assumption of pastoral: ". . . You can say everything about complex people by a complete consideration of simple people." To put it another way, simple people fully considered are no longer simple. So it is with the Müllers whose lives are something more than tranquil, orderly, and perfectly consistent.

The apparent simplicity and neatness of the Müllers' lives leads the narrator to flee there and make a haven of their home, but she soon finds out life in both its manifest forms and unpredictable nature continues any and everywhere, despite man's best efforts to avoid it. The mystery of the human experience remains, whether he be in tenement or field, townhouse or cottage. One thinks at the outset that the life of the Müllers inheres in the good since it is straightforward, free of duplicity and cunning, and since it is, for all intents and purposes, wholly successful. But it turns out that not a little of the old German atavism is present: we catch hints of dynastic rule and heavy-handed politics. If Mr. Müller is not Marx's *Kapital* (as he says), he still smacks of the German tribal chieftain and rules his house and lands with the close grip of the beneficent dictator.

Because Miss Porter quite characteristically qualifies her sympathy, the Müllers are believable and interesting: they have human failings as well as human virtues. That is one reason why the reader assents to the donnée of the story and is caught up in its action. There is primitivism in "Holiday," but not of the romantic sort: the view of man in the natural world is hard—not soft—and is tough-minded and realistic. As J. F. Powers has said, "Nobody else could have written the story 'Holiday,' " a story which is an example of what he calls "the nearest thing yet to reality in American fiction." The reality emerges because Katherine Anne Porter "has approached life reverently in her stories, and it lives on in them." And, in the words of Robert Penn Warren, the story is "paradoxically, both a question asked of life and a celebration of life; and the author of it knows in her bones that the more corrosive the question asked, the more powerful may be the celebration."

The version of pastoral in "Holiday" is neither propaganda nor idyll: it is realistic in its depiction of a world which is both elemental and communal, and the sharpness of detail and accuracy of picture contribute in no small way to our understanding of this microcosm of the human

community. If to the unwary reader this world seems narrow and artificial, then he should examine it more closely. As Empson has shrewdly
remarked,

> The feeling that life is essentially inadequate to the human spirit, and
> yet that a good life must avoid saying so, is naturally at home with most
> versions of pastoral; in pastoral you take a limited life and pretend it is
> the full and normal one, and a suggestion that one must do this with all
> life, because the normal itself is limited, is easily put into the trick. . . .

Within these boundaries (which are in some respects those of all art) the
action of "Holiday" embodies a full and convincing world, invested with
all the appurtenances of life and charged with visceral (and cerebral)
forces: indeed the still center of the story involves the senses and emotions in an almost-painfully real and palpable way: it is the intense yet
sure feeling one encounters often in the best Russian fiction—in *A
Sportsman's Sketches* and in parts of *Anna Karenina*. All in all "Holiday" is an utterly believable confluence of elements which are caught
and held—radiantly—in the living tapestry of the art—a pastoral in
which form, the shape of the art, and substance, the fable within the
art, are one: the form of the wrought thing is the thing itself—and the
configuration of the whole is both beautiful and blest.

IV

Lodwick Hartley

The Lady
and the
Temple

IN SPITE OF the fact that at least one of her books has been reissued in a popular edition and that many of her short stories have appeared in anthologies, Katherine Anne Porter remains chiefly a writer's writer. Such a circumstance is a pity, for in her short stories and novels she has a great deal to say to all intelligent readers; and she says it with clarity and beauty. She is by no means difficult to read; and, though her overzealous critics have made a few of her short stories seem over-wrought with symbolism, there is actually little of the occult in her work. She has always lacked patience with the literary faddists—those people who affect newness of manner when they are actually destitute of matter. She writes in the main stream of English prose style and of English fiction without being imitative: a great achievement in itself. Her diffi-culty is an ironic one, though it involves no irony peculiar to her own time. In brief, she is a perfectionist, and perfectionists have rarely en-joyed popular success in any age. Furthermore, in the pursuit of her ideal she has evolved a theory of art that might reasonably be expected to limit her range. Even among the literary highbrows she has not entirely escaped ridicule for preciosity, as a few delicately pointed barbs in Mary McCarthy's *The Groves of Academe* will attest.

The Days Before, a recent collection of Miss Porter's essays and fugitive pieces written over a period of some thirty years, provides an illuminating index to the excellencies of her criticism and her art, as well as an index to some of her limitations. Though the book contains a great deal of material on other subjects—for example, a long essay on the rose as an actuality and as a symbol, a warmly vivid description of the Audubon country, colorful and sensitive commentaries on the author's several periods of residence in Mexico, an evocation of the "Old South" through a sketch of her fabulous grandmother—the collection as a whole is really concerned with writing, the one subject to which Miss Porter has devoted the greatest part of her life and thought. And she manages to reveal her own philosophy of art most penetratingly by discussing the achievement of Henry James, Thomas Hardy, Katherine Mansfield, Willa Cather, Virginia Woolf, Edith Sitwell, Ezra Pound, Gertrude Stein, E. M. Forster, D. H. Lawrence, and Eudora Welty.

Throughout her critical essays Miss Porter writes with such precision, compactness, and fine fluency that no perceptive reader can fail to be charmed by what she has to say. Whether everyone will want to accept her rigidly pure concept of the art of writing is another matter. Certainly, it will be easy to conclude that art is the nearest thing to a be-all and end-all in her existence. The bases of her position she has clearly marked out—so clearly, in fact, that the whole position may seem to approach rationalization. In short, one may be led to feel that her own peculiar experience has developed in her such a profound distrust of institutional religion and of human relationships that she has felt compelled to seek certainties elsewhere and that, consequently, her theory of art, beautiful and praiseworthy though it is, arises out of a peculiar personal necessity rather than out of a completely universal one.

From her days in convent schools (where, she once said with delightful candor, she was "precocious, nervous, rebellious, and unteachable") she has reacted against authoritarianism and totalitarianism in any form —in government, morals, religion—including the faith of her youthful training and either the Southern brand of conservatism of her social milieu or the survival of Puritanism that still determines the American moral climate. Religion itself she, of course, does not reject. "The idea of God" she acknowledges to be "the most splendid single act of the creative human imagination"; and she agrees with E. M. Forster (himself hardly a champion of orthodoxy) that "there are only two possibilities for any real order: art and religion." (The order is significant.) But, although she plainly makes a distinction intellectually, she is rarely capable emotionally of detaching religion from its institutions, the history of which she thinks of as being "calamitous." The mystical concept of God, she contends warmly,

> has been harnessed rudely to machinery of the most mundane sort, and has been made to serve the ends of an organization which, ruling under divine guidance, has ruled very little better, and in some respects, worse, than certain rather mediocre but frankly man-made systems of government. And it has often lent its support to the worst evils in secular government, fighting consistently on the side of the heavy artillery.

The social results of institutional religion, Miss Porter further suggests, have been equally calamitous. "Of all evil emotions generated in the snake-pit of human nature," she writes apropos of the Bishop of Wakefield's unfortunate attack on Thomas Hardy, "theological hatred is perhaps the most savage." And she praises the elder James for inculcating in his children not Puritan notions of religion and morality but "a horror of priggishness and conscious virtue" and for guarding them "from that vulgarity he described as 'flagrant morality.'" The deleterious effects of religion are to be found not only in morality but also in criticism and in the arts. T. S. Eliot's enthusiastic conversion to Anglo-Catholicism becomes a case in point. Having turned "preacher," Mr. Eliot's "great gifts as a critic . . . do not flow with their old splendor and depth," Miss Porter asserts.

In the field of religion Miss Porter's admiration is, therefore, quite logically only for the "great tradition of dissent," which "will remain, persistent, obdurate, a kind of church in itself, with its leaders, teachers, saints, martyrs, heroes; a thorn in the flesh of orthodoxy." But, from this point of view, dissent seems admirable largely for its nuisance value rather than for its contribution to spiritual growth.

If religion as she finds it offers Miss Porter no essential and permanent satisfaction, neither do human relationships. I do not mean to suggest that she is a misanthropist in the usual sense of the term. As an artist she finds human life to be full of interest:

> I have never known an uninteresting human being, and I have never known two alike. . . . I am passionately involved with these individuals who populate all these enormous migrations, calamities; who fight wars and furnish life for the future; these beings without which, one by one, all the "broad movements of history" could never take place. One by one —as they were born.

However, she is acutely conscious of the isolation of the individual, the "locked-in ego." Everywhere she sees the "lovelessness in which most people live." She implies agreement with Willa Cather's conclusion that "human relationships are the tragic necessity of life . . . never . . . wholly satisfactory"; and she even concludes that, as friends, cats might prove more valuable than the common two-legged creature without feathers. "I leave cats to the last," Miss Porter wrote recently in the *New York Herald-Tribune Books*. "I love them above all animals, and my friendship with them has been the most charming, constant thing, all my life." The statement is, of course, humorous; but its serious aspect is undeniable.

From disillusionment of this kind the artist can take refuge only in the temple of art itself. Hardy, Miss Porter points out, had "the mathematical certainty of music and architecture." And Henry James, who plainly furnishes an ideal for her, sought for truth "not in philosophy nor in religion, but in art, and found his own." And then there was Willa Cather, who held that "knowledge of great art and great thought was a good in itself not to be missed for anything." Moreover, as the record shows, when Miss Porter's own world seemed so definitely to be disintegrating with the fall of France in 1940, the author herself could find hope for permanence in art alone. But even the search for truth in the arts, as Miss Porter sees it, hardly promises an apocalyptic vision. The "triumph" of that "born artist," Virginia Woolf, is simply that, beyond her love for all the arts, she "had no plan whatever for her personal salvation; or the salvation of someone else; brought no doctrine; no dogma"; and she concluded merely that life is a "great mystery."

Miss Porter's pervading dislike of dogma and authoritarianism effectually prevents her acceptance of anything like neoclassical ideals in literature. Yet it leads her neither into a form of nineteenth-century Romanticism nor into sympathy with any of the various "revolutionary" schools of literature that have flourished so profusely in the twentieth century. The plain fact is that she wishes to be a classicist in the Greek tradition both in her practice and in her theory; and what she admires in the literary work of her contemporaries often sounds remarkably like what an enthusiastic scholar like Edith Hamilton admires in the literature of the Age of Pericles.

For the floodtide of experimentalism that came in the twenties, Miss Porter has patent contempt. "Every day in the arts," she writes, "as in schemes of government and organized crime, there was, there had to be something new," a principle that operated in crass failure to recognize that in reality there is nothing new except that which conforms to the true classical ideal of being "outside of time and beyond the reach of change." The false ideals of "The Lost Generation" Miss Porter sees as being epitomized in the "hoarse, anxious, corrupted mysticism" of the magazine *transition* and in the colossal illogic of Gertrude Stein. Miss Stein's judgments, writes Miss Porter,

> were neither moral nor intellectual, and least of all aesthetic, indeed they were not even judgments, but simply her description from observation of acts, words, appearances giving her view; limited, personal in the extreme, prejudiced without qualification, based on assumptions founded in the void of pure reason.

For the serious young men who had found writing difficult (the critic continues) the idea of automatic writing was a comfortable delusion. Ultimately, of course, these same young men who tried at first to write as if they had never read a book discovered that they had to read books before they could write.

Naturally, it would be erroneous to feel that Miss Porter's fundamental quarrel has been with the spirit of experimentalism itself. Rather is it, indeed, with what she considers to be the superficiality and unreason of most innovators and with the use of "tricky techniques and disordered syntax" to disguise "poverty of feeling and idea." For the innovations of an artist like Edith Sitwell the matter is quite different. In Miss Sitwell's early work, for example, Miss Porter finds a "challenging note of natural arrogance" that is completely admirable, because it was "boldly experimental" and "inventive from a sense of adventure" rather than from a paucity of ideas.

But even in Miss Sitwell it is rather a classical quality than her experimentalism *qua* experimentalism that Miss Porter genuinely admires. "A primrose by the river's brim was always a simple primrose and nothing more," writes Edith Hamilton of the Greek poets. "Birds were birds and nothing else, but how beautiful a thing was a bird." Of Miss Sitwell, Katherine Anne Porter is moved to write in a similar vein: "Rain is rain in these poems, it rains on the page and you can smell and feel it." Indeed, it is this classical quality of "realism" that Miss Porter seeks in both poetry and prose and that provides reason for her praise of the "objectivity" of Henry James or Willa Cather or Katherine Mansfield or Eudora Welty. It is always the concrete detail and the exact statement that matters. In this regard, Miss Porter writes of Katherine Mansfield: "She was magnificent in her objective view of things, her real sensitiveness to climate, mental or physical, her genuinely first-rate equipment in the matter of the five senses."

In the whole matter of style, then, it is not surprising to find Miss Porter writing of an artist like Willa Cather in almost the same language in which Edith Hamilton writes of Euripides. "It is plain writing, direct, matter-of-fact," Miss Hamilton remarks of the great dramatist in *The Greek Way*. "The words [are] so literal, so grave, so unemphatic [that they] hardly assist our attention to see the beauty in them." Miss Porter maintains the same necessity for the union of content and style. "The style should never attract the attention from what the writer is saying," she comments concerning Willa Cather's work; and it is Miss Cather's "fine pure direct prose . . . [and her] well-tempered voice saying very good, sensible things with complete authority" that give her superiority over most of her contemporaries.

Though Miss Porter's complete conception of the artist is not exactly vatic, it is a lofty one, indeed. She sees, first of all, the necessity of "that indispensable faculty of aspiration of the human mind called, in morals and the arts, nobility." The true artist will, like Flaubert, have "astronomical standards" and will be unyielding to the death in his literary principles, even though he may be in danger, as Miss Porter honestly admits, of developing "a coldness of heart." If the artist is "a lover of the sublime and a seeker after perfection," he may be, like Ezra Pound, a true poet, no matter how badly informed he is. His chief natural virtue must be sensitivity: the capability of "soaking in impressions at every pore." ("The whole scene of his childhood existed in his memory in terms of the lives lived in it," Miss Porter remarks of Henry James, "with his own growing mind working at it, storing it, transmuting it, reclaiming it.") The artist's chief acquired virtue must be objectivity, which is the ability to see life with "clearness, warmth of feeling, calmness of intelligence, and ample human view of things" (an idea not unlike Matthew Arnold's pronouncement on Sophocles) or the ability to achieve such an aloofness from life that allows him to "bare a moment of experience" without the necessity of stating beliefs, theories, motives (an idea that suggests Keats's comment on the "negative capability" of Shakespeare).

Art will set the artist apart from the conventional relationships and criteria: "Greatness in art is like any other greatness in religious experience, in love, it is great because it is beyond the reach of the ordinary, and cannot be judged by the ordinary, nor be accountable to it." Therefore, there is a necessity that the work of art and the personality of the artist should be kept distinct by the critic. "I have not much interest in anyone's personal history after the tenth year," Miss Porter asserts, "not even my own." In another place she insists: "Katherine Mansfield's work is the most important thing about her, and she is in danger of the worst fate that the artist can suffer—to be overwhelmed by her own legend, to have her work neglected for her 'personality.' " And with the same logic Miss Porter decries the "hysterical nonsense" that has been written about Rilke and D. H. Lawrence.

Whatever "separateness" Miss Porter may claim for the artist, she cannot very well deny his social responsibility as a person. Thus she writes: "The responsibility of the artist toward society is the plain and simple responsibility of any other human being, for I refuse to separate the artist from the human race." But arguing on the premise that edification is the highest form neither of the intellectual nor of the religious experience, she allows to art no propagandist function. On this matter her opinion finds clear and sharp statement:

> There exist documents of political and social theory which belong, if not to poetry, certainly to the department of humane letters. They are reassuring statements of the great hopes and dearest faiths of mankind and they are acts of high imagination. But all working, practical political systems, even those professing to originate in moral grandeur, are based upon

and operate by contempt of human life and the individual fate; in accepting any one of them and shaping his mind and work to that mold, the artist dehumanizes himself, unfits himself for the practice of any art.

And thus the concept of the functions and limitations of the artist is rounded out.

Miss Porter's serene consistency in her philosophy and her tolerance of nothing less than the highest standards of performance for herself as well as for others deserve the highest admiration. It is true, however, that, beneath the almost perfect poise of her manner, her rigid purism and her championship of art as effectually comprehending both morality and religion may at times seem less like a confession of faith than an act of desperation. Moreover, like the brave generalization about truth and beauty made by Keats in the presence of physical disintegration, her solution has never been a universally satisfactory one. Though this philosophy, however explicitly stated in the critical essays, may appear only implicitly in Miss Porter's fiction, its limitation curiously suggests a possible restriction of her total appeal. "All the conscious and recollected years of my life," she writes in the 1940 Preface of *Flowering Judas,* "have been lived to this day under the heavy threat of world catastrophe, and most of the energies of my mind and spirit have been spent in the effort to grasp the meaning of these threats, to trace them to their sources and to understand the logic of this majestic and terrible failure of life in the Western world." But these efforts to understand the failure of life in the Western world, however important they may be in her heart and mind, could hardly be said to be the major subject of her art. Indeed, her writing—imaginative and critical—seems more nearly an attempt to escape from the central problem. Perhaps the reason that her work, for all its beauty, does not etch itself indelibly on our consciousness is that it ultimately does not illuminate the supreme tragedy of which she speaks. Thus, whatever may be the acuity, the vitality, and even the nicely calculated violence of some of her stories, and whatever may be the strength of her utterance in other fields, she may continue to be regarded essentially as a lovely, white-robed priestess of the shrine of Apollo—a role that she seems deliberately and expertly to have written for herself.

Edward G. Schwartz

The Way
of Dissent

THE WAY OF DISSENT and the way of orthodoxy are apt to be one
and the same. Although Katherine Anne Porter consistently attacks
"the military police of orthodoxy" in her essays, she does so not
out of lack of faith but by "compulsion of belief," because she, like
Thomas Hardy, is committed to the faith of "the Inquirers." [1] The articles of this faith, which, I suppose, is what Miss Porter means when
she speaks of the "continuous, central interest and preoccupation of
[my] lifetime," [2] include insistence that the artist be concerned with the
fate of individual human beings, with the individual's need for recognizing, understanding, and accepting his human opportunities, responsibilities, and limitations as an animal in nature; emphasis upon the use
of reason, tempered by a suspicion that mysterious, irrational forces
working in man's unconscious mind may invalidate reason and cause
him to rationalize, to delude himself; awareness of the seething internal

[1] "Notes on a Criticism of Thomas Hardy," *Southern Review*, VI (1940), 150–161.
[2] *The Days Before* (New York: Harcourt, Brace and Co., 1952), p. vii.

realities which often are obscured by external appearances; rejection of dogmas that provide easy answers to problems that may, after all, have no solutions; tolerance of the inquisitive spirit in man which enables him to participate with joy in everyday life and which causes him to attempt to see through his illusions, to discover what is "true" for him. Concomitants of Miss Porter's creed are her devotion to truth-telling (i.e., the art of fiction), her skepticism of abstract theories, and her exalted view of the devout artist, who, though he is only human, endued with the responsibilities of other men, is as worthy as the saint. Because Miss Porter's preoccupation is essentially religious, it is appropriate that such expressions as "saints and artists," the "vocation" of the artist, and the poet's songs to the "greater glory of life" recur in her essays.[3]

※ ※

Katherine Anne Porter's acceptance of her literary calling—"the basic and absorbing occupation, the line intact of my life, which directs my actions, determines my point of view, profoundly affects my character and personality, my social beliefs and economic status, and the kind of friendships I form"[4]—led to her early rejection of the orthodox religious and social beliefs accepted for generations by her family. Born in Indian Creek, Texas, on May 15, 1890, Miss Porter belongs to "the last generation" that reached maturity in the twenties, the jazz age. The world she knew as a child was governed by a fixed code administered by her Kentucky grandmother, her father, her uncles and aunts. This old order, nurtured during the Victorian age, knew what to expect from a young girl of good family and proper upbringing. But Miss Porter, a proud great-great-great granddaughter of Daniel Boone, confounded the family's expectations: when she was sixteen, she ran away from a Catholic convent school and was married.[5] The following year she left Texas, as she later commented, to escape "the South because I didn't want to

---

[3] *The Days Before, passim.*

[4] "Autobiographical Sketch," *Authors Yesterday and Today,* ed. S. J. Kunitz (New York: H. W. Wilson Co., 1933), p. 538.

[5] Three years later, she was divorced. She was subsequently married (in 1933) to Eugene Pressly, an American career diplomat, and (in 1938) to Albert R. Erskine, Jr., an English teacher at Louisiana State University. These marriages also ended in divorces.

be regarded as a freak. That was how they regarded a woman who tried to write. I had to make a rebellion. . . . When I left, they were all certain I was going to live an immoral life. It was a confining society in those days." [6]

But Miss Porter's rebellion was not complete; she did not intend it to be. Wherever she lived, whether in New Orleans, Chicago, Denver, New York, Hollywood, Bermuda, Mexico City, France, Spain, Germany, or Switzerland, she discovered within herself a past which somehow seemed to shape her present life, to determine her character and her fate. She desired to understand that past, to rediscover that childhood world and the familiar, though, enigmatic, human beings who peopled it. In a far-off country where she could be fascinated by a new landscape with its mysterious inhabitants, Miss Porter found the "constant exercise of memory . . . to be the chief occupation of my mind, and all my experience seems to be simply memory with continuity, marginal notes, constant revision and comparison of one thing with another." [7] Neither abstract speculation nor rationalization about the meaning of life, but exact memory of past events concerned her. She set about to resist "one of the most disturbing habits of the human mind . . . its willful and destructive forgetting of whatever in its past does not confirm or flatter its present point of view." [8] Like Henry James, Miss Porter was determined to obtain "knowledge at the price of finally, utterly 'seeing through' everything" [9]—everything, even a sheltered childhood, which by most standards was fortunate and happy.

Critical as Miss Porter is of the inadequacies of the old order, she does not completely reject it or despise it. She understands what it can mean to live in a world in which people do not share ideas, intuitions, habits, and customs; so she values the stable society in which "there is no groping for motives, no divided faith: [the Mexican peons] love their past with that uncritical, unquestioning devotion which is beyond logic and above reason. Order and precision they know by heart. Instinctive

[6] Archer Winsten, "The Portrait of an Artist," *New York Post*, May 6, 1937, p. 17. (An early interview.)

[7] "Notes on Writing," *New Directions, 1940*, ed. James Laughlin (Norfolk, Conn.: New Directions, 1940), p. 203.

[8] *Ibid.*, p. 203.

[9] "The Days Before," *Kenyon Review*, V (Autumn, 1943), 492.

obedience to the changeless laws of nature, strait fidelity to their inner sense mark all they do." [10] And she admires Henry James partly because

> nothing came to supplant or dislocate in any way [his] early affections and attachments and admirations. This is not to say he never grew beyond them, nor that he did not live to question them, for he did both; but surely no one ever projected more lovingly and exactly the climate of youth, of budding imagination, the growth of the tender, perceptive mind, the particular freshness and keenness of feeling, the unconscious generosity and warmth of heart of the young brought up in the dangerous illusion of safety; and though no writer ever 'grew up' with more sobriety and pure intelligence, still there lay at the back of his mind the memory of a lost paradise; it was in the long run the standard by which he measured the world he learned so thoroughly. . . .[11]

For Miss Porter, too, the old stable order provides the standard by which the failures (and the occasional successes) of modern man in a chaotic, mechanized world are measured. But for her the old order shares the responsibility for some of the failures of the new. And Miss Porter's memories of the matriarchal world of her childhood did not permit her to describe it as a lost paradise, because the old order had its serious failures, too, its abnegation of important human needs and desires.

※　※

Victorian morality, the bulwark of the old, settled Southern society of Miss Porter's childhood, was based on such orthodox dogmas as original sin, the existence of a personal God, the purposiveness of all human life, the need for regarding man's life on earth as preparation for a refined spiritual life after death. When Miss Porter left the care of her family and moved out of the South, she revolted against not only the customs of the old order but also its fundamental convictions. The traditional dogmas of orthodox Christianity, Miss Porter came to believe, could only hinder the artist, who must find his own answers, his own truths. In a violent attack upon T. S. Eliot for his criticism of Thomas Hardy, Miss Porter renounces the tradition of orthodoxy and

---

[10] *Outline of Mexican Popular Arts and Crafts* (Los Angeles: Young & M'Callister, Inc., 1922), p. 39.
[11] "The Days Before," p. 494.

moves, with Hardy, "into another tradition of equal antiquity, equal importance, equal seriousness, a body of opinion running parallel throughout history to the body of law in church and state: the tradition of dissent." [12]

Recognizing "the unbridgable abyss" between the questions posed by Hardy and the answers offered by the orthodox Mr. Eliot, Miss Porter asserts that "the yawning abyss between question and answer remains the same, and until this abyss is closed the dissent will remain, persistent, obdurate, a kind of church in itself, with its leaders, teachers, saints, martyrs, heroes; a thorn in the flesh of Orthodoxy, but I think not necessarily of the devil on that account." [13] Intent upon probing her own world for the meaning of what she sees, hears, feels, thinks, Miss Porter is unwilling to relinquish her calling, the art of fiction, by accepting the catechism she was taught at the convent school; but she concedes that "there is at the heart of the universe a riddle no man can solve, and in the end God may be the answer." [14]

Perhaps what Miss Porter most deplores about organized religion is its misdirection of men, its cynicism and false otherworldly orientation. Man's mysticism, Miss Porter complains, "has been harnessed rudely to machinery of the most mundane sort, and has been made to serve the ends of an organization which ruling under divine guidance, has ruled very little better, and in some respects, worse, than certain frankly man-made systems of government." [15] Organized religion, she continues, has justified "the most cynical expedients of worldly government by a high morality" and committed "the most savage crimes against human life for the love of God." [16] Furthermore, the leaders of the church, often "God-intoxicated mystics and untidy saints with only a white blaze of divine love where their minds should have been," are "perpetually creating as much disorder within the law as outside it." [17] Miss Porter, aware of man's self-deception, distrusts mystics because "the most dangerous people in the world are the illuminated ones

---

[12] "Notes on a Criticism of Thomas Hardy," p. 153.
[13] *Ibid.*, pp. 153–154.
[14] *Ibid.*, p. 155.
[15] *Ibid.*, p. 155.
[16] *Ibid.*, p. 155.
[17] *Ibid.*, p. 154.

through whom forces act when they themselves are unconscious of their own motives." [18]

The proper concern of man, according to Miss Porter, is the visible world. She rejects the theological notion that "the world [is] a testing ground for the soul of man in preparation for eternity, and that his sufferings [are] part of a 'divine' plan, or indeed, so far as the personal fate of mankind [is] concerned, of any plan at all." [19] Instead, she insists upon a humanistic, this-worldly orientation, for "both malevolence and benevolence originated in the mind of man, and the warring forces [are] within him alone; such plan as [exists] in regard to him he [has] created for himself, his Good and his Evil [are] alike the mysterious inventions of his own mind." [20] The tangible world was the one Miss Porter would have, so she, like Henry James, "strained and struggled outward to meet it, to absorb it, to understand it, to be part of it." [21]

Since Miss Porter believes that men bring evil upon themselves by attributing human ills to divine providence and by preparing for a spiritual after-life instead of concerning themselves with the everyday world, she insists upon the efficacy of social reform: "man could make the earth a more endurable place for himself if he would." [22] She believes, with Hardy, in the use of "reasonableness: the use of intelligence directed towards the best human solution of human ills." [23] But, while Miss Porter expects men to use reason to ameliorate human suffering, she qualifies whatever optimism might be implicit in her faith in reasonableness by her conviction that "the refusal to acknowledge the evils in ourselves which therefore are implicit in any human situation is as unworkable a proposition as the doctrine of total depravity." [24] These

[18] "James's *The Turn of the Screw*," *New Invitation to Learning*, ed. Mark Van Doren (New York: Random House, 1942), p. 230. Cf. "A Bright Particular Faith," *Hound and Horn*, VII (January, 1934), 246–257; and "A Goat for Azazel," *Partisan Review*, VII (May, 1940), 188–199. In these chapters from an unfinished biography of Cotton Mather, Miss Porter seems most impressed with the egotism, pride, and self-deception of the early American "saint."

[19] "Notes on a Criticism of Thomas Hardy," p. 157.

[20] *Ibid.*, p. 157.

[21] "The Days Before," p. 492.

[22] "Notes on a Criticism of Thomas Hardy," p. 156.

[23] *Ibid.*, p. 156.

[24] "Love and Hate," *Mademoiselle*, October, 1948, p. 204.

evils are inherent in man's unconscious life; they belong to that part of human nature which is "not grounded in commonsense, [that] deep place . . . where the mind does not go, where the blind monsters sleep and wake, war among themselves and feed upon death." [25] This irrational element in human nature is "not subject to mathematical equation or the water-tight theories of dogma, and this intransigent, measureless force [is] divided against itself, in conflict with its own system of laws and the unknown laws of the universe." [26]

༘ ༘

Respect for the dignity of the individual, whose complicated life, both conscious and unconscious, cannot be explained away by ingenious theories or impressive abstract words, enables Miss Porter to reject the dogmatic line of political parties as well as religious sects. The artist, Miss Porter believes, cannot restrict his view by adhering to a party line because "all working practical political systems . . . are based upon and operate in contempt of human life and the individual fate; in accepting any one of them and shaping his mind and work to that mold, the artist dehumanizes himself, unfits himself for the practice of an art." [27] Commending Eudora Welty for escaping "a militant social consciousness," Miss Porter observes that Miss Welty is supported by "an ancient system of ethics, an unanswerable, indispensable moral law," which has "never been the particular property of any party or creed or nation," but which relates to "that true and human world of which the artist is a living part; and when he dissociates himself from it in favor of political, which is to say, inhuman, rules, he cuts himself away from his proper society—living men." [28]

The artist's job of work is to deal with the "true and human world" he himself knows. He does this not as that "parochial visitor," Mr.

[25] "Notes on a Criticism of Thomas Hardy," p. 157.

[26] *Ibid.*, p. 157.

[27] Introduction, *A Curtain of Green*, by Eudora Welty (New York: Doubleday, Doran and Co., 1941), pp. xiii–xiv.

[28] *Ibid.*, p. xiii. Cf. "Corridos," *Survey*, LII (May, 1924), 158. "Such things [as revolution] are ephemerae to the maker of ballads. He is concerned with the eternal verities."

Eliot, legislates, for the edification of his audience; "in the regions of art, as religion, edification is not the highest form of intellectual or spiritual existence." [29] The artist's creations, Miss Porter believes, "are considerably richer, invoked out of deeper sources in the human consciousness, more substantially nourishing than this lukewarm word can express." [30] Thus, her own work has been an attempt "to discover and understand human motives, human feelings, to make a distillation of what human relations and experiences my mind has been able to absorb." [31] And her admiration is for the writer who, like Katherine Mansfield, with "fine objectivity" bares "a moment of experience, real experience, in the life of some human being; [Miss Mansfield] states no belief, gives no motives, airs no theories, but simply presents to the reader a situation, a place, and a character, and there it is; and the emotional content is present implicitly as the germ is in the wheat." [32] This comes very close to being a description of Miss Porter's own method of composition, which is to record objectively her exact memory of life as she knows it, to avoid rationalizations, to trust her reader to find within the story or short novel the unifying and informing theme or symbol. Miss Porter begins with an image, an incident, a character: "a section here and a section there has been written—little general scenes explored and developed. Or scenes or sketches of characters which were never intended to be incorporated in the finished work have been developed in the process of trying to understand the full potentiality of the material." [33] At the critical moment, "thousands of memories converge, harmonize, arrange themselves around a central idea in a coherent form, and I write a story." [34]

Since Miss Porter's "aesthetic bias, [her] one aim is to tell a straight story and to give true testimony," [35] she is convinced that the artist must retain a close, vital connection with society. She agrees with Diego Rivera's objection to early Mexican artists who "were still thrall to the

[29] "Notes on a Criticism of Thomas Hardy," p. 154.
[30] *Ibid.*, p. 154.
[31] "The Situation in American Writing," *Partisan Review*, VI (Summer, 1939), 38.
[32] "The Art of Katherine Mansfield," *Nation*, CXLV (October 23, 1937), 436.
[33] "Notes on Writing," p. 203.
[34] *Ibid.*, p. 203.
[35] "Autobiographical Sketch," p. 539.

idea that the artist is an entity distinct from the human world about him, mysteriously set apart from the community; . . . they still regarded painting as a priestly function. This is an old superstition, and though the artist did not invent it, he became ultimately its victim." [36] While Miss Porter looks upon her work as a "vocation," a "calling," [37] and sometimes feels that "only the work of saints and artists gives us any reason to believe the human race is worth belonging to," [38] she distrusts the romantic, illuminated artist: "I think the influence of Whitman on certain American writers has been disastrous, for he encourages them in the vices of self-love (often disguised as love of humanity, or the working classes, or God), the assumption of prophetic powers, of romantic superiority to the limitations of craftsmanship, inflated feeling, and slovenly expression." [39] Like Rivera, she feels that "when art becomes a cult of individual eccentricity, a meager precious and neurasthenic body struggling for breath; when it becomes modish and exclusive, the aristocratic pleasure of the few, it is a dead thing." [40] Miss Porter considers the artist's obligations to society to be "the plain and simple responsibility of any other human being, for I refuse to separate the artist from the human race." [41] The artist should expect no special privileges from society, no "guarantee of economic security"; for he "cannot be a hostile critic of society and expect society to feed [him] regularly. The artist of the present is demanding (I think childishly) that he be given, free, a great many irreconcilable rights and privileges." [42]

Preferring the kind of art that aims at "a perfect realism, a complete statement of the thing [the artist] sees," Miss Porter expects the artist to write about his own familiar country, the world and people he knows

[36] "The Guild Spirit in Mexican Art" (as told to Katherine Anne Porter by Diego Rivera), *Survey*, LII (May, 1924), 175.

[37] Cf. "Homage to Ford Madox Ford," *New Directions, Number 7*, ed. James Laughlin (Norfolk, Conn.: New Directions, 1942), p. 175.

[38] "Transplanted Writers," *Books Abroad*, XVI (July, 1942), 274.

[39] "The Situation in American Writing," p. 36.

[40] "The Guild Spirit in Mexican Art," p. 175. Cf. "Gertrude Stein: A Self-Portrait," *Harper's*, CXCV (December, 1947), 519–528.

[41] "The Situation in American Writing," p. 39. Cf. "Transplanted Writers," p. 274.

[42] *Ibid.*, p. 38.

best.[43] She early took issue with critics who complained that the guild art of Mexico was provincial and lacked sophistication: "a peasant art," she wrote, "is what it is, what it should be." [44] Miss Porter also disagreed with the editors of *Partisan Review* who (when it was fashionable) were critical of the renewed emphasis in American literature on the specifically native elements in contemporary culture; she thought "the 'specifically American' things might not be the worst things for us to cultivate, since this is America and we are Americans, and our history is not altogether disgraceful." [45] Thus, her enthusiasm could be aroused by such a writer as Willa Cather, who was

> a provincial, and I hope not the last. She was a good artist, and all true art is provincial in the most realistic sense: of the very time and place of its making, out of human beings who are so particularly limited by their situation, whose faces and names are real and whose lives begin each one at an individual unique center. Indeed, Willa Cather was as provincial as Hawthorne, or Flaubert, or Turgenev, or Jane Austen.[46]

Besides reflecting Miss Porter's special interest in her own particular region, her strong defense of provincialism is an extension of her skepticism of modern industrial progress, which, she fears, destroys individuality and results in an empty uniformitarianism. Miss Porter further suspects that should the artist be removed from his "fructifying contact with his mother earth, condemned daily to touch instead the mechanics and artifices of modern progress, he might succumb as do the aristocratic arts, . . . to the overwhelming forces of a world turned dizzyingly by a machine." [47] While Miss Porter directs her irony at the "myth creativeness which has always marked the ideas of man pitiably eager to explain himself to himself, to open the door to eternity with the

[43] *Outline of Mexican Popular Arts and Crafts*, p. 42. Cf. "Defoe's *Moll Flanders*," *New Invitation to Learning*, p. 143. "I like the introspective novel very much,... but I do think that the weakness of it is that when a novelist gets inside a character, he finds only himself, and the great art really is to be able to look at the world and individuals and present characters that readers will recognize and will know or feel they know." Cf. "The Days Before," p. 491.

[44] *Ibid.*, p. 33.

[45] "The Situation in American Writing," p. 38.

[46] "The Calm, Pure Art of Willa Cather," *New York Times Book Review*, Sept. 25, 1949, p. 1.

[47] *Outline of Mexican Popular Arts and Crafts*, p. 38.

key of his human imagination," she values the "symbols of the racial mind" that the artist can discover by concerning himself with individuals of a particular time and place.[48]

Related to Miss Porter's taste for provincial literature is her conviction that really good art, like the early twentieth-century peasant art of Mexico, must be natural, organic—"a living thing that grows as a tree grows, thrusting up from its roots and saps, knots and fruits and tormented branches, without an uneasy feeling that it should be refined for art's sake." [49] The writer, too, must come by his art organically; artistic technique "is an internal matter." [50] A writer is "dyed in his own color; it is useless to ask him to change his faults or his virtues; he must . . . work out his own salvation." [51] The art of fiction "cannot be taught, but only learned by the individual in his own way, at his own pace and his own time." [52] Or, as Miss Porter once advised young writers, "if you have any personality of your own, you will have a style of your own; it grows, as your ideas grow, and as your knowledge of your craft increases." [53]

Although Miss Porter seems to accept an organic theory of art, she prefers Henry James to such an "organic" writer as Whitman, because she holds with "the conscious disciplined artist, the serious expert against the expansive, indiscriminately 'cosmic' sort." [54] Her skepticism moves in two directions—against the academic teacher and the literary cult that obstructs the artist from following his calling in his own individual way, and against the egotistical artist who wants to express himself, to become (as Emerson wanted to) the mystical eyeball of the universe. Miss Porter considers the artist's job to be the creation of order, of form, but she does not value technical virtuosity for its own sake: "unless my material, my feelings, my problems on each new . . . work are not well ahead of my technical skill at the moment, I should distrust the whole thing. When virtuosity gets the upper hand of your theme, or is better than your idea, it is time to

---

[48] *Ibid.*, pp. 5, 9.
[49] *Ibid.*, p. 33.
[50] "Notes on Writing," p. 195.
[51] "The Situation in American Writing," p. 35.
[52] Introduction, *A Curtain of Green*, p. xii.
[53] "No Plot, My Dear, No Story," *Writer*, LV (1942), 168.
[54] "The Situation in American Writing," p. 34.

quit." [55] Miss Porter's concern with problems of style, then, stems from her desire to curb the artist's emotional tendencies and to make his ideas more precise.

Miss Porter's interest in the technical problems of her craft also results from her affinity for "the new way of writing." [56] But the new movement in literature involved much more than a change of style; it included a view of reality that (its adherents thought) was radically different from that of Arnold Bennett or H. G. Wells or other Edwardian writers. The Edwardians described the fabric of things, the externals, but the new writers were to be concerned with the internal reality, the truth of the human heart. Miss Porter found in Virginia Woolf's first novel, *The Voyage Out*, "the same sense of truth I had got in early youth from Laurence Sterne . . . , from Jane Austen, from Emily Brontë, from Henry James." [57] These and W. B. Yeats, James Joyce, T. S. Eliot, and Ezra Pound seemed "in the most personal way . . . to be my contemporaries; their various visions of reality merged for me into one vision, one world view." [58]

To express this vision of reality adequately a writer needed new techniques, new forms; he needed to develop an exact, nondiscursive fiction which could simultaneously contain detailed, objective description and intricate patterns of symbols. In his own way, each writer Miss Porter admires had developed the necessary tools. Miss Porter values James's "extreme sense of the appearance of things, manners, dress, social customs, [through which] he could convey mysterious but deep impressions of individual character." [59] She also could admire in Katherine Mansfield's stories "the sense of human beings living on many planes at once with all the elements justly ordered and in right proportion." [60] Miss Porter's acceptance of the new world view and her desire to find a proper vehicle to contain it result in her "deeply personal interest" in the kind of story "where external act and the internal voiceless life of the imagination almost meet and mingle on the mysterious threshold between

---

[55] "Notes on Writing," p. 196.
[56] "Example to the Young," *New Republic*, LXVI (April 22, 1931), 279.
[57] "Virginia Woolf's Essays," *New York Times Book Review*, May 7, 1950, p. 3.
[58] *Ibid.*, p. 3.
[59] "The Days Before," p. 491.
[60] "The Art of Katherine Mansfield," p. 436.

dream and waking, one reality refusing to admit or confirm the existence of the other, yet both conspiring toward the same end."[61]

¤ ¤

Like Willa Cather, Katherine Anne Porter never has been primarily concerned with literary theory. And so Miss Porter's critical position may sometimes seem ambiguous, at times even contradictory. Her preference for the conscious artist who is alert to the technical problems of his craft, for instance, may seem to contradict her advocacy of an organic theory apparently akin to that of Whitman, whose "expansive, indiscriminate 'cosmic'" impulse the skeptical, rational Miss Porter distrusts. And her concept of the poet as a "seer" set apart and to be trusted more than other men may not be entirely compatible with her notion of the poet as being like other men, with the usual social responsibilities and privileges.[62]

But the most striking paradox in Miss Porter's position emerges from her consistent definition of the nature of her devotion to her "basic and absorbing occupation," for Miss Porter's language suggests religious devotion and faith: she speaks of art as a "calling," of "saints and artists," of giving "true testimony," of the "indispensable moral law," of the necessity for "order and precision," of the "only two possibilities for any real order: art and religion." The paradox of Miss Porter's negation of the orthodoxy of her Catholic family, of her denial of social and political authoritarianism, is that its end is affirmation: extremes meet; "the way up and the way down is one and the same," as Heraclitus was wont to say and as the orthodox T. S. Eliot seems to agree (in "Burnt Norton"). For Miss Porter—ironically, in view of her skepticism—declares her faith in the continuity of human life through art. The arts, Miss Porter declares,

> do live continuously, and they live literally by faith; their names and their shapes and their uses and their basic meanings survive unchanged in all that matters through times of interruption, diminishment, neglect; they outlive governments and creeds and the societies, even the very civilizations that produced them. They cannot be destroyed altogether

---

[61] Introduction, *A Curtain of Green*, p. xviii.

[62] Cf. "Quetzalcoatl," *New York Herald Tribune Books*, March 7, 1926, p. 1; and "The Situation in American Writing," p. 39.

because they represent the substance of faith and the only reality. They are what we find again when the ruins are cleared away. And even the smallest and most incomplete offering at this time can be a proud act of faith in defense of that faith.[63]

Like Henry James, Miss Porter's quest for moral definition led not to philosophy or religion but to art. She thus became the inheritor of a great tradition—the tradition of dissent and inquiry, of selfless devotion to the search for meaning and order in the world of fiction.

[63] Introduction, *Flowering Judas and Other Stories* (New York: Modern Library, 1940), p. ii.

V

M. M. Liberman

The Responsibility of the Novelist

THE TITLE of this essay is, I suppose, somewhat misleading, in the way that a title can be, when it seems to promise a discourse on an arguable concept. In this instance it suggests a certain premise: namely, that the question, "What does the author owe society?" is one which still lives and breathes. In fact, I think it does not. I suspect, rather, that its grave can be located somewhere between two contentions: André Gide's that the artist is under no moral obligation to present a useful idea, but that he is under a moral obligation to present an idea well; and Henry James's, that we are being arbitrary if we demand, to begin with, more of a novel than that it be interesting. As James uses the word *novel* here, I take it to mean any extended, largely realistic, narrative fiction, but his view is applicable as well to fiction in other forms and modes.

If a literary work is more than immediately engaging, if, for example, it stimulates the moral imagination, it is doing more than is fairly required of it as art.

Why, then, if I think it is in most respects dead, do I choose to raise the question of the writer's responsibility? The answer is that I do not choose to raise the question. The question is continually being raised for me, and because literature is my profession, it haunts my house. Thus, I am moved to invoke certain commonplaces, as above, of a sort I had supposed to be news only to sophomore undergraduates. This was the case markedly on the occasion of the publication of Katherine Anne Porter's *Ship of Fools* in 1962. Twenty years in the making, a book club selection even before it was set up in type, restlessly awaited by a faithful coterie, reviewed widely and discussed broadly almost simultaneously with its appearance on the store shelves, this book caused and still causes consternation in the world of contemporary letters to a degree which I find interesting, curious, and suspect. The focus of this paper will be on the critical reception of this book and I hope that the relevance of what remains of the responsibility question will issue naturally from it. Finally, I must quote at awkward length, in two instances, in order to be fair to other commentators.

The first brief waves of reviews were almost unanimous in their praise of *Ship of Fools* and then very shortly the many dissenting opinions began to appear, usually in the most respectable intellectual journals where reviewers claim to be, and often are, critics. These reviews were characterized by one of two dominant feelings: bitter resentment or acute disappointment. A remarkable instance of the former appeared in the very prestigious journal, *Commentary* (October, 1962), as its feature article of the month, under the byline of one of its associate editors. That Miss Porter's book should have been originally well-received so rankled *Commentary*'s staff that a lengthy rebuttal was composed, taking priority over other articles on ordinarily more-pressing subjects, such as nuclear destruction and race violence. The article progresses to a frothing vehemence in its later pages. I will quote from the opening of the piece which begins relatively calmly, as follows:

> Whatever the problems were that kept Katherine Anne Porter's *Ship of Fools* from appearing during the past twenty years, it has been leading a charmed life ever since it was published last March. In virtually a single voice, a little cracked and breathless with excitement, the reviewers annnounced that Miss Porter's long-awaited first novel was a "triumph," a "masterpiece," a "work of genius . . . a momentous work of fiction." "a

phenomenal, rich, and delectable book," a "literary event of the highest magnitude. . . ."

Riding the crest of this wave of acclaim, *Ship of Fools* made its way to the top of the best-seller lists in record time and it is still there as I write in mid-September. During these four months, it has encountered virtually as little opposition in taking its place among the classics of literature as it did in taking and holding its place on the best-seller lists. A few critics . . . wound up by saying that *Ship of Fools* fell somewhat short of greatness, but only after taking the book's claim to greatness with respectful seriousness. Some of the solid citizens among the reviewers, like John K. Hutchens, found the novel to be dull and said so. Here and there, mainly in the hinterlands, a handful of independent spirits . . . suspected that the book was a failure. But who was listening?

Prominent among the circumstances which have helped to make a run-away best-seller and a *succés d'estime* out of this massive, unexciting, and saturnine novel was the aura of interest, partly sentimental and partly deserved, that Miss Porter's long struggle with it had produced. Most of the reviews begin in the same way: a distinguished American short-story writer at the age of seventy-one has finally finished her first novel after twenty years of working on it. As this point was developed, it tended to establish the dominant tone of many reviews—that of an elated witness to a unique personal triumph, almost as though this indomitable septuagenarian had not written a book, but had done something even more remarkable—like swimming the English Channel.

The *Commentary* critic goes on to charge Miss Porter with having written a novel contemptible in two decisive ways: (1) badly executed in every conceivable technical sense, particularly characterization and (2) unacceptable on moral grounds, being pessimistic and misanthropic. "But the soul of humanity is lacking," he says, quoting still another reviewer sympathetic to his own position. Why Dostoevsky, for example, is permitted to be both massive and saturnine and Miss Porter not is a question spoken to later only by implication. The critic's charge that her writing is "unexciting" is curious considering his own high emotional state in responding to the work. The charge of misanthropy is, of course, directly related to the alleged technical failure of the characterization, which he says "borders on caricature" in the way it portrays nearly every human type as loathesome and grotesque, with hardly a single redeeming feature. In considering the charge of misanthropy we are, perforce, confronted with the question of the writer's social responsibility in the moral sphere, for the attribution of misanthropy to a writer by a critic is typically a censure and is seldom merely a description of the writer's stance. The writer is usually, as in this case, denied the right to be misanthropic on the ground that it is immoral to hate and, given the writer's influential function, it is deemed irresponsible of him to clothe such a negative sentiment as hate in intellectually attractive garb. In my efforts at synthesis, I will get back to these questions. But for the moment I should like to point out that *Commentary*'s view of *Ship of Fools* as depicting mankind in a hatefully distorted, therefore, untruthful, therefore, immoral way, is in fact the view of the book commonly held by the normally intelligent and reasonably well-educated reader of fiction, if my impressions are accurate.

I turn now to the other mode of reception: acute disappointment. One of the most clearly and intelligently presented of this group was Professor Wayne Booth's critique in the *Yale Review* (Summer, 1962) from which I quote, in part, as follows:

> Katherine Anne Porter's long-awaited novel is more likely to fall afoul of one's bias for finely-constructed, concentrated plots. In this respect her own earlier fiction works against her; part of the strength of those classics, *Pale Horse, Pale Rider* and *Noon Wine,* lies in their concision, their economy, their simplicity. *There* is *my* Katherine Anne Porter, I am tempted to protest, as she offers me, now, something so different as to be almost unrecognizable—a 225,000-word novel (more words, I suppose, than in all of the rest of her works put together) with nearly fifty characters. What is worse, the manner of narration is fragmented, diluted. Her plan is to create a shipload of lost souls and to follow them, isolated moment by isolated moment, in their alienated selfishness, through the nasty, exasperating events of a twenty-seven day voyage, in 1931, from Veracruz to Bremerhaven. She deliberately avoids concentrating strongly on any one character; even the four or five that are granted some sympathy are kept firmly, almost allegorically, subordinated to the portrayal of the ship of fools ("I am a passenger on that ship," she reminds us in an opening note).
>
> Her method is sporadic, almost desultory, and her unity is based on theme and idea rather than coherence of action. We flash from group to group, scene to scene, mind to mind, seldom remaining with any group or observer for longer than three or four pages together. While the book is as a result full of crosslights and ironic juxtapositions, it has, for me, no steady center of interest except the progressively more intense exemplification of its central truth: men are pitifully, foolishly self-alienated. At the heart of man lies a radical corruption that can only occasionally, fitfully, be overcome by love. . . .

Once the various groupings are established—the four isolated, self-torturing Americans, two of them lovers who hate and fear each other when they are not loving; the sixteen Germans, most of them in self-destructive family groups, and all but two of them repugnant almost beyond comedy; the depraved swarm of Spanish dancers with their two demon-children; the carefree and viciously irresponsible Cuban students; the half-mad, lost Spanish countess; the morose Swede; and so on—each group or lone traveler is taken to some sort of climactic moment, most often in the form of a bungled chance for genuine human contact. These little anti-climaxes are scattered throughout the latter fourth of the book, but for most of the characters the nadir is reached during the long "gala" evening, almost at the end of the journey. . . .

Such a work, lacking, by design, a grand causal, temporal sequence, depends for complete success on the radiance of each part; the reader must feel that every fragment as it comes provides proof of its own relevance in its illustrative power, or at least in its comic or pathetic or satiric intensity. For me only about half of the characters provide this kind of self-justification. There are many great things: moments of introspection, including some masterful dreams, from the advanced young woman and the faded beauty; moments of clear and effective observation of viciousness and folly. But too often one finds, when the tour of the passenger list is undertaken again and again, that it is too much altogether. Why, why did Miss Porter feel that she should try to get everything in?

Since a useful version of Aristotle's *Poetics* has been available to us, there have been critics who have been engaged in what has been called criticism proper, the task of determining what literature in general is, and what a given work of literature in particular is. One fundamental assumption of criticism proper is that by a more and more refined classification, according to a work's properties, all literature can be first divided into kinds and sub-kinds. Ideally, and as such a process becomes more and more discriminating and precise, and as the subdivisions become small and smaller, criticism will approach the individual work. Accordingly the proper critic assumes that all questions of evaluation, including, of course, moral evaluation, are secondary to and issue from questions of definition. Or to put yet otherwise, the proper critic asks: How can we tell what a work means, let alone whether it's good or bad, if we don't know what it is to begin with?

At this turn, I call attention to the fact that in none of my own references to *Ship of Fools* have I spoken of it as a novel. The *Com-*

mentary editor calls it a novel and Mr. Booth calls it a novel, and in the very process of describing what it is about this alleged novel that displeases them, they go a long way toward unintentionally defining the work as something else altogether. But instead of evaluating *Ship of Fools* on the grounds of their own description of its properties, both insist on ignoring this analytical data, making two substitutions in its stead: (1) the publisher's word for it that *Ship of Fools* is a novel and (2) their own bias as to how the work would have to be written to have been acceptable as a novel. Mr. Booth is both candid and disarming in making explicit his bias for finely-constructed, concentrated plots. To entertain a preference for *Pride and Prejudice* or *The Great Gatsby* over, say, *Moby Dick* or *Finnegans Wake* is one thing and legitimate enough in its way. To insist, however, that the latter two works are inferior because their integrity does not depend on traditional plot structure would be to risk downgrading two admittedly monumental works in a very arbitrary and dubious way. Finally, to insist that every long work of prose fiction should be as much like *Pride and Prejudice* as possible is to insist that every such work be not only a novel, but a nineteenth-century one at that.

The *Commentary* critique has its own bias which is not, however, stated explicitly. It is the bias of the journal itself as much as of the critic, and is one it shares with many another respectable publication whose voice is directed at an audience it understands to have a highly developed, independent, post-Freudian, post-Marxist, humanitarian social consciousness. Neither especially visionary, nor especially doctrinaire, such a publication has, typically, nevertheless, a low tolerance for anything that smacks of the concept of original sin, having, as this concept does, a way of discouraging speculation about decisively improving the human lot. Miss Porter's book appears to take a dim view of the behavior of the race and that is enough for the intellectual journal, despite its implied claim to broad views and cultivated interests, including an interest in fiction. The aggrieved critic cannot come down from high dudgeon long enough to see that a view of literature as merely an ideological weapon is in the first place a strangely puritanical one and wildly out of place in his pages. Secondly, there are a few more commonplaces about literature which are usually lost sight of in the urgency to claim that people are not all bad and therefore can and must be portrayed in fiction as likely candidates for salvation. Most works of fiction, *as anyone should know,* are not written to accomplish anything but themselves, but some works of fiction are written to demonstrate to the innocent that there is much evil in the world. And others are written to demonstrate to the initiated, but phlegmatic, that there is more evil than even they had supposed and that, moreover, this evil is closer to home than they can comfortably imagine. In any case, since fiction is by definition artificial, the author is within his rights in appearing to overstate the case for the desired results. It is nowhere everlastingly written that literature must have a sanguine, optimistic, and uplifting effect. Is there not sometimes something salutary in a work which has the effect of inducing disgust and functioning therefore as a kind of emetic? Had the critic given Miss Porter her due as an artist he might have seen that *Ship of Fools* condemns human folly, but it never once confuses good and evil. It is one thing to be a writer who smirks at human decency and argues for human destruction (Marquis de Sade)—it is another to be a writer who winces at human limitations and pleads by her tone, her attitude towards her readers, for a pained nod of agreement.

Said Dr. Johnson to the Honourable Thomas Erskine some 200 years ago: "Why, sir, if you were to read Richardson for the story, your impatience would be so much fretted that you would hang yourself. But you must read him for the sentiment." In the case of *Ship of Fools,* this sentiment is so consistent and so pervasive as to make us wonder how anyone could have scanted or mistaken it. It is the very opposite of misanthropy in that far from taking delight in exposing human foibles, in "getting" her characters' "number," Miss Porter's narrative voice has the quality of personal suffering even as it gives testimony. It seems to say: "This is the way with the human soul, as I knew it, at its worst, in the years just prior to the Second World War. And alas for all of us that it should have been so." By way of illustration, recall the characters Ric and Rac. I select them because Miss Porter's readers of all stripes agree that these two children, scarcely out of their swaddling clothes, are probably as thoroughly objectionable as any two fictional characters in all literature in English. Twin offspring of a pimp and a prostitute, they lie, steal, torture, attempt to murder a dumb animal, cause the death of an innocent man and fornicate incestuously; they are not very convincing as ordinary real children and for a very good reason. They are not meant to be. I cite a passage from that section where, having made a fiasco of their parents' larcenous schemes, they are punished by those parents:

> Tito let go of Rac and turned his fatherly discipline upon Ric. He seized his right arm by the wrist and twisted it very slowly and steadily until the shoulder was nearly turned in its socket and Ric went to his knees with a long howl that died away in a puppy-like whimper when the terrible hold was loosed. Rac, huddled on the divan nursing her bruises, cried again with him. Then Manolo and Pepe and Tito and Pancho, and Lola and Concha and Pastora and Amparo, every face masking badly a sullen fright, went away together to go over every step of this dismaying turn of affairs; with a few words and nods, they decided it would be best to drink coffee in the bar, to appear as usual at dinner, and to hold a rehearsal on deck afterwards. They were all on edge and ready to fly at each other's throats. On her way out, Lola paused long enough to seize Rac by the hair and shake her head until she was silenced, afraid to cry. When they were gone, Ric and Rac crawled into the upper berth looking for safety; they lay there half naked, entangled like some afflicted, misbegotten little monster in a cave, exhausted, mindless, soon asleep.

For 357 pages a case has been carefully built for the twins' monstrous natures. The reader has been induced to loathe the very sound of their names. Suddenly the same reader finds himself an eye witness to the degree of punishment he has privately imagined their deserving. But even as they are being terribly chastised they demonstrate an admirable recalcitrance and suddenly it is the adult world which appears villainous, monstrous and cruel. Finally, in the imagery of our last view of them, they are not demons altogether, or even primarily, but in their nakedness, which we see first, they are also merely infants and this is what does—or should—break the reader's heart. The reader is meant to sympathize, finally, with these hideous children, but more than that, his moral responses have been directed to himself. He has been led to ask himself: Who am I that I should have for so long despised these children, however demonic they are. Am I, then, any better than their parents?

When I contend that Ric and Rac are not meant to be taken as real children, I am agreeing for the moment with the *Commentary* critic who spoke of Miss Porter's method of characterization as caricature, as if to speak of this method so, were, *ipso facto*, to condemn it, as if realism were the only possible fictional mode and the only category into which a long fiction can be cast. But if *Ship of Fools* is not a novel, what would a novel be? I rely on the recent study by Sheldon Sacks, *Fiction and the Shape of Belief*, to define it as follows: a novel would be an action organized so that it introduces characters about whose fates the reader is made to care, in unstable relationships, which are then further complicated, until the complication is finally resolved, by the removal of the represented instability. This plainly is not *Ship of Fools*. Our most human feelings go out to Ric and Rac, but we cannot care further about them precisely *not* because we are made to hate them, but because they are clearly doomed to perpetual dehumanization by the adult world which spawned and nurtured them. In the same image in which Miss Porter represents them as helpless infants, she also declares them "mindless." The generally unstable relationships which define the roles of most of the other characters in the book remain unstable to the very end and are not so much resolved as they are revealed. The resolution of the manifold conflicts in the work is part of the encompassing action of the work, that which the reader can logically suppose will happen after the story closes. The Germans will march against Poland and turn Europe into a concentration camp. The others will, until it is too late, look the other way. This is a fact of history which overrides in importance the fact that no one on the ship can possibly come to good.

Nor is *Ship of Fools* a satire which is organized so that it ridicules objects external to the fictional world created in it. Rather, it is, I believe, a kind of modern apologue, a work organized as a fictional example of the truth of a formulable statement or a series of such statements. As such it owes more than its title to the didactic Christian verses of Sebastian Brant, whose *Das Narrenschiff*, *The Ship of Fools*, was published sometime between 1497 and 1548. Brant's work was very influential and no one thinks of it as misanthropic when he reads:

> The whole world lives in darksome night,
> In blinded sinfulness persisting,
> While every street sees fools existing
> Who know but folly, to their shame,
> Yet will not own to folly's name.
> Hence I have pondered how a ship
> Of fools I'd suitably equip—

A galley, brig, bark, skiff, or float,
A carack, scow, dredge, racing-boat,
A sled, cart, barrow, carryall—
One vessel would be far too small
To carry all the fools I know.
Some persons have no way to go
And like the bees they come a-skimming,
While many to the ship are swimming,
Each one wants to be the first.
A mighty throng with folly curst,
Whose pictures I have given here.
They who at writings like to sneer
Or are with reading not afflicted
May see themselves herewith depicted
And thus discover who they are.
Their faults, to whom they're similar.
For fools a mirror shall it be,
Where each his counterfeit may see.

As an apologue Miss Porter's work has more in common with John-son's *Rasselas* than with *Gone with the Wind*. As an apologue it not only has the right, it has the function by its nature to "caricature" its actors, to be "saturnine," to have a large cast, to be "fragmented" in its narration and above all, to quote Mr. Booth again, to achieve "unity based on theme and idea rather than coherence of action . . . [to have] no steady center of interest except the progressively more intense ex-emplification of its central truth. . . ."

In addition to calling attention to its formal properties for evaluating Miss Porter's book not as a novel but as something else, one ought to stand back a bit to see how the work fits a reasonable definition of the novel historically, that is, according to traditional and conventional themes and types of action. Recall that though the English word novel, to designate a kind of fiction, is derived from the Italian *novella*, mean-ing "a little new thing," this is not the word used in most European countries. That word is, significantly, *roman*. One forgets that a work of fiction, set in our own time, and thus bringing us knowledge of our own time, that is, news, is not, however a novel by that fact alone, but may be a literary form as yet undefined and, therefore, unnamed. For, in addition to bringing us news, the novel, if it is such on historical principles, must pay its respects to its forebears in more than a nominal way. It must do more than bear tales and look like the *Brothers Kara-mazov.* It must, I suspect, as a *roman,* be in some specific ways romantic.

We understand that the novel is the modern counterpart of various earlier forms of extended narrative. The first of these, the epic, was succeeded in the middle ages by the *romance* written at first like the epic, in verse, and later in prose as well. The romance told of the adventures of royalty and the nobility, introduced a heroine and made love a central theme. It relocated the supernatural realm from the court of Zeus to fairyland. The gods were replaced by magical spells and enchantments. When magical spells and enchantments were replaced, in the precursors of contemporary fiction, by the happy accident, the writer took unto himself a traditional given and the romantic tradition continued in the novel. When Henry James arranged for his heroine, Isabel Archer, to inherit a substantial sum of money from a relative who didn't know her, this was very Olympian of him; at any rate it was a piece of modern magic, legitimately granted to the novelist. Realist though he was, James recognized that the romantic element gets the novel going, frees the hero or heroine from those confinements of everyday life which make moral adventure undramatic. When in the most arbitrary way James makes Isabel an heiress he launches her on a quest for self-realization. He gives her her chance. Now in this connection, I quote again from *Ship of Fools:*

> While he [Freytag] shaved he riffled through his ties and selected one, thinking that people on voyage mostly went on behaving as if they were on dry land, and there is simply not room for it on a ship. Every smallest act shows up more clearly and looks worse, because it has lost its background. The train of events leading up to and explaining it is not there; you can't refer it back and set it in its proper size and place.

When Miss Porter, who could have put her cast of characters anywhere she wanted, elected to put them aboard ship, she made as if to free them, in the manner of a romance, for a moral quest; that is, they are ostensibly liberated, as if by magic, precisely because they *are* aboard ship—liberated from the conventions of family background, domestic responsibility, national custom, and race consciousness. Theoretically, they can now emerge triumphant at the end of the journey, over duplicity, cruelty, selfishness and bigotry. But they do not.

Freedom they are incapable of utilizing for humane ends. Freedom

Miss Porter can grant them, but since they are men of our time, they cannot, in her view, accept it responsibly. That is, they cannot make good use of their lucky accident because their freedom is only nominal. On the one hand, history has caught up with them; on the other hand, psychology has stripped their spiritual and emotional lives of all mystery. In Miss Porter's world the past is merely the genesis of neurosis (there is no point in pretending we've never heard of Freud) and the future, quite simply, is the destruction of Isabel Archer's Europe of infinite possibilities (there is no point in pretending we've never heard of Neville Chamberlain). *Ship of Fools* argues that romantic literary conventions do not work in the modern world, and emerges as even more remote from the idea of the novel than a study of its formal properties alone would suggest. One can see it finally as anti-novel.

In her 1940 introduction to *Flowering Judas,* Miss Porter says that she spent most of her "energies" and "spirit" in an effort to understand "the logic of this majestic and terrible failure of man in the Western world." This is the dominant theme of *Ship of Fools* as it is of all her writing. Nearly every character in the work is a staggering example of an aspect of this failure. And here is the only passage in the work emphasized by italics:

> What they were saying to each other was only, *Love me, love me in spite of all! Whether or not I love you, whether I am fit to love, whether you are able to love, even if there is no such thing as love, love me!*

Robert B. Heilman

Ship of Fools
Notes
on Style

KATHERINE ANNE PORTER is sometimes thought of as a stylist.
"Stylist" is likely to call up unclear images of coloratura, acrobatics,
elaborateness of gesture, a mingling of formalism probably euphuistic
with conspicuous private variations, like fingerprints. It might call to
mind Edward Dahlberg's peremptory dense texture of crusty archaism
and thorny image, a laboriously constructed thicket so well guarding
the estate of his mind that it often becomes that estate. It is not
so with Miss Porter. There is nothing of arresting facade in her style,
nothing of showmanship. Though on the lecture platform she can
be all showman, and slip into the prima donna, in her proper medium
both the public personality and the private being vanish from the stage.
At least they are not easily detectable presences. In *Ship of Fools* [1] the
style is a window of things and people, not a symbolic aggression of
ego upon them. It seems compelled by the objects in the fiction; it is

---

[1] I am arbitrarily limiting this essay to the latest work. One cannot talk about
style without using many examples; to bring in the stories and novellas would
expand the study to inordinate length.

their visible surface, the necessary verbal form that makes their identity perceivable. It seems never the construction of an artist imposing, from her own nature, an arbitrary identity upon inert materials, but rather an emanation of the materials themselves, finding through the artist as uninterfering medium the stylistic mold proper to their own nature. Miss Porter is ruling all, of course, but she seems not to be ruling at all: hence of her style we use such terms as "distance," "elegance," and of course the very word for what she seems to have ceded, "control." She is an absentee presence: in one sense her style is no-style. No-style is what it will seem if style means some notable habit of rhythm or vocabulary, some uninterchangeable (though not unborrowable) device that firmly announces "Faulkner" or "Hemingway." Miss Porter has no "signal" or call letters that identify a single station or wave length. She does not introduce herself or present herself. Much less does she gesticulate. She does not pray on street corners; wrestle with her subject in public as if she were barely managing to throw a troublesome devil; or lash her tail and arch her back like a cat demonstrating expertise with a mouse. She does not cry "Look, ma, no hands"; she just leaves hands out of it. Her style has neither birthmarks nor those plaintive rebirthmarks, tattoos. Not that she disdains embellishment; in her there is nothing of unwashed Kate in burlap ("I am life"). Nor, on the other hand, is there anything of frilly femininity tendering little dainties from a fragile sensibility ("I am beauty," "I am feeling").

彩　彩

No-style means a general style, if we may risk such a term, a fusion of proved styles. She can do ordinary documentary whenever it is called for: the ship's passengers "advertised on little thumbtacked slips of paper that they had lost or found jeweled combs, down pillows, tobacco pouches, small cameras, pocket mirrors, rosaries." Here she sticks to nouns; yet she has no fear of the adjectives somewhat in disrepute now: "In the white heat of an early August morning a few placid citizens of the white-linen class strolled across the hard-baked surface of the public square under the dusty shade of the sweet-by-night trees. . . ." She relies without embarrassment on the plain, direct, ordinary, explicit. Veracruz "is a little purgatory"; Amparo decided "prematurely" that trouble was over. "Herr Lowenthal, who had been put at a small table by himself, studied the dinner card, with its list of unclean foods, and asked for a soft omelette with fresh green peas. He drank half a bottle of good wine to comfort himself. . . ."

On such sturdy foundations of style she can build in several ways. Without altering the everyday, matter-of-fact manner, she gets below the surface. Glocken, the hunchback, "scared people off; his plight was so obviously desperate they were afraid some of it would rub off on them." "Rub off": imaging casually a world of prophylactic finickiness. Captain Thiele paces the deck "alone, returning the respectful salutations of the passengers with reluctant little jerks of his head, upon which sat a monumental ornate cap, white as plaster." The commonplace comparison, dropped in without commotion at the end, unobtrusively deflates the large official figure. Of a shipboard communion service: "The priest went through the ceremony severely and hastily, placing the wafers on the outstretched tongues expertly and snatching back his hand." The plain adverbs suggest a minor public official in a distasteful routine: "snatching," the fear of contamination. Mrs. Treadwell leaves a self-pitying young man: "If she stayed to listen, she knew she would weaken little by little, she would warm up in spite of herself, perhaps in the end identify herself with the other, take on his griefs and wrongs, and if it came to that, feel finally guilty as if she herself had caused them; yes, and he would believe it too, and blame her freely." The easy lucidity never shirks depths or darks, which to some writers seem approachable only by the involute, the cryptic, or the tortuous.

Using the kind of elements that she does, she can organize them, elaborately if need be, with control and grace. The local papers "cannot praise too much the skill with which the members of good society maintain in their deportment the delicate balance between high courtesy and easy merriment, a secret of the Veracruz world bitterly envied and unsuccessfully imitated by the provincial inland society of the Capital." Under the gentle irony and the rhythm that serves it, lie in easy and well articulated order a remarkable number of modifiers—such as Hardy would have fouled into knotty confusion, and James, pursuing precision, would have pried apart with preciosity in placement. She manages with equal skill the erection of ordinary terms, both concrete and analytical, into a periodic structure in which all elements converge unspectacularly on a climax of sudden insight: "The passengers, investigating the cramped airless quarters with their old-fashioned double tiers of bunks and a narrow hard couch along the opposite wall for the unlucky third comer, read the names on the doorplates—most of them German—eyed with suspicion and quick distaste luggage piled beside their own in their cabins, and each discovered again what he had believed lost for a while though he could not name it—his identity." A compact sketch of outer world and inner meaning, it is never crowded or awkward or rambling.

Luggage as guarantor of identity: it is the kind of true perception regularly conveyed in terms modest and unstraining, but fresh and competent. Of the troubles of boarding ship: "This common predicament did not by any means make of them fellow sufferers." Each kept "his pride and separateness within himself"; "there crept into eyes meeting unwillingly . . . a look of unacknowledged, hostile recognition. 'So there you are again, I never saw you before in my life,' the eyes said." Of David Scott's special capacity for triumph as a lover: "Feeling within him his coldness of heart as a real power in reserve, he . . . laid his hand over hers warmly"—with just a shadow of oxymoron to accent the reality without calling attention to itself. Jenny Brown, his girl, had a "fondness for nearness, for stroking, touching, nestling, with a kind of sensuality so diffused it almost amounted to coldness after all": the plain tactile words preparing for the shrewd analysis in which the paradox is not thrust triumphantly at one but offered almost experimentally. There is a good deal of this relaxed movement between the physical and the psychic or moral, each grasped directly and surely. The Spanish dancers "would look straight at you and laugh as if you were an object too comic to believe, yet their eyes were cold and they were not enjoying themselves, even at your expense." The vocabulary is hardly more than elementary, and the words are arranged in a classic compound structure, almost as in an exercise book, yet they communicate a disturbing hardness. The next sentence is of the same stamp but is trimmed back sharply to an almost skeletal simplicity: "Frau Hutten had observed them from the first and she was afraid of them." The fear is ours, but not through a tensed-up stylistic staging of fear.

Miss Porter can combine words unexpectedly without becoming ostentatious: for instance, an adjective denoting mood or value with a neutral noun—"serious, well-shaped head," "weak dark whiskers," or, more urgently, "strong white rage of vengeful sunlight"; or sex words with gastric facts—"They fell upon their splendid full-bodied German food with hot appetites." She pairs partly clashing words: "softened and dispirited" (of a woman affected by childbirth), "with patience and a touch of severity" (of people waiting for the boat to leave), "oafish and devilish at once" (of a nagging inner voice), "at once crazed and stupefied" (of the air of a bad eating place): and gets inner contradictions in sharp phrases: "this pugnacious assertion of high breeding," "classic erotic-frowning smile" (of a dancer), "shameless pathos" (of an angry face). She can surprise, and convince, with a preposition: a newly married couple's "first lessons in each other."

She has strong, accurate, but not conspicuous, metaphors: "soggy little waiter," "pink-iced tea-cake of sympathy," "hand-decorated hates," "making conversation to scatter silence," a "laugh was a long cascade of falling tinware." But metaphors are less numerous than similes, that now less fashionable figure to which Miss Porter turns with instinctive ease, rarely without amplifying the sense or shading the tone, and always with the added thrust of imagistic vitality. She may fix the object visually: Elsa Lutz had a "crease of fat like a goiter at the base of the throat"; on her canvases Jenny Brown painted cubistic designs "in primary colors like fractured rainbows." She has a sense of how the inanimate may creep up on or take over the human: the steerage passengers "slept piled upon each other like dirty rags thrown out on a garbage heap"; or how a human attribute may be dehumanized: the Spanish dancers' voices "crashed like breaking crockery." When a woman, confident of her worldly knowingness, is publicly snubbed by the Captain, she first turns red; then her blush "vanished and left her pale as unborn veal"—colorless, unknowing, pre-innocent, pre-calf. When his wife bursts forth with a public expression of views contrary to his own, Professor Hutten "sat like something molded in sand, his expression that of a strong innocent man gazing into a pit of cobras." It is a complete picture of mood and man. Miss Porter confers her own incisive perception of character upon Jenny Brown when she has Jenny thinking about David Scott, ". . . I'll be carrying David like a petrified fetus for the rest of my life." Jenny's sense of rigidity and immaturity in her lover is really an echo of her creator's sense of many of her human subjects: she sees them with easy clarity and goes right to the point. Her images for them come solidly out of life; they are not stylistic gestures, literary exercises, but unlabored responses to need, responses from experience against which the doors of feeling and knowing have never been closed.

The difficulty of describing a style without mannerisms, crotchets, or even characteristic brilliances or unique excellences leads one constantly to use such terms as *plain, direct, ordinary, unpretentious, lucid, candid.* These are neither derogatory nor limiting words, nor words that one is altogether content with. The qualities that they name are not inimical to the subtle or the profound, to the penetrating glance or the inclusive sweep. Whether Miss Porter's basic words are a multitude of documentary nouns or adjectives, are literally descriptive or pointedly or amplifyingly imagistic, are terms that report or present or comment or analyze, she composes them, without evident struggle, in a great variety of ways—in combinations of revelatory unexpectedness; tersely or compactly or with unencumbered elaboration, either in a succession of ordered dependencies or in structured periods where everything builds to a final emphasis; with an apparently automatic interplay of force and fluency; meticulously but not pickily or gracelessly; with a kind of graceful adjustment to situation that we call urbanity, yet by no means an urbanity that implies charm or agreeableness at the expense of firmness or conviction.

※ ※

Certain of Miss Porter's arrangements disclose characteristic ways of perceiving and shaping her materials. She describes Veracruz as a "typical port town, cynical by nature, shameless by experience, hardened to showing its seamiest side to strangers: ten to one this stranger passing through is a sheep bleating for their shears, and one in ten is a scoundrel it would be a pity not to outwit." The traditional rhetoric—the triad series; the first half balanced against the second, which is balanced internally; the antithesis and chiasmus—is the instrument of clarity, analytical orderliness, and detachment. Miss Porter has a notable talent for the succinct summarizing sequence; she often employs the series, which combines specification with despatch; through it a packing together of near synonyms may master by saturation, or a quick-fingered catalogue may grasp a rush of simultaneous or consecutive events. A dancer's "pantomime at high speed" to an infatuated pursuer communicates "pity for him or perhaps his stupidity, contempt for the Lutzes, warning, insult, false commiseration, and finally, just plain ridicule." A series may define by a concise anatomy: William Denny's "mind seemed to run monotonously on women, or rather, sex; money, or rather his determination not to be gypped by anybody; and his health." Such series remind one of Jane Austen, who can often look at people and things as logically placeable, sometimes dismissable by a quick list of traits, or naturally amenable to a 1–2–3 kind of classification. Miss Porter has a marked Jane Austen side, which appears, for instance, in the dry summation of a girl and her parents: their "three faces were calm, grave, and much alike," with the anticlimax offhand instead of sharpened up into a shattering deflation. Miss Porter's comic sense is like Austen's both in the use of pithy geometrical arrangements and in the presentment of observed ironies, sometimes suffusing a whole scene, sometimes clipped down as in neoclassical verse: Elsa Lutz spoke "with a surprising lapse into everyday common sense" (cf. "But Shadwell seldom deviates into sense"); Herr Lowenthal felt "he was living in a world so dangerous he wondered how he dared go to sleep at night. But he was sleepy at that very moment." (Cf. "And sleepless lovers, just at twelve, awake.") The irony is Austen-like when, though piercing, it is less censorious than tolerantly amused: "With relief he seized upon this common sympathy between them, and they spent a profitable few minutes putting the Catholic Church in its place." It may catch a social group, gently replacing the group's sense of itself by another: at the Captain's table Frau Rittersdorf "turned her most charming smile upon the Captain, who rewarded her with a glimpse of his two front teeth and slightly upturned mouthcorners. The others ranged round him, faces bent towards him like sunflowers to the sun, waiting for him to begin conversation." It may go beneath the surface to capture habits of mind, setting them up in a neat balance that comments on their insufficiency: Jenny Brown thinks wryly of " 'the family attitude'—suspicion of the worst based on insufficient knowledge of her life, and moral disapproval based firmly on their general knowledge of the weakness of human nature."

Yet to a passage with a strong Austen cast Miss Porter may make an inconspicuous addition that will elusively but substantially alter it. When

Lizzi Spöckenkieker runs carelessly into pompous Captain Thiele, he "threw an arm about her stiffly," and she, "blushing, whinnying, cackling, scrambling, embraced him about the neck wildly as if she were drowning." There is the Austen series crisply hitting off the ludicrous behavior, but there is more visual imagery than Austen uses, more of the physically excessive, and "whinnying" and "cackling," dehumanizing words, carry the joke beyond the usual limit of the Austen mode. It is more like Charlotte Brontë, who could often plunge into the comic, but was likely to do it more fiercely and scornfully. With Brontë, the absurd more quickly edged into the grotesque and even the sinister; she had an awareness of potential damage not easily contained within a pure comic convention. Miss Porter is much closer to Brontë than to Austen in her description of Dr. Schumann when he catches the evil Spanish twins in another destructive practical joke: he "examined the depths of their eyes for a moment with dismay at their blind, unwinking malignance, their cold slyness—not beasts, though, but human souls."

Or consider this comment on a group of first-class passengers looking down on a steerage meal and feeling that the poor people there were being treated decently: "Murmuring among themselves like pigeons . . . [they] seemed to be vaguely agreed that to mistreat the poor is not right, and they would be the first to say so, at any time. Therefore they were happy to be spared this unpleasant duty, to have their anxieties allayed, their charitable feelings soothed." With the subdued ironic contemplation of the group, and with the series that dexterously encompasses their mood, this could be Austen's; and yet behind the smile-provoking self-deceit there is a kind of moral frailty, a trouble-breeding irresponsibility, and in the steerage sights a degree of wretchedness, that extends beyond the borders of the comic perspective. Here, as elsewhere, Miss Porter's manner is reminiscent of George Eliot's—of a carefully, accurately analytical style that is the agent of a mature psychic and moral understanding. David Scott observes the non-dancers: "the born outsiders; the perpetual uninvited; the unwanted; and those who, like himself, for whatever sad reason, refused to join in." The series serves no comic end, speaks for no rationally organizing mind; it makes nice distinctions among the members of a class, somberly, with a mere touch of restrained sympathy to soften the categorical lines. Freytag mentally accuses boat travelers, who "can't seem to find any middle ground between stiffness, distrust, total rejection, or a kind of invasive, gnawing curiosity." The general precision is especially notable in the fresh, climactic joining of the learned "invasive" with the common "gnawing," the latter used uncharacteristically of an external trouble. There is an Eliot-like perceptiveness in Freytag's discovery "about most persons—that their abstractions and generalizations, their Rage for Justice or Hatred of Tyranny or whatever, too often disguised a bitter personal grudge of some sort far removed from the topic apparently under discussion" and in the matter-of-fact postscript that Freytag applied this only to others, never to himself. Miss Porter has repeated need for a vocabulary of emotional urgency, of tensions beyond comedy, as in Jenny Brown's concluding observation on the split with her family: "But that didn't keep you from loving them, nor them from loving you, with that strange longing, demanding, hopeless tenderness and bitterness, wound into each other in a net of living nerves." Here the terms for human contradictions are different in kind from those which present simply laughable incongruities. There is an Eliot note both in this and in another passage on the same page in which we are given a saddened sense of necessities which might, but does not, drift into bitterness: "She did not turn to them at last for help, or consolation, or praise, or understanding, or even love; but merely at last because she was incapable of turning away."

The language and syntax reveal Miss Porter's eye for precision, specification, and distinctions. There is the same precision in the definition of Freytag's "hardened expression of self-absorbed, accusing, utter righteousness" and of a stewardess's "unpleasant mixture of furtive insolence and false abasement, the all too familiar look of resentful servility." Freytag himself distinguishes the phases of another personality: "overfamiliar if you made the mistake of being pleasant to him; loud and insolent if he suspected timidity in you; sly and cringing if you knew how to put him in his place." David prefers, he thinks, "Mrs. Treadwell's unpretentious rather graceful lack of moral sense to Jenny's restless seeking outlaw nature trying so hard to attach itself at any or all points to the human beings nearest her: no matter who." Miss Porter confers her own flair for distinctions upon certain characters. Thus Dr. Schumann, planning to go to confession: ". . . he felt not the right contrition, that good habit of the spirit, but a personal shame, a crushing humiliation at the disgraceful nature of what he had to confess." And it is near the end of the book that Jenny, the most sentient and spontaneous character, reflects upon her griefs over love that did not fulfill expectations: "—and what had it been but the childish refusal to admit and accept on some term or other the difference between what one hoped was true and what one discovers to be the mere laws of the human condition?" The clarity in words comes here from the character's clarity of thought, and this in turn from the writer's clarity of mind. Thus an examination of style in the narrower sense of verbal deportment leads, as it repeatedly does, to the style in conceiving—to the "styling" of, we might say—episode and character, and from this on to the ultimate style of creative mind: the grasp of fact and the moral sense.

We have been following Miss Porter's range: from wit to wisdom, from the sense of the laughable slip or flaw to the awareness of graver self-deception and self-seeking, and to the feeling for reality that at once cuts through illusion and accepts, among the inevitable facts of life, the emotional pressures that lead to, and entangle, fulfillment and discord. Now beside this central sober work of reflective intelligence and alert conscience put the gay play of the Captain's being driven, by a "lethal cloud of synthetic rose scent" at dinner, to sneeze: "He sneezed three times inwardly, one forefinger pressed firmly to his upper lip as he had been taught to do in childhood, to avoid sneezing in church. Silently he was convulsed with internal explosions, feeling as if his eyeballs would fly out, or his eardrums burst. At last he gave up and felt for his handkerchief, sat up stiffly, head averted from the room, and sneezed steadily in luxurious agony a dozen times with muted sounds and streaming eyes, until the miasma was sneezed out and he was rewarded with a good nose-blow." This is farce, the comedy of the physical in which mind and feelings are engaged either not at all, or only mechanically: of the perversity of things and circumstances that render one absurd or grotesque with merely formal suffering, not the authentic kind that by stirring sympathy cuts off outrageous laughter. To say that it is in the vein of Smollett is to emphasize both its present rareness outside the work of committed funnymen and the extraordinariness of having it juxtaposed with writing of sensitiveness and thoughtfulness. Farce may have a satirical note, as in this note on Lizzi Spöckenkieker's disappointment with Herr Rieber, her would-be lover: "Every other man she had known had unfailingly pronounced the magic word *marriage* before ever he got into bed with her, no matter what came of it in fact." A little earlier, Herr Rieber, a short fat man, having gone through suitable amatory preliminaries, decided that his hour had come and, "with the silent intentness of a man bent on crime," maneuvered Lizzi, a tall thin woman, "to the dark side of the ship's funnel. He gave his prey no warning. . . . It was like embracing a windmill. Lizzi uttered a curious tight squeal, and her long arms gathered him in around his heaving middle. . . . She gave him a good push and they fell backward clutched together, her long active legs overwhelmed him, she rolled him over flat on his back, . . . Lizzi was spread upon him like a fallen tent full of poles. . . ." Herr Rieber's passion for flesh and conquest is defeated, turned into grief, by the vigorous surrender that has swept him into unorthodox subordination, and he can get rid of his victorious victim, who is in a "carnivorous trance," only by gasping to her in agony that they are watched by Bébé, the fat and generally seasick dog of Professor Hutten. Bebe, only three feet away, "the folds of his nose twitching, regarded them with an expression of animal cunning that most embarrassingly resembled human knowledge of the seamy side of life." After all the modern solemnities about sex, this sheer farce—with the farcical morality of the dog as grave censor—is reassuring evidence that a fuller, more flexible, less doleful sense of sexual conduct can be recovered.

For a final note on Miss Porter's great range, we can contrast this hilarious Smollettian jest with two quite dissimilar passages. One is the vivid imaging, in her visible gestures, of the inner unwellness of a Spanish countess: "Thumbs turned in lightly to the palm, the hands moved aimlessly from the edge of the table to her lap, they clasped and unclasped themselves, spread themselves flat in the air, closed, shook slightly, went to her hair, to the bosom of her gown, as if by a life of their own separate from the will of the woman herself, who sat quite still otherwise, features a little rigid, bending over to read the dinner card beside her plate." Though here there is a more detailed visualization of the symbolizing object, the feeling for the troubled personality is like Charlotte Brontë's. To this Countess, Dr. Schumann feels attracted, guiltily. After seeing her, "He lay down with his rosary in his fingers, and began to invite sleep, darkness, silence, that little truce of God between living and dying; he put out of his mind, with deliberate intention to forget forever, the last words of that abandoned lost creature; nettles, poisoned barbs, fish hooks, her words clawed at his mind with the terrible malignance of the devil-possessed, the soul estranged from its kind." In the meditative element, in the imaging of a remembered frenzy, and most of all in the particular moral sense that leads to the words "soul estranged from its kind," the account is reminiscent of Conrad.

Range means contrasts such as these. Often, too, there is direct juxtaposition of different styles. Miss Porter can write page after page of sonorous periods—plausible, not overplayed—for Professor Hutten's dinner disquisitions to a captive audience, and then shift bluntly to Frau Hutten's perspective: "He was boring them to death again, she could feel it like vinegar in her veins"—another trenchant simile. Here are two ways of commenting on intelligence: the cultivated irony of "[Elsa's] surprising lapse into everyday common sense," and, on the next page, Jenny's breezy colloquial hyperbole for the Cuban students, "The trouble . . . is simply that they haven't been born yet." David Scott solemnly claims a high disgust for sexual binges: "He had felt superior to his acts and to his partners in them, and altogether redeemed and separated from their vileness by that purifying contempt"; Jenny retorts, with pungent plainness, "Men love to eat themselves sick and then call their upchuck by high-sounding names." Or there is the innocent, flat-voiced irony of Miss Porter's comment on the "lyric prose" of newspapers reporting parties "lavish and aristocratic—the terms are synonymous, they believe" and on newly boarded passengers wandering "about in confusion with the air of persons who have abandoned something of great importance on shore, though they cannot think what it is"; and beside this the vulgar force appropriate to a tactical thought of Herr Rieber's: "A man couldn't be too cautious with that proper, constipated type, no matter how gamey she looked."

※ ※

In their slangy vigor or insouciance, their blunt and easy immediacy, their spurning of the genteel, their casual clinicality, their nervous grip on strain and tension, some of these passages have an air that, whether in self-understanding or self-love, we call "modern." The novel has

Lodwick Hartley

Dark Voyagers

THE ENTRY on Katherine Anne Porter in the 1962 edition of Chambers's *Biographical Dictionary* lists among her publications *No Safe Harbor*, dated 1949. No such book appeared in that year. This error is not unique, for other reference works have included the title as a published work of Miss Porter, though the date has not always been the same. The editorial carelessness involved may be quite indefensible; but what is of real interest is not the error but the circumstances producing it. These provide a remarkable story, the whole of which only the author herself could tell.

As most readers of Miss Porter now know, her novel, once given the title of *No Safe Harbor* and finally published as *Ship of Fools*, has very likely been the longest and most eagerly awaited fictional work of the century. For over two decades it has been subsidized by foundations and by publishers; and, since it was first advertised as forthcoming in 1942, its publication has subsequently been announced so often and so firmly that its existence has understandably been assumed sight unseen. Perhaps, too, the fact that segments of the work have appeared from time to time in magazines has contributed to the illusion of completed publication.

Part of the history of the book, Miss Porter has indicated with succinctness and candor in two dates appended to the version that is now generously substantive. One is "Yaddo, August, 1941," and the other is "Glen Cove, August, 1961." Though simple arithmetic indicates less time, the process of the writing and the rewriting (of which there has been much) has gone on for over a quarter of a century. If one remembers that the date of the generating circumstance was 1931, one may safely say that Miss Porter has been engaged with the idea half as long as Goethe devoted himself to *Faust;* and if one can accept with any sort of seriousness Miss Porter's statement in an interview that some of the ideas of the book were in her mind when she was five years old, then the periods of gestation for *Faust* and the *Ship of Fools* are almost identical. Perhaps this comparison does not put Miss Porter's statement or her intentions quite in the proper perspective; but it is plain enough that, though she originally intended only a short novel, she ultimately decided to attempt something big in scope, something different from what her readers had come to accept as her hallmark—the elegantly polished short story or short novel, limited but perfect. And for the mere reason that the novel has 497 pages as against the total of slightly over a thousand pages in four books that contain her entire critical and fictional output, it is in bulk alone something other than a brilliant gem to be displayed on the black velvet of a jeweler.

Since the appearance of *Flowering Judas* in 1930, Miss Porter has achieved a reputation and developed an adulation that are in themselves almost legendary. On college campuses, on the lecture platform, and in the summer circuit of the creative writing schools she has had a career that has made her a kind of high priestess of the short story whose cool poise, soft voice, and genuine grace have been combined with an ineffable histrionic talent of wide appeal. Moreover, the fact of her frequently astonishing workmanship has lent substantial credence to the myth that she can do no wrong and has provided a charming mask for any artistic and critical shortcomings that she might have. (Glenway Wescott once said that her writing was like "translation by an angel.")

Furthermore, the publication of her stories and sketches has been so beautifully spaced and so carefully prepared for that the thrill of anticipation and rediscovery has been perennial. Certainly, the appearance in the *Atlantic Monthly* of "Holiday" (included also in the *O. Henry Memorial Prize Stories of 1962*), has provided ample evidence that her skill in the short narrative is as firm and assured as ever and that the beauty of her prose style is, if anything, superior.

What the short story is, of course, nobody knows. The only thing we are able to do, with the proper discrimination, is to recognize genuine achievement in the medium when we see it. From the first, Miss Porter has not wanted to be confined within the limits of the short-story form; and she has accepted them warily, even when she has done so most expertly. Thus she has sought variety through writing sketches and short novels—sometimes manifesting in the latter superbly tight control, as in "Noon Wine," and at others looser and less assured mastery as in "Old Mortality" or "The Leaning Tower." Refusing to give herself over to so-called experimental writing either in imitation of her contemporaries or of her own devising, she has sought with the dedication of a true artist for the best media of expression generally within the main stream of traditional literary forms, always bolstered by the assurance of a stylistic competence beyond question.

The necessity of the search, however, cannot have led her willingly to a commitment to the full-length novel. The reluctance of twenty years argues both that the choice all along was hard and that it was no small matter finally to agree to the *imprimatur*. In an introduction for Eudora Welty's *A Curtain of Green*, published in 1941, Miss Porter in writing ostensibly about Miss Welty told more about herself than was immediately apparent:

> ... there is a trap lying just ahead, and all short-story writers know what it is: The Novel. That novel which every publisher hopes to obtain from every short-story writer of any gifts at all, and who finally does obtain it, nine times out of ten.

Miss Welty's successful negotiation of the "trap" came sooner than Miss Porter seems to have anticipated. Her own dilemma was destined to last far longer.

Before *Ship of Fools* was published, some critics found it possible to argue that the composite of Miss Porter's fiction in a sense comprised her "novel"—to which the "Miranda" stories gave a kind of loose structural framework and to which a philosophical unity was provided by the writer's pervading concern for the loneliness and dignity of the human spirit faced with a destiny for which it was ill prepared. In fact, support seemed evident for such an argument in the author's own statement made in the gloomy summer of 1940 as an introduction to *Flowering Judas:*

> They [the stories in the collection] are fragments of a much larger plan which I am still engaged in carrying out, and they are what I was then able to achieve in the way of order and form and statement in a period of grotesque dislocations in a whole society when the world was heaving in the sickness of millennial change.... All the conscious and recollected years of my life have been lived to this day under the heavy threat of world catastrophe, and most of the energies of my mind and spirit have been spent in the effort to grasp the meaning of these threats, to trace them to their sources and to understand the logic of this majestic and terrible failure of the life of man in the Western world.

But nowhere does Miss Porter actually indicate that she would regard the "fragments" as constituting anything like a "novel," and anyone who has argued that they do has been at least guilty of a quibble. Moreover, though Miss Porter's pronouncement about the failure of Western man may be eloquently sincere as an expression of her own personal feeling, it becomes pretentious if applied too closely to her literary production prior to 1940. This failure she must be said at least to have treated obliquely rather than directly.

On the other hand, "the larger plan" of her statement may well include the novel that she finally published; and, since her engagement with the project covers a period when other writing was in progress, the novel can easily be assumed to be closely related to her other work.

The genesis of *Ship of Fools*, factual and literary, is stated in the foreword explaining the title. If the basic circumstance was the author's first voyage to Europe in the summer of 1931, a secondary one was her encounter with *Das Narrenschiff—*

> a moral allegory by Sebastian Brant (1458?–1521) first published in Latin as *Stultifera Navis* in 1494. I read it in Basel in the summer of 1932 when I had still vividly in mind the impressions of my first voyage to Europe. When I began thinking about my novel, I took for my own this simple almost universal image of the ship of this world on its voyage to eternity. It is by no means new—it was very old and durable and dearly familiar when Brant used it; and it suits my purpose exactly. I am a passenger on that ship.

The idea of the *Ship of Fools* is, indeed, very old and it has been used many times. Unfortunately, however, Brant's image is not quite what Miss Porter assumes it to be, since it involved not one ship of fools but several and since these ships set out not for eternity but for the native country of the passengers, the Land of Fools. Miss Porter's description could aptly apply to quite a numerous progeny of literary works old and new, an example of which might be Sutton Vane's highly successful *Outward Bound* of 1924; but, certainly, it suits neither Brant's work nor her own.

Anyway, Brant's "moral allegory," for all its contemporary popularity as a *Volksbuch* and for all its numerous translations, imitations, and adaptations, is now a pretty dull volume; moreover, the best known version in English, *The Ship of Fools* (1509) of Alexander Barclay (1475?–1552), is longer and duller than Brant's original, of which it is an adaptation rather than a strict translation. One could readily forgive a discriminating reader like Miss Porter if she actually spent more time with the racy cleverness of the woodcuts than with the pedestrian moral satire of the text. Ironically, however, Brant's actual purpose better suits at least part of Miss Porter's own than her inaccurate statement of it indicates.

No one is forced to take *Ship of Fools* to be an allegory in the basic meaning of a prolonged metaphor with dual meanings carefully worked out through personifications of abstract qualities and of universal applications—as in *The Faerie Queene*, or Bunyan's *Pilgrim's Progress*, or even *Gulliver's Travels*. The name of the ship was not inevitably chosen because in derivation it suggests Truth; nor must we regard the pasengers on the *Vera* as being as broadly representative of twentieth-century life as Chaucer's pilgrims (to take a handy example) were representative of fourteenth-century life. But the most important group on board the ship are Germans returning in 1931 to their native land; and from Miss Porter's presentation of them, it is plain that she is dealing with a species of fools returning to a native land that is just on the brink of cataclysmic folly. The fact that she represents her fools as being contemptible and loathsome rather than merely foolish in the usual sense is close enough to Brant's purpose. Moreover, her portraits have the sharpness of the Brant woodcuts.

Miss Porter's statement, "I am a passenger on that ship," is from one point of view as old as the borrowed image itself. In an interview for a literary magazine she said of her identification with the characters of the novel—

> I am nowhere and everywhere. I am the captain and the seasick bulldog and the man in the cherry-colored shirt who sings and the devilish children and all of the women and lots of the men.

This, of course, is no negotiable revelation. Perhaps the author *intended* it that way. Indeed, her public utterances as revealed in a number of press interviews that she has necessarily given from time to time have seemed rather like cheerful evasions of inquiry into her personal life and her art than reliable material for a consideration of her biography or her craft.

The search for the author in the cast of characters is obliged to go on—almost by invitation. And one will be sure to find some aspects of her in at least two passengers: Jenny Brown, the young American painter, and Mrs. Treadwell, the middle-aged divorcée. Jenny's resemblance to the Miranda of *Pale Horse, Pale Rider* is to be sensed rather than documented; but it can hardly be missed. Mrs. Treadwell, whose early marriage ended in disillusionment, suggests Miranda at a later age. (Miranda, as we learn from an earlier story, was eighteen in 1912; thus she would have been thirty-seven at the time of the sailing of the *Vera*. Mrs. Treadwell was forty-five.) The restlessness of Mrs. Treadwell and her inability to find fulfillment in either love or life is explicit in the novel:

> ... never for any price will I be able to buy a ticket that will set me down in the place I wish to be. Maybe the place does not exist, or if it does, it's much too late to go there.

In an early autobiographical statement, Miss Porter wrote:

> My personal life has been the jumbled and apparently irrelevant mass of experiences which can only happen, I think, to a woman who goes with her mind permanently absent from the place she is ... I have no time sense and almost no sense of direction and have seen a great deal of the world by getting completely lost and simply taking in the scenery as I roamed about getting my bearings.

The similarity is striking. Here may be documentation enough. But the matter should not be pressed too far. The author and her characters are from the very nature of fiction never really the same, no matter how closely they at times seem to resemble each other. And Miss Porter is finally no more Jenny or Mrs. Treadwell than she is, for example, La Condesa, the fascinating decayed noblewoman who in spite of her age manages still to be a *femme fatale* (and for whom the author has unconcealed admiration), or Frau Rittersdorf who keeps supercilious and venomous notes on the voyage as Miss Porter must have kept sensitive and perceptive ones. Jenny and Mrs. Treadwell, it is true, do furnish such lenses as to make Miss Porter's "I am a passenger" somewhat analogous to Christopher Isherwood's "I am a camera." Thus far one can go safely.

The cast of the novel is large, and the possibilities of classification and interpretation are endless. Indeed, as Mark Schorer has suggested, a field day for the analogy- and symbol-seekers among graduate students in contemporary literature is an inevitable prospect. Though nobody has yet tried to force the novel into the mould of the medieval allegory through the application of something like the stock device of the Seven Deadly Sins, a general claim has already been staked for the Freudians: namely, the Captain represents the Super-Ego; the cabin passengers stand for the Ego; and the steerage, the Id. Perhaps the matter should be dropped while the generalization still glitters.

The opening scenes take place in August, 1931, in the port town of Veracruz, described as "a little purgatory between land and sea for the traveler." The heat, the color, the squalor, the beggars, the Indians are rendered with the same kind of expertness that a considerable residence in Mexico had enabled Miss Porter to demonstrate earlier in such stories as "María Concepción" and "Hacienda," to which the section seems closely related.

The confusion of the dock, of the ship itself at the time of the sailing, and of the beginning of the voyage allows for only glimpses of the passengers. Some of these, however, are sharply visualized; and in the instance of the eight hundred seventy-six wretched Spanish migrant workers who embarked when the *Vera* docked in Havana and who were in process of being shipped back to the Canaries and to Spain because of a failure in the sugar market, the depiction presages something more than mere purgatorial horror awaiting these damned souls—men, women, and children—in the steerage of the mixed freighter and passenger ship:

> The air was not air any more, but a hot, clinging vapor of sweat, of dirt, of stale food and befouled litter, of rags and excrement: the reek of poverty. The people were not faceless: they were all Spanish, their heads had shape and meaning and breeding. . . . Their skins were the skins of the starved who are also overworked, a dark dirty pallor with green copper overtones, as if their blood had not been sufficiently renewed for generations. Their bare feet were bruised, hardened, cracked, knotted in the joints, and their hands were swollen fists.

As the ship continues its voyage, the other passengers sort themselves out and take shape.

Since the ship is German, one naturally expects the German nationals to dominate. They do so—and in a manner quite apart from any question of numerical strength. Any reader of "The Leaning Tower" is acquainted with the loathing for certain aspects of the national character that Miss Porter displayed in it, at times with more justification from the facts of history than from the canons of artistic detachment. The same sort of portraiture reappears here, with the same kind of subtle distortion.

There is a difference, however, in the tone. The atmosphere of "The Leaning Tower" tends toward the tragic. It sets out to show how in the last days of the Weimar Republic not only Berlin but all Germany was a prison house, full of poverty, fear, and frustrations out of which Nazism was inevitably bred. Hans, the Heidelberg student with the festered saber scar, is youthfully arrogant; Herr Bussen, the University student, is proud in his poverty; and Frau Rosa Reichl, a bitterly nostalgic Viennese aristocrat reduced to keeping a pension, takes out her frustration by tyrannizing over her paying guests. In the dilemmas of all these Miss Porter sees the desperate hopelessness of an excessively nationalistic people. The central symbol of the story is a little plaster cast model of the Leaning Tower, a memento of Frau Reichl's honeymoon, that Charles Upton, an American student, accidentally breaks and later finds pitifully restored in a patched up condition—a representation (as others have pointed out) of the determination of the German people to restore their past, however shoddily, after the ruin of World War I, a ruin perversely attributed to the Americans.

Though they represent some of the same forces and frustrations, the Germans of *Ship of Fools* are not tragic. Frau Rittersdorf with her spiteful note taking and her pathological self-deception is a repulsively stupid purveyor of the kind of race pride that was at the core of Nazism. ("—What was there about Americans that made them *only* that? the gradual mongrelization of that dismaying country by the mingling of the steerage sweepings of Europe. . . .") The author leaves little room for sympathy for her. The German character suffers even more in pig-snouted little Herr Rieber, publisher of a ladies' garment trade maga-zine, whose amorous pursuit of the ridiculous Lizzi Spöckenkieker (the names themselves at times indicate the quality of the satire) is obscenely grotesque. A grotesque of a different sort is Herr Wilibald Graf, a dying religious enthusiast who has hallucinations of divine healing pow-ers and who is murderously hated by his blond nephew Johann, forced to attend him as a male nurse. Still another variety is represented in Herr and Frau Professor Hutten, a middle-aged childless couple who disgustingly lavish their affection on an English bulldog named Bébé. Then there is the chronic alcoholic Herr Karl Baumgarten, a lawyer from Mexico City, with his tortured wife, and his frightened and baffled little boy. The soft, round, and sickeningly sentimental aspect of the German character is incarnated in Frau Schmidt, returning to Nürnberg with the corpse of her husband. Physical degeneracy—so despised by the Master Race—is represented in Herr Karl Glocken, the self-pitying little hunchback who has sold his tobacco and newsstand in Mexico ironically to return to Germany just at a time when his uselessness to the Nazi ideology could not be more evident.

The Jew, Herr Julius Löwenthal, tends (perhaps unexpectedly but quite in keeping with the author's plan) to be anything but a sympathetic character. A manufacturer of Catholic church furnishings and religious objects, he distrusts and hates gentiles and isolates himself from them whenever possible.

William Freytag, a handsome young business man with oil interests in Mexico and a Jewish wife whom he hopes to remove from the rising tide of anti-Semitism in Germany, is a typical German in most of his reactions, notably in his feeling that the world would have been a better place if America had sided with Germany in World War I. And though he seems to luxuriate in the beauty of his wife for whose affection he has consciously placed himself at a disadvantage, he is quite satisfied to travel unambiguously as a gentile and he is capable of making a revaluation of his love after the secret of the marriage has been revealed

—a fact that fully justifies his discovery in a shipboard affair that he has a faculty for "pure lust without one trace of love or tenderness."

The Captain is Prussian in his stiff adherence to discipline, in his perfectly symmetrical morality, and in his lofty disdain for inferiority of any sort. Mitty-like he has his dreams of "lawless murderous fury breaking out . . . in some place he could not even fix on the map . . . with himself . . . always in command and control"; but he is scarcely successful in controlling his own passengers. He does not clearly come to life as a real person. The ship's physician, Dr. Schumann, however, is another matter. Conscious both of a ruined life and of the ever-present threat of death from a heart disease, handsome at sixty with a jaunty *Mensur* scar in the tradition of the fencing clubs of German universities, he is still capable of romance and gallantry. In his attachment to La Condesa and in his involvement in love that comes too late, he stands conspicuously apart from his compatriots in the book. However, his worldly bitterness removes him from the truly tragic.

The Swiss are represented by a hotel keeper named Lutz, his wife, and their hopelessly gawky and unattractive daughter, Elsa, whose one slender possibility of shipboard romance ends in pathetic frustration. There is a lanky Swede, Arne Hansen—virile, moody, lusty, and typecast for chasing the Spanish dancers and feuding with Herr Rieber.

Among the Americans besides Mrs. Treadwell and the painter, Jenny Brown ("Jenny Angel"), there is another young painter, David Scott ("David darling"), who has been living with Jenny in a relationship alternating between love and torture. There is also the chemical engineer from Texas, William Denny, a bore permanently poised between narcissism and satyriasis. ("His mind seemed to run monotonously on women, or rather, sex; money, or rather his determination not to be gypped by anybody; and his health.")

Whatever may be the arrogance, stupidity, drunkenness, cupidity, and lechery of the other pasengers, the vices of the Latins aboard are still of another sort. Sleazy, thieving, irresponsible, dissolute, dirty, destructive, they operate within a kind of anarchic amorality in contrast to the perverted and misdirected morality of the Teutonic passengers. The most numerous of this group are the zarzuela company of Spanish singers and dancers, calling themselves gypsies and returning to Granada after being stranded in Mexico. The women are brazen prostitutes;

the men, equally brazen pimps. They are all petty cheats and thieves. Bracketing the sheer outrageousness of the lot are six-year-old male and female Ric and Rac—incredible imps of evil and annihilation, constantly running amok on the decks and in the companionways.

On the side of irresponsibility and juvenility are also six Cuban medical students on their way to Montpellier. Taking *La Cucharacha* as their theme song, these form, as if by natural instinct, the train of the most romantic of the Latins: La Condesa, a decayed Spanish noblewoman being deported from Cuba to Tenerife for political intrigue. An addict of ether and drugs, she is a ravaged beauty who can seduce the young and extract gallantry from the old, and who can still preserve the illusion of individual grandeur in the midst of ruin and perversity. ("I do not intend to reconcile myself with a society I despise.")

The Mexicans (strangely enough, since Miss Porter has elsewhere shown herself able to make excellent fictional use of them) count for little more than color and atmosphere. There are the bride and groom from Guadalajara who tend to be structural symbols rather than people, two perfunctory priests on their way to Spain, and a political agitator in steerage—"a fat man in cherry-colored shirt, who sings."

Finally, in the hold are the returning migrant workers, existing like swine in their revolting squalor, mere human detritus to the scions of the Master Race above—eating, sleeping, making love, giving birth, praying, hating in a small hell of subhuman existence.

This is, indeed, a motley panorama, observed in something less than detachment and recorded quite often in loathing and indignation rather than in pity.

The thesis of the novel, Miss Porter has been quoted as saying, is "the responsibility people must share for evil." And she continues, "I do not want to be uncharitable, but the good and virtuous people of the world are often in collusion with evil." This kind of statement is sufficiently general. Even so, it seems too specific for what the novel accomplishes. The evil is abundantly evident. This no one can doubt—just as one cannot doubt that the *Vera* is a ship of fools. But the matter of the collusion of the good and virtuous people with the evil is hardly made explicit. In fact, the basic frustration produced by the book is its refusal to shape up either dramatically or thematically to a point where the reader can take hold of it with assurance.

Both in "The Leaning Tower" and *Ship of Fools* Miss Porter indicates that she at an early stage unerringly sensed in the German character the destructive elements that would produce the holocaust of World War II. But in both instances, the zeal shown for revealing the germ of the disease precludes attention to those who neglected to apply the clyster.

At one point in *Ship of Fools*, for example, the story seems ready to shape up into a significant and sustained revelation of the insidious and virulent poison of race hatred. The complication begins in the conversation between Mrs. Treadwell and Freytag in which in friendly intimacy Freytag reveals that his wife is Jewish. In an offguard moment of less well justified intimacy, Mrs. Treadwell innocently repeats the conversation to her cabin mate, Lizzi Spöckenkieker. A chain reaction of anti-Semitism quickly begins. Resentment over the possibilities of "pollution" spreads among the Germans who share the Captain's table with Freytag, and the fever pitch rises so high that he is asked to leave, to share unhappily a table with the unattractive Löwenthal.

One expects the incident to become central and dramatic, for its galvanic effect upon the attention at this point promises something significant and illuminating. Yet the incident is dissipated in succeeding events, to be picked up only subliminally in the matter of Freytag's subtle change of attitude toward his wife. In a sense, Mrs. Treadwell may have been in "collusion" with the evil dissemination of race hatred and ultimate genocide in failing to comprehend the effect that her revelation would have on Lizzi. The charge of collusion against the "good" people outside Germany who for too long failed to sense the evils of Nazism is valid enough. But to see in Mrs. Treadwell a symbol of this tragic error requires more effort and ingenuity than it should require if such is the author's intent.

The sins of society symbolized by the steerage passengers, it is true, are viewed with classic disinterest by the more fortunate passengers, but the viewers are not exactly "good and virtuous people":

> At the other end of the ship, they found the Lutz family, the Huttens, the Cuban students, and Herr Glocken in a row looking down into the pit, where the canvas covering had been removed from the grating to give light and air to the quarters where the steerage passengers ate ... The six students lined up and shouted something friendly and barbarous in their unfathomable argot; several of the men turned their faces upward, mouths full, cheeks bulging, and jerked a hand at them, good-naturedly

... The sight-seers moved on, a little bored with relief, their eased minds reflected in their slightly vacuous expressions. Murmuring among themselves like pigeons, the Lutzes and the Huttens and Herr Glocken seemed to be vaguely agreed that to mistreat the poor is not right, and they would be the first to say so, at any time. Therefore they were happy to be spared this unpleasant duty, to have their anxieties allayed, their charitable feelings soothed.

The evil of the Spaniards is pure evil, pure amorality, removed—it would seem—from any question of voluntary collusion on the part of anybody. Two related incidents in which the devil-possessed Ric and Rac are involved provide bizarre and even macabre episodes, matched only by the utterly stultifying circumstances created by their elders in their diabolically absurd scheme to fleece their fellow pasengers. In the first episode, the twins cavalierly toss the Hutten's bulldog Bébé over the rail, an event evoking a curious reaction from a shadowy woodcarver among the steerage passengers who either quixotically or desperately jumps overboard to the rescue—"the only purely distinterested act the novel records," as Granville Hicks has remarked. The dog is saved, and the woodcarver drowns. The picture of the peasant women below deck hovering with their clicking rosaries over the gaunt body of the drowned man is set in bitter irony against the scene above with the Huttens "bowed like a sculptured Pietà" over the prostrate but live dog. The second episode—of less obvious dramatic quality—involves the incident of the twins' snatching the Condesa's pearls (part of the small bastion that defends her from abject poverty) and dropping the necklace with fiendish irresponsibility into the sea.

The wildly presumptuous scheme of the zarzuela company to sell tickets to the Captain's gala—a promised fiesta with dancing, entertainment, and prizes—is an incredible intrusion and imposition that can be resisted only ineffectually. The effort is pursued with wheedling and even a species of blackmail; and, as if the evil of the affair had developed like a mephitic infection, the scheme has its climax in a *Walpurgisnacht* of sickeningly pathological implications. During the course of it, Arne Hansen clobbers the despicable Herr Rieber over the head with a beer bottle and an attempted seduction of Jenny by Freytag comes to a feckless anticlimax. Far more shocking is the behavior of the usually ladylike Mrs. Treadwell. Having made herself up to look like one of the Spanish dancers, she is accosted by Denny in an alcoholic stupor before the door of a dancer named Pastora who has denied him entrance. In an incredibly insane outburst of sex starvation impelled by her own drunkenness, she savagely beats the face of the Texan into a swollen mass of half moons with the metal heel of her gilded dancing sandal.

After the party, the crescendo of folly diminishes—as, indeed, it must. The effect is diffused in the concluding details of the voyage.

No further proof need be adduced that evil has been pervasive. Here and there can be found hints of personal courage and intimations of tragedy. But nowhere is there strength but in decay; nor is there real love or palpable happiness. Sexuality is tasteless, ridiculous, gross. The Spaniards love in sheer animalism; the Germans, in thinly disguised perversity; the Americans, in torture or futility. Even the children are defeated or depraved.

In *No Exit* Sartre makes Garcin say, "Hell is—other people." In spite of Miss Porter's expressed distaste for Sartre, she had described in the *Vera* a floating hell that abundantly corroborates the statement. "*Mein Liebchen,*" says the sodden Herr Baumgarten to his wife at one point, "have you forgotten? We have been married ten years today." "What is there to remember?" is the reply. "What has it been? A hell, a little hell on earth from the beginning."—"I am thinking," says Arne Hansen at another point, "about all the things people everywhere do to make each other miserable."—"We're all on our way somewhere else," says Jenny, "and we'll be glad to see the last of each other. God, I'd hate to think I'd ever get even a postcard from anybody on this ship again, as long as I live!" So the drear rubric runs.

At the very end of the voyage Jenny, having once more patched up her uneven love affair with David, concludes, "I am a sleepwalker, and this is a dream." "Dreams are real too," said David, "nightmares, everything."

Perhaps, after all, this is the best approximation of the novel's theme, for the quality of the nightmare is the dominant impression left by the book. In this respect, the "allegory" of Miss Porter stands somewhere between the fifteenth-century allegory of Brant and that of the twentieth-century Kafka. In most respects, Miss Porter is as unlike the latter as she is unlike the former. Her characters are more than Kafkaesque wraiths. She rarely sails quite so much windward of fantasy as Kafka. Her symbols are not so elusive, intangible, or equivocal. Her reliance is on her own powers of exact observation rather than on intuition. But she is assuredly successful like Kafka in convincing her readers that nightmares are reality—at the same time that she shows reality to be a nightmare.

Since the intention of the novel is what it is, no one should be surprised that it has no plot in the usual sense. There is, naturally, the pattern provided by the voyage itself out of which grows an orchestration of themes and motives. The characters emerge rather than develop, and their movements in and out are rather like details in a flat design than like instrumentalities of cause and effect in a logical progression of action. In this respect they are like allegorical figures. Although violence and change in one form or another come to some, most of the voyagers leave the ship very much as they were when they embarked. Since there is no fixed scheme of rising and falling action, there is no crisis to point toward a conclusion—not even the important sequence involving Freytag and anti-Semitism. And though the climax may very well be the orgy instigated by the zarzuela company it is not solidly related to the whole by the logic of inevitability.

The episodic structure of the novel, then, is demanded and predetermined by the subject. But though the writing itself has in the main the beauty and efficiency that one has always found in Miss Porter, some of the handling of the subject matter is monotonous and repetitious. At points, false leads into what at first seem to be important thematic developments are frustrating. Then, too, there is a subtly sustained indecision in method between the objective and the subjective view of the characters and their involvement.

In an essay on Thomas Hardy countering a criticism of T. S. Eliot, Miss Porter wrote in 1940:

> Hardy seems almost to agree with Mr. Eliot for once: "The best tragedy—highest tragedy in short—is that of the WORTHY encompassed by the INEVITABLE. The tragedies of immoral and worthless people are not of the best." My own judgment is that Hardy's characters are in every way superior to those of Mr. Eliot, and for precisely the reason the two writers are agreed upon. Hardy's people suffer the tragedy of being, Mr. Eliot's of not-being. The strange creatures inhabiting the wasteland of Mr. Eliot's particular scene are for the most part immoral and worthless, the apeneck Sweeneys, the Grishkins, and all. . . . They have for us precisely the fascination the poet has endowed them with,

and they also have great significance: they are the sinister chorus of the poet's vision of human beings without God and without faith, a world of horror, surrounding this soul thirsting for faith in God. E. M. Forster has remarked that *The Waste Land* is a poem of real horror. . . . For how else can one explain the self-absorbed despair of Eliot's point of view, even in religion? That uncontrolled emotion of loathing for his fellow pilgrims in this mortal life? Was there not one soul worth tender treatment, not one good man interesting enough to the poet to inhabit his tragic scene? Hardy feels no contempt for his characters at all; he writes of them as objectively as if they existed by themselves, they are never the background, the chorus, for the drama of his own experience.

If in the passage one substitutes Miss Porter for Eliot, Rieber and Lizzi Spöckenkieker for Sweeney and Grishkin, and *Ship of Fools* for *The Waste Land*, and in addition makes some adjustments in the religious implications, the relevance is illuminating.

In the light of the author's total work, *Ship of Fools* will seem increasingly like a chorus "for the drama of her own experience." Certainly, if throughout she has been concerned with the "majestic and terrible failure" of Western man, the majesty of the failure has remained at best a secondary consideration. Whereas her individual stories may indicate tragic insights into the human character, she has not finally elected the tragic approach. In spite of her enduring and highly perceptive interest in people, she has expressed a profound distrust of human relationships and of human potentialities for happiness, love, and selfless action; and though it is not exactly uncontrolled, her emotion of loathing for her fellow voyagers in this mortal life is left as her latest bequest. The one good man interesting enough to inhabit her tragic scene is, in the familiar phrase, hard to find.

Indeed, part of the irony of Jenny Brown's expressed desire never to see any of her fellow passengers again is the fact that her feeling must be shared by the reader. Why should not we, then, reject them and the ugly implications about the human condition that they reveal, and thus reject the book itself? The answer may be that, if the majesty of human failure is missing from Miss Porter's picture, the terror is there, a terror powerfully and hypnotically revealed in such imperfections and indecisions in characters and in design as reflect not (as some of the greatest tragedies do) the possibility of a universal order above the chaos of life, but rather the dark chaos of life itself.

After all, there is perhaps for a ship of fools no safe harbor.

A Selective
Bibliography

Editorial Note:

This bibliography is divided into six sections: stories (first publication); major books; poems; uncollected miscellaneous pieces and forthcoming books; interviews and discussions; and books, articles, and reviews about Katherine Anne Porter. Foreign language items are not listed, and minor biographical and bibliographical articles are generally not included.

I. Stories: First Publication

"The Circus," *Southern Review*, o. s., I (Summer 1935), 36–41.
"The Cracked Looking-Glass," *Scribner's Magazine*, XCI (May 1932), 271–276, 313–320.
"A Day's Work," *Nation*, CL (February 10, 1940), 205–207.
"The Downward Path to Wisdom," *Harper's Bazaar*, MMDCCXXXI (December 1939), 72–73ff.
"The Fig Tree," *Harper's Magazine*, CCXX (June 1960), 55–59.
"Flowering Judas," *Hound and Horn*, III (Spring 1930), 316–331.
"The Grave," *Virginia Quarterly Review*, XI (April 1935), 177–183.
"Hacienda," *Virginia Quarterly Review*, VIII (October 1932), 556–569.
"He," *New Masses*, III (October 1927), 13–15.
"Holiday," *Atlantic Monthly*, CCVI (December 1960), 44–56.
"The Jilting of Granny Weatherall," *transition*, XV (February 1929), 139–146.
"The Leaning Tower," *Southern Review*, o. s., VII (Autumn 1941), 219–279.

"Magic," *transition*, XIII (Summer 1928), 229–231.
"María Concepción," *Century*, CV (December 1922), 224–239.
"The Martyr," *Century*, CVI (July 1923), 410–413.
"Noon Wine," *Story*, X (June 1937), 71–103.
"Old Mortality," *Southern Review*, o. s., II (Spring 1937), 686–735.
"The Old Order," *Southern Review*, o. s., I (Winter 1936), 495–509. This title
    was later used by Miss Porter for *The Old Order*, a collection of Southern
    stories published in 1955 by Harcourt, Brace & World, Inc. The short story
    was then retitled "The Journey."
"Pale Horse, Pale Rider," *Southern Review*, o. s., III (Winter 1938), 417–466.
"Rope," *The Second American Caravan*, ed. A. Kreymborg. New York:
    Macaulay Co., 1928, 362–368.
"The Source," *Accent*, I (Spring 1941), 144–147.
"That Tree," *Virginia Quarterly Review*, X (July 1934), 351–361.
"Theft," *The Gyroscope*, November 1929, 21–25.
"Two Plantation Portraits" ("The Witness" and "The Last Leaf"), *Virginia
    Quarterly Review*, XI (January 1935), 85–92.
"Virgin Violeta," *Century*, CIX (December 1924), 261–268. Reprinted as
    "Violeta" in *Redbook*, December 1964, 36, 93, 96–97.

II. Books

The Collected Stories of Katherine Anne Porter. New York: Harcourt, Brace
    & World, Inc., 1965. ["Every story I ever finished and published is here."]
The Days Before. New York: Harcourt, Brace & Company, 1952. Contents:
    Critical—"The Days Before," "On a Criticism of Thomas Hardy,"
    "Gertrude Stein: Three Views," "Reflections on Willa Cather," " 'It Is
    Hard to Stand in the Middle,' " "The Art of Katherine Mansfield,"
    "Orpheus in Purgatory," " 'The Laughing Heat of the Sun,' " "Eudora
    Welty and 'A Curtain of Green,' " "Homage to Ford Madox Ford,"
    "Virginia Woolf," "E. M. Forster"; Personal and Particular—"Three
    Statements about Writing," "No Plot, My Dear, No Story," "The Flower
    of Flowers," "Portrait: Old South," "Audubon's Happy Land," "A
    House of My Own," "The Necessary Enemy," " 'Marriage Is Belonging,' "
    "American Statement: 4 July 1942," "The Future Is Now"; Mexican—
    "Notes on the Life and Death of a Hero," "Why I Write about Mexico,"
    "Leaving the Petate," "The Mexican Trinity," "La Conquistadora,"
    "Quetzalcoatl," "The Charmed Life."
Flowering Judas and Other Stories. New York: Harcourt, Brace & Company,
    1930. Contents: "María Concepción," "Magic," "Rope," "He," "The
    Jilting of Granny Weatherall," "Flowering Judas." Reprinted by Harcourt,
    Brace & Company, 1935, with four new stories; "Theft," "That Tree."

"The Cracked Looking-Glass," and "Hacienda." 1935 edition reprinted by Modern Library in 1940.

Hacienda. [New York:] Harrison of Paris, 1934.

The Leaning Tower and Other Stories. New York: Harcourt, Brace & Company, 1944. Contents: "The Source," "The Witness," "The Circus," "The Old Order," "The Last Leaf," "The Grave," "The Downward Path to Wisdom," "A Day's Work," and "The Leaning Tower."

Noon Wine. Detroit: Schuman's, 1937.

Pale Horse, Pale Rider: Three Short Novels. New York: Harcourt, Brace & Company, 1939. Contents: "Old Mortality," "Noon Wine," and "Pale Horse, Pale Rider." Reprinted by Modern Library in 1949.

Ship of Fools. Boston: Little, Brown, and Company, 1962. Parts of *Ship of Fools* were published separately as follows: "Embarkation," *Sewanee Review*, LV (1947), 1–23; "The Exile," *Harper's*, CCI (November 1950), 70–78; "The High Sea," *Partisan Review*, XII (1945), 514–549; "Kein Haus, Keine Heimat," *Sewanee Review*, LII (1944), 465–482; "The Prisoner," *Harper's*, CCI (October 1950), 89–96; "Seducers," *Harper's*, CCVII (November 1953), 33–38; "Ship of Fools," *Atlantic*, CXCVII (March and April 1956), 33–38, 56–63; "Ship of Fools," *Mademoiselle*, XLVII (July 1958), 26–43; "Ship of Fools," *Texas Quarterly*, II (1959), 97–151; "The Strangers," *Accent*, VI (1946), 211–229; "Under Weigh," *Harper's*, CCI (November 1950), 80–88.

III. Poems

"After a Long Journey," *Mademoiselle*, XLVI (November 1927), 142–143.

"Anniversary in a Country Cemetery," *Harper's Bazaar*, MMDCCXLIV (November 1940), 139, and in book form, New York: Independent Music Publisher, 1940. [With music by David Diamond.]

"Bouquet for October," *Pagany*, III (Winter 1932), 21–22.

"Enchanted," *Literary Review*, III (August 25, 1923), 921.

"Measures for Song and Dance," *Harper's* CC (May 1950), 80–81.

"November in Windham," *Harper's*, CCXI (November 1955), 44.

"Requiescat," *The Measure: A Journal of Poetry*, No. 38 (April 1924), 11.

"Two Songs from Mexico," *The Measure: A Journal of Poetry*, No. 35 (January 1924), 9.

"Winter Burial," *New York Herald Tribune Books*, November 14, 1926, 2.

IV. Uncollected Miscellaneous Pieces and Forthcoming Books

The Collected Essays and Occasional Writings of Katherine Anne Porter. Boston: Seymour Lawrence Incorporated, 1969. This volume will include all of *The Days Before*, poems, reviews, and essays. (See section III for a listing of Miss Porter's poetry.) Some of the more important uncollected essays follow, most of which will appear in the book:

"Adventures of Hadji," *Asia*, XX (August 1920), 683–684. ["A Tale of A Turkish Coffee-House, retold by Katherine Anne Porter."]

"A Christmas Story," *McCall's*, XCV (December 1967), 90–91, and in book form, New York: A Seymour Lawrence Book/Delacorte Press, 1967.

"A Defense of Circe," *Mademoiselle*, XXXIX (June 1954), 46–48, 96–97.

From a work in progress, *The Devil and Cotton Mather*: "Affectation of Praehiminincies," *Accent*, II (1942), 131–138, 226–232, and in the *Accent Anthology*, ed. Kerker Quinn and Charles Shattuck (New York, 1946), pp. 220–240; "A Bright Particular Faith," *Hound and Horn*, VII (1934), 246–257; "A Goat for Azazel," *Partisan Review*, VII (1940), 188–199.

"From the Notebooks of Katherine Anne Porter—Yeats, Joyce, Eliot, Pound—," *Southern Review*, n. s., I (1965), 570–573.

"Gracious Greatness," *Esprit*, VIII (1964), 50–58. [On Flannery O'Connor.]

" 'Noon Wine': The Sources," *Yale Review*, XLVI (1956), 22–39.

"Ole Woman River: A Correspondence with Katherine Anne Porter," *Sewanee Review*, LXXIV (1966), 754–767.

"On First Meeting T. S. Eliot," *Shenandoah*, XII (1961), 25–26.

"Paris: A Little Incident in the Rue de l'Odeon," *Ladies Home Journal*, LXXXI (August 1964), 54–55.

"A Sprig of Mint for Allen," *Sewanee Review*, LXVII (1959), 545–546.

"St. Augustine and the Bullfight," *Mademoiselle*, XLI (July 1955), 28–34.

"Where Presidents Have No Friends," *Century*, CIV (July 1922), 373–384.

"The Winged Skull" (review of *This Is Lorence* by Lodwick Hartley), *Nation*, CLVII (July 17, 1943), 72–73.

"A Wreath for the Gamekeeper," *Shenandoah*, XI (1959), 3–12, and *Encounter*, XIV (February 1960), 69–77.

The Selected Letters of Katherine Anne Porter, ed. Glenway Wescott. Boston: Seymour Lawrence Incorporated, 1970.

V. Interviews and Discussions

Doblier, Maurice. "I've Had a Good Run for My Money," *New York Herald-Tribune Books*, April 1, 1962, pp. 3, 11.

Janeway, Elizabeth. "For Katherine Anne Porter, *Ship of Fools* Was a Lively Twenty-Two Year Voyage," *New York Times Book Review*, April 1, 1962, pp. 4–5.

Lopez, Hank. "A Country and Some People I Love," *Harper's*, CCXXXI (September 1965), 58, 62, 65, 68.

From *Invitation to Learning*, a series of radio broadcasts:

"Alice in Wonderland," *The New Invitation to Learning*, ed. Mark Van Doren. New York: The New Home Library, 1942, pp. 208–220. (A discussion with Bertrand Russell and Van Doren.)

"*Moll Flanders,*" *The Invitation to Learning,* ed. Huntington Cairns, Allen Tate, and Mark Van Doren. New York: The New Home Library, 1942, pp. 137–151. (With the editors.)

"*Tom Jones,*" *The New Invitation to Learning,* pp. 194–205. (With Tate and Van Doren.)

"*The Turn of the Screw,*" *The New Invitation to Learning,* pp. 223–235. (With Tate and Van Doren.)

"An Interview with Katherine Anne Porter," *McCall's,* XCII (August 1965), 88–89, 137–143.

Ruoff, James. "Katherine Anne Porter Comes to Kansas," *Midwest Quarterly,* IV (1963), 205–234.

Ruoff, James and Del Smith. "Katherine Anne Porter on *Ship of Fools,*" *College English,* XXIV (1963), 396–397.

Thompson, Barbara. "The Art of Fiction XXIX—Katherine Anne Porter: An Interview," *Paris Review,* No. 29 (1963), 87–114. Reprinted in *Writers at Work: "The Paris Review" Interviews* (New York, 1963), 137–163.

Winsten, Archer. "The Portrait of an Artist," *New York Post,* May 6, 1937, p. 17.

VI. Books, Articles, and Reviews About Katherine Anne Porter

Aldridge, John W. "Art and Passion in Katherine Anne Porter," *Time to Murder and Create: The Contemporary Novel in Crisis* (New York, 1966), pp. 178–184.

Alexander, Jean. "Katherine Anne Porter's Ship in the Jungle," *Twentieth Century Literature,* XI (1966), 179–188.

Allen, Charles A. "Katherine Anne Porter: Psychology as Art," *Southwest Review,* XLI (1956), 233–250.

———. "The Nouvelles of Katherine Anne Porter," *University Review,* XXIX (1962), 87–93.

———. "Southwestern Chronicle: Katherine Anne Porter," *Arizona Quarterly,* II (1946), 90–95.

Auchincloss, Louis. "Katherine Anne Porter," *Pioneers and Caretakers: A Study of Nine American Women Novelists* (Minneapolis, 1965), pp. 136–151.

Baker, Howard. "The Upward Path: Notes on the Work of Katherine Anne Porter," *Southern Review,* n.s., IV (1968), 1–19.

Bates, H. E. *The Modern Short Story.* London and Boston, 1941, pp. 185–187.

Baumgartner, Paul R. *Katherine Anne Porter.* American Authors and Critics Series. New York, 1969.

Beach, Joseph W. "Self-Consciousness and Its Antidote" (review of *The Leaning Tower* and Steinbeck's *Canary Row*), *Virginia Quarterly Review,* XXI (1945), 289–293.

Beck, Warren. Review of *Ship of Fools*, *Chicago Sunday Tribune Magazine of Books*, April 1, 1962, p. 1.

Becker, Laurence A. " 'The Jilting of Granny Weatherall': The Discovery of Pattern," *English Journal*, LV (1966), 1164–1169.

Bedford, Sybille. "Voyage to Everywhere," *Spectator*, November 16, 1962, pp. 763–764.

Bell, Vereen M. " 'The Grave' Revisited," *Studies in Short Fiction*, II (1965), 39–45.

Bluefarb, Sam. "Loss of Innocence in 'Flowering Judas,' " *College Language Association Journal*, VII (1964), 256–262.

Bode, Carl. "Katherine Anne Porter," *The Half-World of American Culture* (Carbondale, Ill., 1965), pp. 212–225.

Bride, Sister Mary. "Laura and the Unlit Lamp," *Studies in Short Fiction*, I (1963), 61–63.

Brooks, Cleanth. "On 'The Grave,' " *Yale Review*, LV (1966), 275–279.

Core, George. " 'The *Best* Residuum of Truth,' " *Georgia Review*, XX (1966), 278–291.

Crume, Paul. " 'Pale Horse, Pale Rider,' " *Southwest Review*, XXV (1940), 213–218.

Cruttwell, Patrick. "Swift, Miss Porter, and the 'Dialect of the Tribe,' " *Shenandoah*, XVII (1966), 27–38.

Curley, Daniel. "Katherine Anne Porter: The Larger Plan," *Kenyon Review*, XXV (1963), 671–695.

————. "Treasure in 'The Grave,' " *Modern Fiction Studies*, IX (1964), 377–384.

Donoghue, Denis. "Reconsidering Katherine Anne Porter" (review of the *Collected Stories*), *New York Review of Books*, November 11, 1965, 18–19.

Emmons, Winifred S. *Katherine Anne Porter: The Regional Stories*. Southwest Writers Series, No. 6. Austin, 1967.

Gordon, Caroline. "Katherine Anne Porter and the ICM" (review of *Katherine Anne Porter and the Art of Rejection* by William Nance), *Harper's*, CCXXIX (November 1964), 146–148.

Gottfried, Leon. "Death's Other Kingdom: Dantesque and Theological Symbolism in 'Flowering Judas,' " *PMLA*, LXXXIV (1969), 112–124.

Gross, Beverly. "The Poetic Narrative: A Reading of 'Flowering Judas,' " *Style*, II (1968), 129–139.

Hafley, James. " 'María Concepción': Life Among the Ruins," *Four Quarters*, XII (1962), 11–17.

Hagopian, John V. "Katherine Anne Porter: Feeling, Form, and Truth," *Four Quarters*, XII (1962), 1–10.

Hartley, Lodwick. "Dark Voyagers: A Study of Katherine Ann Porter's *Ship of Fools*," *University Review*, XXX (1963), 83–94.

————. "Katherine Anne Porter," *Sewanee Review*, XLVIII (1940), 216–226.

———. "The Lady and the Temple: The Critical Theories of Katherine Anne Porter," *College English*, XIV (1953), 386–391.

———. "Stephen's Lost World: Katherine Anne Porter's 'The Downward Path to Wisdom,' " *Studies in Short Fiction*, VI (July 1969).

Herbst, Josephine. "Miss Porter and Miss Stein," *Partisan Review*, XV (1948), 568–572.

Heilman, Robert B. "*Ship of Fools*: Notes on Style," *Four Quarters*, XII (1962), 46–55.

Hendrick, George. *Katherine Anne Porter*. Twayne's United States Authors Series, New York, 1965.

Hertz, Robert N. "Sebastian Brant and Porter's *Ship of Fools*," *Midwest Quarterly*, VI (1965), 389–401.

Hicks, Granville. "Voyage of Life" (review of *Ship of Fools*), *Saturday Review*, XLV (March 31, 1962), 15–16.

Hoffman, Frederick J. *The Art of Southern Fiction: A Study of Some Modern Novelists*. Carbondale and Edwardsville, 1967, pp. 39–50.

Isherwood, Christopher. Review of *Pale Horse, Pale Rider*, *New Republic*, XCVIII (April 19, 1939), 312–313.

Johnson, James William. "Another Look at Katherine Anne Porter," *Virginia Quarterly Review*, XXXVI (1960), 598–613.

Joselyn, Sister M. O.S.B. "Animal Imagery in Katherine Anne Porter's Fiction," in *Myth and Symbol: Critical Approaches and Applications*, ed. Bernice Slote (Lincoln, Neb., 1963), pp. 101–115.

———. " 'The Grave' As Lyrical Short Story," *Studies in Short Fiction*, I (1964), 216–221.

———. "On the Making of *Ship of Fools*," *South Dakota Review*, I (1964), 46–52.

Kaplan, Charles. "True Witness: Katherine Anne Porter," *Colorado Quarterly*, VII (1959), 319–327.

Kiely, Robert. "The Craft of Despondency—the Traditional Novelists [Greene, Waugh, Porter]," *Daedalus*, XCLI (1963), 220–237.

Kirkpatrick, Smith. "Ship of Fools," *Sewanee Review*, LXXI (1963), 94–98.

Kramer, Dale. "Notes on Lyricism and Symbols in 'The Grave,' " *Studies in Short Fiction*, II (1965), 331–336.

Liberman, M. M. *Her Cool Instrument: A Study of Katherine Anne Porter*. Detroit: Wayne State University Press, 1971. [Forthcoming.]

———. "The Responsibility of the Novelist: The Critical Reception of *Ship of Fools*," *Criticism*, VIII (1966), 377–388.

———. "The Short Story as Chapter in *Ship of Fools*," *Criticism*, X (1968), 65–71.

———. "Some Observations on the Genesis of *Ship of Fools*: A Letter from Katherine Anne Porter," *PMLA*, LXXIII (1968), 136–137.

McIntyre, John P. "*Ship of Fools* and Its Publicity," *Thought*, XXXVIII (1963), 211–220.

Marshall, Margaret. "Writers in the Wilderness: Katherine Anne Porter," *Nation*, CL (April 13, 1940), 473–475.

Marsden, M. M. "Love as a Threat in Katherine Anne Porter's Fiction," *Twentieth Century Literature*, XIII (1967), 29–38.

Matthiessen, F. O. Review of *The Leaning Tower and Other Stories*, *Accent*, V (1945), 121–123. Reprinted as "That True and Human World" in the *Accent Anthology*, ed. Kerker Quinn and Charles Shattuck (New York, 1946), pp. 619–623.

Miller, Paul W. "Katherine Anne Porter's *Ship of Fools*: A Masterpiece Manqué," *University Review*, XXXII (1965), 151–157.

Mizener, Arthur. "A Literary Self-Portrait" (review of *The Days Before*), *Partisan Review*, XX (1953), 244–246.

Mooney, Harry John, Jr. *The Fiction and Criticism of Katherine Anne Porter*. University of Pittsburgh Critical Essays in English and American Literature, No. 2. Pittsburgh, 1962.

Moss, Howard. "No Safe Harbor" (review of *Ship of Fools*), *New Yorker*, XXXVIII (1962), 165–173.

———. "A Poet of the Story" (review of the *Collected Stories*), *New York Times Book Review*, September 12, 1965, pp. 1, 26.

Nance, William L., S. M. *Katherine Anne Porter and the Art of Rejection*. Chapel Hill, 1964.

Plante, Patricia R. "Katherine Anne Porter: Misanthrope Acquitted," *Xavier University Studies*, II (1963), 87–91.

Perry, Robert L. "Porter's 'Hacienda' and the Theme of Change," *Midwest Quarterly*, VI (1965), 403–415.

Pierce, Marvin. "Point of View: Katherine Anne Porter's 'Noon Wine,' " *Ohio University Review*, III (1961), 95–113.

Poss, S. H. "Variations on a Theme in Four Stories of Katherine Anne Porter," *Twentieth Century Literature*, IV (1958), 21–29.

Powers, J. F. "She Stands Alone," *Four Quarters*, XII (1962), 65.

Prager, Leonard. "Getting and Spending: Porter's 'Theft,' " *Perspective*, XI (1960), 230–234.

Pritchett, V. S. "Stories and Stories" (review of the *Collected Stories*), *New Statesman*, LXIII (1964), 47–48.

Rockwell, Jeanne. "The Magic Cloak," *Michigan Quarterly Review*, V (1966), 283–284.

Ryan, Marjorie. "*Dubliners* and the Stories of Katherine Anne Porter," *American Literature*, XXXI (1960), 464–473.

———. "Katherine Anne Porter: *Ship of Fools* and the Short Stories," *Bucknell Review*, XII (1964), 51–63.

Schorer, Mark. "We're All on the Passenger List" (review of *Ship of Fools*), *New York Times Book Review*, April 1, 1962, pp. 1, 5.

Schwartz, Edward G. "The Fictions of Memory," *Southwest Review*, XLV (1960), 204–215.

————. "Katherine Anne Porter: A Critical Bibliography." With an Introduction by Robert Penn Warren. *Bulletin of the New York Public Library*, LVII (1953), 211–247.

————. "The Way of Dissent: Katherine Anne Porter's Critical Position," *Western Humanities Review*, VIII (1954), 119–130.

Smith, J. Oates. "Porter's 'Noon Wine': A Stifled Tragedy," *Renascence*, XVII (1965), 157–162.

Solotaroff, Theodore. "*Ship of Fools* and the Critics," *Commentary*, XXXIV (1962), 277–286. See also the discussion in *Commentary*, XXXV (1963), 247–250.

Stein, William Bysshe. " 'Theft': Porter's Politics of Modern Love," *Perspective*, XI (1960), 223–228.

Tate, Allen. "A New Star" (review of *Flowering Judas*), *Nation*, CXXXI (October 1930), 352–353.

Troy, William. "A Matter of Quality" (review of *Flowering Judas*), *Nation*, CXLI (October 30, 1935), 517–518.

Van Gelder, Robert. "Katherine Anne Porter at Work," *New York Times Book Review*, April 14, 1940, p. 20, and *Writers and Writing* (New York: Charles Scribner's Sons, 1946), pp. 42–44.

Waldrip, Louise D. B. *A Bibliography of the Works of Katherine Anne Porter.* Ann Arbor: University Microfilms, Inc., 1967. A University of Texas Ph.D. dissertation soon to be published in revised form by the Scarecrow Press, Inc., Metuchen, N.J.

Walsh, Thomas F. "The 'Noon Wine' Devils," *Georgia Review*, XXII (1968), 90–96.

Walton, Gerald. "Katherine Anne Porter's Use of Quakerism in *Ship of Fools*," *University of Mississippi Studies in English*, VII (1966), 15–23.

Warren, Robert Penn. "Irony with a Center: Katherine Anne Porter," *Selected Essays* (New York, 1958), pp. 136–156. This is a revised version of "Katherine Anne Porter (Irony with a Center)" which appeared in the *Kenyon Review*, IV (1942), 29–42.

————. "Uncorrupted Consciousness: The Stories of Katherine Anne Porter," *Yale Review*, LV (1966), 280–290.

Welker, Robert L. and Hershel Gower. " 'The Grave': Investigation and Comment," *The Sense of Fiction* (Englewood Cliffs, N.J., 1966), pp. 150–154.

Welty, Eudora. "The Eye of the Story," *Yale Review*, LV (1966), 265–275.

Wescott, Glenway. "Katherine Anne Porter Personally," *Images of Truth: Remembrances and Criticism* (New York, 1962), pp. 25–58.

————. "Praise," *Southern Review*, o. s., V (1939), 161–173.

West, Ray B., Jr. *Katherine Anne Porter.* University of Minnesota Pamphlets on American Writers, No. 28. Minneapolis, 1963.

————. "Katherine Anne Porter: Symbol and Theme in 'Flowering Judas,' " *Accent*, VII (1947), 182–187.

Wiesenfarth, Brother Joseph, F.S.C. "Illusion and Allusion: Reflections in 'The Cracked Looking-Glass,'" *Four Quarters*, XII (1962), 30–37.

Wilson, Angus. "The Middle-Class Passenger" (review of *Ship of Fools*), *The Observer*, October, 28, 1962, p. 27.

Wilson, Edmund. "Katherine Anne Porter," *Classics and Commercials* (New York, 1950), pp. 219–223.

Winters, Ivor. "Major Fiction," *Hound and Horn*, IV (1931), 303–305.

Wolfe, Peter. "The Problems of Granny Weatherall," *CLA Journal*, XI (1967), 142–148.

●Young, Vernon A. "The Art of Katherine Anne Porter," *New Mexico Quarterly*, XV (1945), 326–341.

Youngblood, Sarah. "Structure and Imagery in Katherine Anne Porter's 'Pale Horse, Pale Rider,'" *Modern Fiction Studies*, V (1959–1960), 344–352.

Index

"The Adventures of Hadji: A Tale of a Turkish Coffee House," xi
Aldridge, John W., xx, xxi, xxiii
Allen, Frederick Lewis, 52
Anderson, Sherwood, 51
Anglo-Catholicism: and Eliot, 163
Apologue: and *Ship of Fools*, 193–194
Aristotle: *Poetics*, 189; 18
Arnold, Matthew, 167
Austen, Jane: *Pride and Prejudice*, 190; 5, 24, 178, 180, 203, 204, 209

Barclay, Alexander: *The Ship of Fools*, 214
Bennett, Arnold, 180
Bishop of Wakefield: and Hardy, 163
Blackmur, R. P., 52
Blake, William, 93

Boone, Daniel, 6, 170
Boone, Jonathan, 6
Booth, John Wilkes, 62
Booth, Wayne: quoted, 188–189; 190, 194
Bowen, Elizabeth, 85
Boyle, Kay, xiii
Brackett, Charles, 47
Brant, Sebastian: *Das Narrenschiff*, 193, 214; 215, 224
Brontë, Charlotte, 204, 207
Brontë, Emily: *Wuthering Heights*, 5, 14; 180
Brooks, Cleanth, xxi
Bunyan, John: *Pilgrim's Progress*, 215
Bushman, Francis X., 8

Cather, Willa, 84, 162–166 *passim*, 178, 181

Catharsis, 14
Chamberlain, Neville, 196
Chambers, Robert: *Biographical Dictionary*, 211
Chase, Mary Ellen, 85
Chaucer, Geoffrey, 215
Chekhov, Anton, xix, xxi, 57, 106
"The Circus," 69–72 *passim*, 89–90, 93–94
Coleridge, Samuel Taylor, 34
Colette, Sidonie Gabrielle: *Gigi*, 37; 24, 33
The Collected Stories of Katherine Anne Porter: Preface, 149; xiii, 97–102
Conrad, Joseph, 95, 208
Constant, Benjamin: *Adolphe*, 37
"Corridos": quoted, 175
"The Cracked Looking-Glass," xviii, 60–61, 88, 91, 94, 139–148, 150

Dahlberg, Edward, 197
Dante, Alighieri: *The Inferno* quoted, 78; 5
"A Day's Work," 88, 94
The Days Before, xiii, 162–180
Dickens, Charles, 5
Donoghue, Denis, xiii, xx
Doré, Gustave, 5
Dostoevsky, Fyodor: *Brothers Karamazov*, 195; *Crime and Punishment*, 96; 187
"The Downward Path to Wisdom," 89, 94, 106

Eisenstein, Sergei, 30
Eliot, George, 19, 85, 204–205
Eliot, T. S.: "Burnt Norton," 181; *Gerontion*, 122, 125, 127; *The Waste Land*, 226; 163, 172–173, 176, 180, 209, 225

Elizabeth I, Queen of England, 31
Emerson, Ralph Waldo, 41, 179
Emmons, Winfred S., xiv
Empson, William: quoted, 156–157, 158; 150
Erskine, Albert R., 170n
Erskine, Thomas, 191
Euripides, 166

Faulkner, William, xiii, 87, 95, 101, 198
"The Fig Tree," 85, 89, 93–94
Fitzgerald, F. Scott: *The Great Gatsby*, 190; *Tender Is the Night*, 12
Flaubert, Gustave, xix, 83, 166, 178
Flowering Judas and Other Stories: Introduction, 22, 168; Introduction quoted, 196, 214; xi, xii, xviii, 97, 127, 212
"Flowering Judas," 15–16, 18, 20, 26, 30, 54–56, 57, 60, 65, 75, 88, 90, 94, 101, 109–110, 120–128
Ford, Maddox Ford, 84
Forster, E. M.: *The Eternal Moment*, 37; *Passage to India*, 14; 162–163, 226
Freud, Sigmund, 64, 196, 217
Freudian, 19, 84, 190, 217
Frost, Robert, 57

Gellhorn, Martha, 85
Gide, André, 185
Glasgow, Ellen, 84
Goethe, Johann Wolfgang: *Die Novelle*, 37; *Faust*, 212
Gordon, Caroline, xiii, xx, 44
"The Grave," xv, 34, 69, 77, 81–82, 89, 93–94, 115–119, 154
"The Guild Spirit in Mexican Art": quoted, 177

"Hacienda," xviii, 30, 36, 65, 90, 150–151, 217

Halleck, Fitz-Greene: "Marco Bozzaris," 144n

Hamilton, Edith: *The Greek Way*, 165, 166

Hardy, Thomas, 5, 95, 162, 163, 172–174, 199, 225

Hawthorne, Nathaniel: *The House of the Seven Gables*, 69; 41, 83, 178

"He," 89, 94

Heilman, Robert B., xxi

Hemingway, Ernest: *A Farewell to Arms*, xviii; xiii, 20, 51, 131, 198

Hendrick, George, xiv

Heraclitus, 181

Hicks, Granville, 223

"Holiday," 149–158, 213

Homer: *The Iliad*, 78; 5, 87

Hughes, Richard: *A High Wind in Jamaica*, 14

Hutchens, John K., 187

Ibsen, Henrik, 57

Isherwood, Christopher: *Goodbye to Berlin*, 87; xi–xii, 217

James, Henry: "The Beast in the Jungle," 139, 146; "In the Cage," 139, 146; *The Portrait of a Lady*, 195; *The Turn of the Screw*, 84; quoted, 75; 5, 83, 146, 149, 162, 164, 166–167, 171, 174, 179, 180, 182, 185, 195, 199

James, William, 163

"The Jilting of Granny Weatherall," 75, 78n, 80, 89, 92, 94, 104–105, 109

John, Book of, 79–80

Johnson, James William, xxi

Johnson, Samuel: *Rasselas*, 194; 17, 191

Jones, John Paul, 6

Joyce, James: *Finnegans Wake*, 190; *Ulysses*, 147; 51, 148, 180

Kafka, Franz, 224, 225

Keats, John, 167

Kunitz, S. J.: *Authors Yesterday and Today*, 170n

Lafayette, Marie Jean Paul, Marquis de, 6

"La Norteña," 30

"The Last Leaf," 86

Lawrence, D. H.: *Lady Chatterly's Lover*, 45; 84, 162, 167

The Leaning Tower and Other Stories, 98, 121

"The Leaning Tower," xv, xviii, 30, 36, 87–88, 91, 94, 121, 127, 150, 213, 218, 222

Liberman, M. M., xxi

Longfellow, Henry Wadsworth: *Psalm of Life*, 72

Lost Generation, 165

MacLeish, Archibald: "The End of the World," 93; *J.B.*, 93

"Magic," xviii, 89–90, 94, 106

Mann, Thomas: *Death in Venice*, 37; 87, 95

Mansfield, Katherine: "At the Bay," 105; xix, 51, 120, 162, 166–167, 176, 180

"María Concepción," xii, xv, 17, 65, 89, 92, 94, 217

Marie Antoinette, 25

Marx, Karl: *Das Kapital*, 152, 157; 64

Marxism, 124–125, 126
Marxist, 127, 190
Mather, Cotton, 174
Maugham, Somerset, 33
Maupassant, Guy de, xix
McCarthy, Mary: *The Groves of Academe*, 162
McCullers, Carson, 84
Melville, Herman: *Billy Budd*, 37; *Moby Dick*, 136, 190; 41
Mérimée, Prosper: *Carmen*, 37
Milton, John: *Paradise Lost*, 37
Miranda stories, xvii, 67–82 *passim*, 86, 151, 213
Mitchell, Margaret: *Gone with the Wind*, 194
Montaigne, Michel Eyquem de, 5
Moore, George, 46
Mooney, Harry John: *The Fiction and Criticism of Katherine Anne Porter*, 85; xiv
Mozart, Wolfgang Amadeus, 29

Nance, William, xiv, xix–xx
"Noon Wine," xviii, 20, 36, 37–41, 57–60, 65, 73, 89, 90, 93, 96, 104, 109, 149, 188, 213
" 'Noon Wine': The Sources," xvi, 40–41, 73
Normand, Mabel, 31
"Notes on Writing": quoted, 171

O'Brien, Margaret, 47
Obrégon Revolution of 1921, 11
"Old Mortality," xv, xviii, xx, 20, 34, 36, 61–65, 69, 71, 72, 86, 90, 91, 92, 94, 101, 103, 107, 109, 149, 151, 156, 213
The Old Order, 151

"The Old Order," 86, 87, 90, 93, 94, 101
O'Neill, Eugene: *Desire Under the Elms*, 88
Outline of Mexican Popular Arts and Crafts: quoted, 178

Pale Horse, Pale Rider: Three Short Novels, xviii, 10, 35, 216
"Pale Horse, Pale Rider," xv, xviii, 34, 35, 36, 65, 69, 72, 75, 76–79, 88–89, 90, 91, 92, 94, 101, 109, 129–138, 149, 151, 156, 188
Petrarch, Francesco, 17
Poe, Edgar Allan, 72
Porter, Horace, 6
Porter, Katherine Anne: on art, 9–23 *passim*; on art and religion, 162, 172–181 *passim*; a classicist, 14, 165; on contemporaries, 17; on experimentalism, 165; and genre, xviii, 36–37, 149–150; and Hollywood, 31; imagery, 105, 108, 129–138; life, 4–48 *passim*; and orthodoxy, 162, 172–173; and religion, 125–126, 162, 163, 172–181 *passim*; and Roman Catholicism, xv; social sensibility, 121, 127, 175, 185–196; and the South (and Southwest), xvi, xx, xxi, 5, 8, 87, 101–102, 108, 162, 170, 172; style, xv, xviii, 16, 18, 27, 46, 53–54, 56–57, 85, 110–111, 166, 179, 188, 197–210, 213; symbolism, 18, 90–93, 123, 128; themes, 86–90. (Works by Miss Porter appear separately by title.)
Porter, William Sidney, 6
"Portrait: Old South," 101
Pound, Ezra, 57, 84, 162, 166, 180
Powers, J. F.: quoted, xix, 157

Pressly, Eugene, **170n**
Proust, Marcel: quoted, 24; xxi, 87
Puritan, **8**, 163
Puritanism, 162–163

Randolph, John, 6
Revelation of St. John, 76, **133**
Richardson, Samuel, 191
Rilke, Ranier Maria, 167
Rivera, Diego, 176–177
Romanticism, 164
Ronsard, Pierre de, 5
"Rope," xviii, 88, 91, 94
Ryder, Albert Pinkham, 76

Sade, Donatin Alphonse, Marquis de, 191
Sand, George, 85
Sans-Gêne, Madame, 32
Sacks, Sheldon: *Fiction and the Shape of Belief*, 193
Sartre, Jean Paul: *No Exit*, 224
Schorer, Mark, xiii
Schwartz, Edward, xiii, xxi
Sennett, Mack, 31
Shakespeare, William: *The Tempest*, 65, 67–68; xxii, 5, 17, 34, 167
Ship of Fools, xviii, xix, xx, 20–23, 24, 30, 36, 42–44, 45–46, 95, 156, 185–226
Sitwell, Edith, 162, 165, 166
Smollett, Tobias George, 5, 206, 207
Sophocles, 167
"The Source," 70, 72, 86
Spenser, Edmund: *The Fairie Queene*, 215
Stein, Gertrude, 45, 84, 162, 165
Stendhal, Henri Beyle: *Le Rouge et Le Noir*, 46

Sterne, Laurence: *Tristram Shandy*, 17; 180
Styron, William: *Set This House on Fire*, 13
Swanson, Gloria, 31
Swift, Jonathan: *Gulliver's Travels*, 215

Tate, Allen, xx
Tennyson, Alfred: "Lady of Shalott," 147
Teresa, Saint, 9
Thackeray, William Makepeace, 5
"That Tree," 88, 94
"Theft," 89, 94, 106
Thomas, Dylan, 84
Thompson, Barbara, xvii
Tolstoy, Count Leo Nikolaevich: *Anna Karenina*, 158
Turgenev, Ivan S.: *A Sportsman's Sketches*, 158; xix, 5, 178
Twain, Mark: *The Adventures of Huckleberry Finn*, 69n

Vane, Sutton: *Outward Bound*, 215
Voltaire, Francois Marie Arouet, 5

Waldrip, Louise, xiii
Warren, Robert Penn: *World Enough and Time*, 84; quoted, 153, 157; xxi, 71–72
Washington, George, 6
Weimar Republic, 218
Weisenfarth, Brother Joseph, xxi
Wells, H. G., 180
Welty, Eudora: *A Curtain of Green*, 213; xiii, xxi, xxii, 84, 162, 175
Wescott, Glenway, xvii, 212
West, Ray B., Jr., xiv, xxi

West, Rebecca, 84–85

Wheeler, Monroe, 33

Whitman, Walt: *Leaves of Grass*, 41; 177, 179, 181

Wilson, Edmund: quoted, 98; 19, 84, 99, 102

"The Witness," 86, 93

Wolfe, Thomas: *You Can't Go Home Again*, 87; 101

Woolf, Virginia: *To the Lighthouse*, 14; *The Voyage Out*, 180; *The Waves*, 111; 33, 85, 95, 162, 164

World War I, xviii, 9, 10, 35, 65, 81, 219

World War II, 31, 191, 222

Yeats, William Butler: quoted, 21; 41, 106, 180

Youngblood, Sarah, xxi